THE
EUROPEAN RECOVERY
PROGRAM

LONDON : GEOFFREY CUMBERLEGE
OXFORD UNIVERSITY PRESS

The European Recovery Program

BY
SEYMOUR E. HARRIS

HARVARD UNIVERSITY PRESS
CAMBRIDGE, MASSACHUSETTS
1948

COPYRIGHT, 1948
BY THE PRESIDENT AND FELLOWS OF HARVARD COLLEGE

PRINTED AT THE HARVARD UNIVERSITY PRINTING OFFICE
CAMBRIDGE, MASS., U.S.A.

TO
SENATOR ARTHUR H. VANDENBERG
FOR HIS STATESMANLIKE CONTRIBUTION
TO THE PASSAGE OF THE FOREIGN ASSISTANCE ACT
OF 1948

ABOUT THIS BOOK

So far there have been two approaches to the European Recovery Program: that of the aroused opponents who object either because they want to wash their hands of Europe or because, sympathetic with Russia, they view the program as an attack on the USSR and her satellites; and that of the host of government experts who are not free to analyze the problems *publicly* with complete objectivity.* In the current volume, the writer, though in agreement with Secretary Marshall's view that the ERP is a prudent risk, nevertheless does not hesitate to criticize the program and to point out its weaknesses. Above all, it is essential that the ERP should not be oversold as the Bretton Woods program was to some extent. Thus government officials are not justified in telling the country that the program is not inflationary or that it may not require the imposition of controls. Miracles should not be expected from expenditures of fifteen to twenty billion dollars over four years; and it is preferable to warn the country now against over-optimism rather than to have the public disillusioned in the next few years. The object of this book is not only to explain the ERP and the major issues involved; but also to offer some points for consideration when the legislation is again reviewed early in 1949 and later years.

* Literature by economists is beginning to appear in substantial quantities. See especially S. Alexander, *The Marshall Plan* (National Planning Association, 1948); G. Haberler in an article scheduled to appear in the September 1948 issue of *American Economic Review*, and B. F. Hoselitz, "Four Reports on Economic Aid to Europe," *J. P. E.*, April 1948; F. A. Lutz, *The Marshall Plan*, International Finance Section (Princeton, N. J., 1948); also essays by S. E. Harris and C. B. Hoover in *The Journal of Finance*, February 1948, and essays by S. Alexander, L. Gordon, C. B. Hoover, K. Mather, and E. S. Mason in my *Foreign Economic Policy for the United States* (Harvard University Press, 1948).

EUROPEAN RECOVERY PROGRAM

World War II cost from six hundred to eight hundred billion dollars. Distortions and maladjustments, resulting from war, do not disappear as suddenly as hostilities are terminated; and it was mistaken policy to assume that the end of hostilities would be accompanied by a simultaneous return to prewar economic conditions. Is it surprising, in view of the vast damage done by war to plant, inventories, and morale, that a war costing about three quarters of a trillion dollars should require United States assistance of twenty billion dollars over the first two and a half years of the postwar period, and an additional fifteen to twenty billion dollars over the four following years? Is it not obvious that Western Europe, having lost the means of paying for one-third of her imports, the product of generations of savings, should face an intractable deficit in her balance of payments?

In view of the perplexing economic and political issues raised by the Marshall Plan and because of the divergent interests supporting it, it was to be expected that the Foreign Assistance Act of 1948 would show serious flaws; but the country should congratulate itself that the act is much better than it might have been.

Among supporters of the legislation were those frightened of Russia and communism and desirous of bolstering capitalism; those who viewed European recovery as an essential condition of prosperity in this country; those who wanted markets for surpluses; and those who would help Europe out of humanitarian motives. The resulting legislation necessarily reflected the views of these groups as well as those of the numerous Americans who, though recognizing the need of legislation, were determined that the costs should be kept down to a minimum and that the project be run on business principles.

In the gestation period of the ERP, the Congress profited not only from the reports of the Paris experts, representing the sixteen participating governments, but also from a most thorough examination of needs and availabilities, by the executive branch.

ABOUT THIS BOOK

(In the evolution of the ERP various government agencies or departments collaborated in preparing materials for the Congress. The important officials have been designated as the "executive branch.") To my knowledge, the executive branch issued forty printed volumes devoted to the problems of deficits in the balance of payments, requirements of European countries by commodities and countries, availabilities of required commodities in the United States and elsewhere, the manner of financing the deficits, and so on. The work was of an unusually high quality; and though forecasts for four and a quarter years are of limited value, they nevertheless are indispensable for a study of the problem.

The Congress was not prepared to accept, without checks of its own, the three able reports by the experts appointed by the President, nor the voluminous materials prepared by the executive branch. Congressman Herter's conscientious Select Committee on Foreign Aid examined the results of the administration studies and, under the able direction of Dr. William Y. Elliott, produced twenty-four independent reports on germane issues. In addition to all this, the House and Senate Foreign Relations Committee held searching hearings which covered 3750 pages, or around one and a half million words. (Hearings before the Appropriations Committee were additional.) That the final act is of a high order is probably due to the conscientious preparatory work, and Senator Vandenberg's statesmanlike handling of the legislation.

The current volume starts with a chapter giving some highlights, then in two chapters in Part I deals with major issues. In the following nine chapters, we elaborate many of the problems discussed in the opening three chapters. He who must run while he reads may be content with the introductory chapter and the brief conclusion; the harassed Congressman, official, or business executive might be expected to read Part I; and the general reader and student unhurried, might be sufficiently interested to read the entire book. Abbreviations, footnotes, and sources of figures are presented at the end — pp. 275 ff.

I am under special obligation to my colleague, Professor William Y. Elliott, to Dr. Charles Kindleberger of the State Department, one of the many able public servants who participated in the formulation of the program, to Mrs. Margarita Willfort for help with the manuscript, and to Mrs. Anna Thorpe for typing it. My wife kindly helped with the proofs.

SEYMOUR E. HARRIS

Cambridge, Massachusetts
September 9, 1948

Contents

EXPLANATION OF TERMS   XV

Highlights

What is the European Recovery Program (ERP)? 3; a program by egalitarianism? 5; a catalyst, 6; pitfalls, 9; recovery? 18; in summary, 24.

PART ONE
MAJOR ECONOMIC AND POLITICAL ISSUES

1. Economic Crisis in Europe

Passage of the Foreign Assistance Act of 1948, 29; the drain over the years, 29; catalyst or ransom? 30; recovery and industrial output, 1945–46, 30; recovery and national output, 31; income and disinvestment abroad, 34; investment: French and British experience, 35; British economists on excessive investment, 36; inflation: suppressed and open, 41; some adverse effects of inflation on government and distribution, 44; inflation and loss of competitive position, 44; inflation: summary, 45; international economic aspects, 46; summary of international economic relations, 57; conclusion, 59.

2. Some Political Aspects

The ERP and communism, 60; is the ERP directed against communism? 61; reaction from the USSR, 63; repercussions on nonparticipating countries, 64; relations with Eastern Europe, 67; the preservation of private enterprise, 71; cooperation, 75; brief note on administration, 80; conclusion, 82.

CONTENTS

PART TWO
EUROPE AND HER BALANCE OF PAYMENTS

3. Deterioration in Europe

The 1947 crisis, 85; prewar and postwar income in the United States and Europe, 86; production figures, 91; conclusion, 93.

4. Dollar Shortage and Foreign Aid

Introduction, 95; dollar scarcity: myth or reality? 96; what is dollar scarcity? 99; theory and practice, 101; scarcity, ephemeral or long-run? 103; credits and grants, 1914 to 1947, 104; conclusions on dollar scarcity, 106.

5. Exchange Rates and Related Problems

Introduction, 109; overvaluation of currencies, 110; establish new parities? 112; the French devaluation of January 1948, 114; exchange rates and terms of trade, 116; stabilization, 119; conclusion, 120.

6. Balance of Payments of the Participating Countries

Introduction, 122; causes of the adverse balance, 122; financing the adverse balance, 1945–1947, 126; the Paris program and successive revisions, 132; final observations on the deficits, 139.

CONTENTS

PART THREE
IMPACT ON THE UNITED STATES

INTRODUCTION 144

7. Determinants of Costs and Allocation of Assistance

Costs, 155; standards of aid, 155; determinants of allocations of funds, 158; loans and capacity to repay, 164; import structure and manner of financing, 166; conclusion, 171.

8. The Financial Costs

Introduction, 173; general observations on burden, 173; the magnitude of the problem, 174; goods or dollars? 177; special problems of finance, 178; use of local currencies, 179; conclusion, 184.

9. Inflation and the ERP

Introduction, 185; over-all factors: income and the cost of the ERP, 185; inflationary effects of the ERP, 189; time for action, 190; three alternative approaches, 190; reduce demand now, 192; resulting injustices, 192; the expansion of money and credit, 193; orthodox monetary control and the government bond market, 194; fiscal policy, 195; other correctives, 197; controls further discussed, 198; the budgetary problem and the ERP, 203; conclusion, 205.

10. Shortages in Relation to the ERP

Introduction, 207; export drains, 208; exports and prices, 214; agricultural markets, 221; energy sources, 228; iron and steel, 232; conclusion, 235.

CONTENTS

PART FOUR
ECONOMIC RECOVERY

11. Economic Recovery?

Introduction, 241; an appraisal of CEEC objectives, 242; accomplishments, 247; over-all trends, 248; individual countries: the United Kingdom, 252; France, 259; Italy, 264; Bizonal Germany, 266; The Netherlands, 269; conclusion, 270.

Concluding Remarks 272

ABBREVIATIONS	275
SOURCES OF FIGURES	277
NOTES	279

Postscript

The first six months of the ECA, 297.

EXPLANATION OF TERMS

For those who are not familiar with economic terms, the following definitions may be helpful:

BALANCE OF PAYMENTS

This term refers to the international transactions of a country. *Credit items* of Country A (say) include exports of commodities and services (for example, shipping, tourist expenditures by foreigners in A), interest and profits on foreign investments received by A, payments on account of money borrowed or received gratis by A from abroad, and repayment to A of funds advanced previously.

Debit items include imports of goods and services, interest and dividends paid to those residing abroad, expenditures by A's government abroad, payments on account of new loans and assistance to interests domiciled abroad by A.

Invisible items include receipts and disbursements on current account, (for example, shipping, income on investments), exclusive of commodity exports, and also exclusive of capital movements.

Should debit items exceed credit items, the difference is made up by gold shipments or release of gold or foreign exchange held abroad, or by borrowing.

DOLLAR SCARCITY

For many years, dollars available to foreigners have been scarce in the sense that the demand for dollars exceeds the supply at the current price of the dollar in terms of pounds sterling, francs, pesos, etc. The scarcity may be reflected in pressure on the exchanges, with the result that the foreign currency depreciates and the dollar appreciates; or in shipments of gold to the United States, the offer of gold, which is exchangeable for dol-

EXPLANATION OF TERMS

lars, reducing the demand for dollars; or (what is usual) control of the demand for dollars and their mobilization by foreign authorities, and replenishment of dollar supplies by obtaining loans or grants.

EXCHANGE EQUILIBRIUM

Some economists accept as an indication of equilibrium the absence of substantial gold movements, or strong pressures on the foreign exchanges which result in downward movements in the external value of a currency and corresponding rises for other currencies. Others presume a position of disequilibrium even if there are no substantial movements of gold or exchange rates if the gold is retained and the exchanges relatively stabilized by restricting monetary supplies at home, and thus inducing unemployment and disequilibrium.

INFLATION

Inflation may be defined simply as a rise of prices brought about by an excess of *general* demand over supplies at the existing price level.

Open inflation prevails when the excess of demand, generally associated with monetary expansion resulting from government deficits, is allowed to exercise its effect on the price level.

Suppressed inflation prevails when government, through control of demand, sterilizes part of the excess purchasing power and thus keeps prices down. In this manner, the government of one European country, despite a supply of money four times as great as before the war, has been able to keep the rise of prices down to about 50 per cent over prewar levels.

OFFSHORE PURCHASES

Under the ERP, this government is to use part of the funds appropriated to purchase supplies and services for the participat-

EXPLANATION OF TERMS

ing countries outside the continental United States. Such purchases are offshore purchases.

OVERVALUED CURRENCIES

Overvaluation occurs when a currency — say the franc — is valued too high in terms of foreign currencies — say the dollar — with the result that foreigners find purchases in France — the country with the overvalued currency — expensive, and French citizens purchase abroad excessively since other currencies are cheap. Countries with overvalued currencies lose gold and foreign exchange, or (and) impose restrictions on the use of foreign exchange (exchange control). In France, for example, the franc was worth more than 2 cents in 1947. At that price, French exports were expensive. Hence the devaluation (reduction of the value of the franc in gold and dollars) by about 40 per cent early in 1948.

TERMS OF TRADE

A country's terms of trade are expressed by the ratio of exports given for a specified quantity of imports. (In this discussion I omit technical difficulties.) An acceptable manner of measuring changes in the terms of trade is a comparison of the ratio of prices of exports and imports in a year (say 1948) with a similar ratio in a base year (say 1939). Should prices of British imports rise by 100 per cent and those of her exports by 80 per cent, then her terms of trade will have deteriorated: she provides more exports for a given quantity of imports.

THE
EUROPEAN RECOVERY
PROGRAM

Highlights

WHAT IS THE EUROPEAN RECOVERY PROGRAM (ERP)?

In the spring of 1948 the United States embarked on a program of aid to sixteen European countries and Western Germany, which may well cost $20 billion over a period of four and a quarter years. The unique feature of the ERP is that the grants and loans are to be conditional upon Western Europe helping itself. This opening chapter inquires into the nature of the program, its objectives, its potential contributions, and the pitfalls. Many of the problems receive fuller treatment later.

Self-interest, rather than charity, inspired the ERP. Frightened by the onward movement of communism, which feeds on distress, the American people rallied to the support of the Marshall Plan, which over a gestation period of eleven months, became the ERP. Americans realized also that economic recovery in Western Europe would rebound favorably on the American economy. Figure 2 indicates the importance of Western Europe: its large proportion of literates, of world output, of steel output, and of trade — all from two to six times its proportion of world population. Yet it would be a mistake to assume that fear of communism and an awareness of the nexus of European recovery and United States economic and political conditions alone accounted for the support of the ERP. Far from it. Narrow, more selfish interests also supported the ERP, not the least of which were groups (for example, farmers), fearful of large surpluses in the years to come and aware of the outlets offered by the ERP. This is not to be interpreted as support of a communist position that the ERP is an attempt to save this country from a depression.

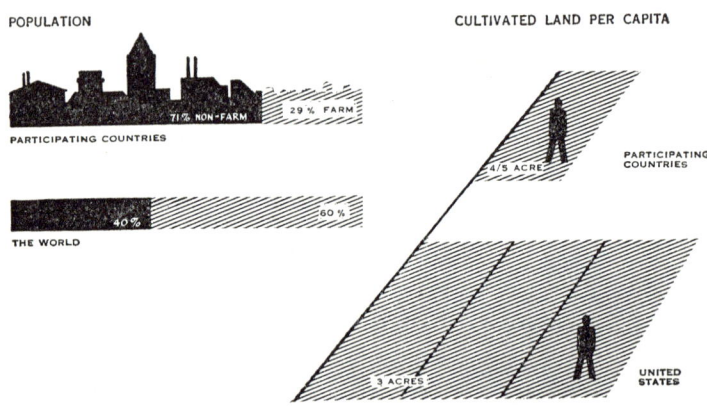

Figure 1

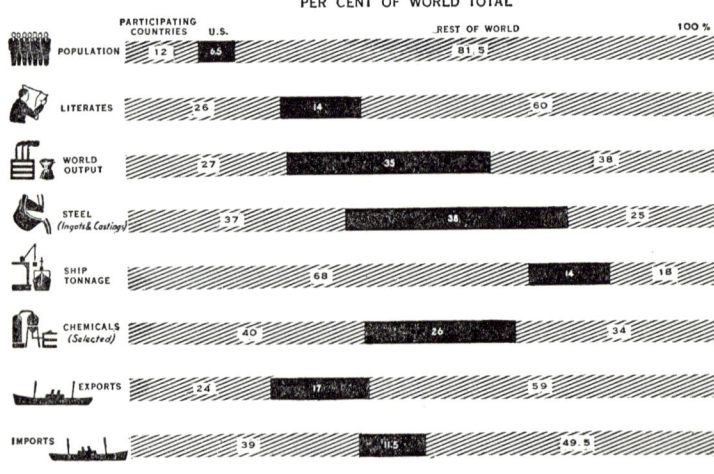

Figure 2

HIGHLIGHTS

Rather my position is that the ERP, justified on other grounds, is being used by special interests to improve their own markets.

In its direct association with projected policies of beneficiary countries, the ERP is unique; but in other respects, it is a continuation of a trend over a period of thirty-five years, during which this country assisted foreigners with about $100 billion of goods and services. For this sum, which equalled about 4 per cent of the income of this country and 40 per cent of the total goods and services exported over the thirty-five years, we received in return about $20 billion in gold, and IOU's, both promising little return in goods. Since most of the exports—the counterpart of loans, assistance, and gold imports—were sent in periods of high employment, the American economy paid largely not out of goods produced with factors otherwise unemployed, but by *diversions* to foreign countries of goods that otherwise would have been used here, with resulting inflationary pressures.

A PROGRAM OF EGALITARIANISM?

Many Americans are disturbed by the large and continued outlays for foreign assistance, and are hopeful that a generous and well planned program over four years will at least put Europe on its own once more. There are hopes that from 1948 to 1952 the ERP will cut Western Europe's annual deficit with the Americas from, say, $5 to $2 billion. This would be a substantial achievement. Yet there are many unknowns; and a persistent deficit in non-ERP countries still requires treatment—even admitting the indirect favorable effects of the ERP on the others.

It will require astute management to prevent the pauperization of Europe and the rest of the world. It is to be hoped, for example, that the future aid under the ERP will not be related to the deficit in the balance of payments shown but rather to the deficit to be expected on the basis of judicious policies and strong efforts by European countries on their own behalf.

EUROPEAN RECOVERY PROGRAM

Our country has about nine times as large an income per capita as the rest of the world. Does the large assistance in the last thirty-five years and through the ERP reflect successful attempts at redistribution of income? Is the threat of communism being used as a gun aimed at the American economy to force it to yield goods and services? Or must the redistribution be effected by World War III and World War IV? These are the thoughts that must occur to our officials in Washington. When Secretary Marshall describes the ERP as a prudent risk, he undoubtedly thinks of it as a means of providing enough economic sustenance to Western Europe to reëstablish prewar standards of living, to make her independent of United States aid, and to assure a milieu in which communism and war will not germinate. The ERP is indeed a further step towards egalitarianism; but a small one relative to that to be achieved through communism or war.

Communists and Mr. Henry Wallace interpret the ERP as a program directed against the iron curtain. That there are strong anticommunist features in the program, few will dispute; and that almost universal support of the ERP and the generous assistance probably to be made available would not have been forthcoming had Molotov cooperated at Paris in the summer of 1947, is equally clear. But this is far from saying that the ERP is merely a program to stop the spread of communism. Those who support this position will have to explain the large assistance to be given the United Kingdom, surely relatively safe from the communist threat, as compared with the amounts to be made available to Italy and France, where the struggle to stop communism is at its height.

A CATALYST

Under the ERP, the annual assistance offered at the most is but 5 per cent of the income of the participating countries. Yet it is

HIGHLIGHTS

anticipated that by 1952 their annual output and income will have risen by several times the annual assistance under the ERP. Even United States experts, more conservative than the Committee of European Economic Cooperation, anticipate the following percentage rise in output from 1947 to 1952: coal, 33; finished steel, 71; hydroelectric power, 36; grains, 39; meat, 31 per cent (see Figure 3). These rises and particularly those for coal, steel, and power, are compatible with a rise of income of at least 25 per cent from 1947 to 1952. Actually from the first quarter of 1946 to the third quarter of 1947, the expansion of *industrial* output for fifteen European countries, for which indexes are available and which account for 75 per cent of Europe's industrial output, was 26 per cent.

We might anticipate an equivalent rise in the years 1948 to 1952. With industrial output about 10 to 15 per cent below that of prewar levels and industrial population equal to the prewar period, with man-hours substantially in excess of prewar times, a gain of these proportions might be realized, should productivity be restored to normal for a growing industrial population.[1] By removing serious bottlenecks, by making dollars available in order to prevent a collapse of international trade, by using aid as a weapon for prevailing upon European countries to introduce judicious fiscal and monetary policies, to cooperate and prudently to deploy their resources, the American Government may well help bring about a long-term *annual* rise of Western Europe's income of five dollars for every dollar made available in each of four years under the ERP. An investment of $20 billion may then serve as a catalyst, raising Western Europe's income by hundreds of billions of dollars (possibly saving trillions, if war is prevented or averted for a generation or two) and also indirectly raising the income of non-ERP countries stimulated by the increased purchasing power made available.

PRODUCTION BY PARTICIPATING COUNTRIES
(U. S. ESTIMATES)

SELECTED YEARS
PREWAR - 1952

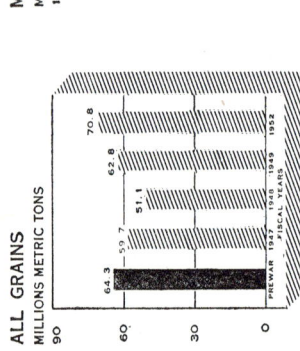

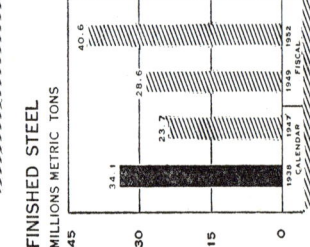

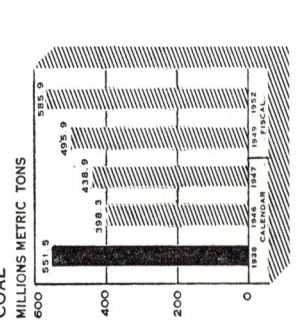

Figure 3

HIGHLIGHTS
PITFALLS

The last paragraph presented an optimistic interpretation of the European Recovery Program, but unfortunately there are many pitfalls.

One: The problem of investment — that is, output of goods not available for consumption. It is difficult to estimate the optimum rate of investment for Europe. American experts, following the lead of orthodox British economists, are disposed to prune European investments drastically. Undoubtedly, the European deficit in the balance of payments over the next four years can be kept down by moderating the rate of investment; with reduced investments, more resources may be made available for exports, and imports may be kept down. But it is not equally clear that the cost to the American taxpayer will not be substantially larger for the next ten to twenty years under a truncated investment program, with adverse effects on output and on the European international accounts. For example, the ambitious investment program of the United Kingdom for 1947, which became the target of criticism, made up only about one-fifteenth of the deficiency of investment incurred over seven years. Even in France investment in 1947 was but 19 per cent of the gross national product (in 1938 it was 14 per cent); at this rate, it would take many years before the deficit was made up. In other countries investment, relative to total product, was less than in 1938. Surely, there is a strong possibility (though we admit that there may be unrealistic programs in some countries) that the American experts may be pressing too hard for a deflation of the investment program.[2]

Two: Reduction of the trade deficit. It is possible that Europe will achieve economic recovery and yet not free herself from dependence on the United States Government. It is well to recall that over thirty-five years capitalism, depending on market reactions and admittedly operating imperfectly, did not prevent periodic breakdowns in the dollar market. Somehow the required resources did not move into export markets, and for this and other reasons, the needed foreign exchange was not forthcoming. Can we expect better results from socialist governments, depending partly on the capitalist adjustments and partly on controls? Socialist governments might do better. They do not have to rely exclusively on market adjustments. Why should they not impose the sacrifices on their people by cutting imports and expanding exports each by a few per cent? But this is not an easy sacrifice to impose, especially where the standard of living is low and governments are weak. With recovery and stronger governments, the ERP will face a crucial test: will European semi-socialist governments, in control (assuming they remain in control) of allocation of resources, raise exports and (or) reduce imports adequately to achieve a balance?

Three: *Control of European economies.* Under the ERP participating countries receive aid on the condition that they carry through approved policies and at least make a strong effort to reach ambitious production and export goals. The conditional nature of the assistance will raise a host of problems, not the least difficult of which will be how far this country can trespass on sovereign rights of foreign countries in order to assure the most effective use of American assistance. Let us consider this point briefly by concentrating on the foreign exchange problem next. (Chapter 5 contains a fuller discussion of this and related problems.)

As the ERP unfolds in the summer of 1948, fear grows in Europe that the United States will impose a revaluation of exchange rates on European countries. High American officials (for example, the National Advisory Council on International and Financial Problems) in the spring of 1948 made strong statements on this issue; and the Foreign Assistance Act of 1948 requires *equitable* rates of exchange.

HIGHLIGHTS

In emphasizing the need of changes in exchange rates, United States authorities put too much faith in the price or market mechanism under European postwar conditions. They assume that a depreciation of the pound sterling, for example, might be as effective in equilibrating the British balance of payments as it proved in 1931. They should be reminded that, much more than practical variations in prices, what determines sales abroad and receipts in foreign exchange is the supply of goods available for exports, the control policies of the relevant countries, the accessibility of markets, and the interchange (convertibility) of currencies. Above all where internal prices and particularly resources are under control, exchange rates are of much less importance than usual. American experts should also be reminded that devaluation means lower world prices, that is, more exports for a given supply of imports — not a highly desirable outcome for impoverished countries. In short, though modifications in exchange rates may be helpful at times, Americans should move cautiously in imposing variations in rates upon European countries. Above all, we emphasize the point that in controlled economies, exchange rates are of less than usual significance. Association of deficits in the balance of payments with unrealistic exchange rates in the Europe of 1948 is somewhat like blaming the gas gauge when there is no gasoline in the tank.

The problem of control of local currencies obtained for goods provided under grants is another perplexing problem. Since this is discussed fully in the body of the volume, it suffices merely to mention this source of friction. A third problem is that of the extent to which controls should be imposed upon Europe. It is interesting that in a discussion with the House Foreign Relations Committee, Secretary of the Treasury Snyder would not indicate how far this country would go in pressing for controls in Europe. He was inclined to support a view which surely has boomeranged in this country: the cure for inflation is higher

EUROPEAN RECOVERY PROGRAM

production. But he also admitted that other anti-inflationary measures, inclusive of tax reform, would be required.[3] The ECA will be embarrassed by the control problem because, although it is generally recognized that controls or allocation of resources and even of prices and wages may be indispensable to achieve the most effective use of American assistance, support of control measures in Europe raises fundamental problems concerning the philosophy of the ERP and the widespread opposition to controls in this country. A program which requires mobilization of controls abroad does not appeal to those who view the ERP as a weapon for salvaging capitalism.

Four: Is the ERP to degenerate into a subsidy system for Americans? No competent observer of the ERP will gainsay the fact that it is in part an organization for dumping surpluses; and that the support for the ERP stemmed partially from those who viewed it as a source of additional markets. It is significant that the attempt to transfer ships to foreign nations or charter them under foreign flags at a potential saving of a few hundred million dollars for the ERP failed; that the machine-tool builders operating at 50 per cent of capacity begged Congress to be generous in the offer of tools under the ERP; that the naval stores associations, with failing export markets, exerted similar pressures for special listing; that the fruit growers, suffering from large excesses, asked for payments in local currencies abroad, with the ERP to guarantee conversion into dollars; that the participating countries are offered more tobacco, dried fruits, and other agricultural products than they requested. Europe asked for scrap and semi-finished iron and steel, of which it will receive little; but this country is to send much more finished iron and steel than was requested. Is the reason the protection and favoring of markets of United States producers? It is not surprising then that farm groups, and even some business groups, fearful of surpluses, gave their enthusiastic support to the ERP.

HIGHLIGHTS

But the American taxpayer had better be sure that in financing the ERP he is not creating artificial markets for surplus products and thus paying concealed subsidies, and he had better be as certain that each ERP dollar does the maximum good, yielding wanted goods, not those that American surplus producers wish to dump on foreign markets. Such dumping is an old weapon of economic warfare, and is favored by certain circles in this country. It would be paradoxical indeed should the ERP, a program introduced to improve international economic relations, become a vehicle for supporting an American subsidy program.

Five: Shall the United States achieve domestic economic policies required for the successful outcome of the ERP? Discussion here will be limited to the problem of supplies in relation to demand. I shall not dwell on short-sighted commercial policies as evidenced in the Congressional views on the Reciprocal Trade Agreements discussed in 1948. The ERP requires sacrifices from this country. To be sure, the executive branch whittled down the amounts asked by the CEEC; and to an important extent also diverted applications for scarce commodities to other countries. Yet the government burdens an already over-employed economy with the ERP and large additional military expenditures. The supplies and men needed for these programs are not likely to come primarily out of resources otherwise unemployed, though as noted above they may come out of surpluses to some extent. It is possible to provide the ERP and the military with the commodities and services needed without further aggravating inflationary pressures. But so far Congress — and in my view the *major* responsibility lies with Congress — has not been disposed to neutralize the inflationary effects of these programs.[4] In its tax reduction program, in its aversion to the minimum controls required to siphon off nonessential demand in several mal-provisioned markets, and in its unwillingness to support unorthodox monetary measures, the Congress seems allergic to the domestic program which must support the ERP. But an over-all attack on the inflation problem is indispensable for the success of the ERP. A price rise of the proportions of 1947 over four and a quarter years would increase the costs of the ERP by from five to ten billion dollars, or reduce the program to a relief basis; and this would seriously jeopardize its success.

Here are the types of problems that confront our government: It may provide veterans with minimum housing and yet sponsor the ERP and the emergency military program; and all this without serious inflationary effects. But in order to exclude inflation, there will have to be allocations of scarce building supplies. Or consider this problem. The outcome of the ERP depends in no small part upon the availability of oil from the Middle East, both because the *total* resources may not become available in time in adequate quantities, and because Europe may not obtain its required share of Middle Eastern oil. This country can, however, make larger contributions of oil. In 1947 the petroleum supply of the United States was 389 million metric tons (hard coal equivalent), while for the participating countries with a population nearly two times as large, it was 51 million metric tons — the per capita supply in the United States was about fifteen times as large as in the ERP countries. From 1938 to 1947 United States petroleum consumption rose by 830 million barrels, or more than two and a half times *the consumption* of all participating countries in 1947; and from 1947 to 1951 the estimated rise of consumption for the United States will amount to three-quarters of the estimated *entire consumption* of the participating countries and their dependent territories in fiscal year 1952. It should be clear from these figures that relatively small economies in this country, obtainable through an allocation system, could save the ERP countries from excessive reliance upon Middle East oil.[5] Excessive relates to the large amounts antici-

HIGHLIGHTS

pated from the Middle East, relative to supplies likely to be available.

Six: Should the ERP be used to support private enterprise? The kind of economic system this country should have must be decided on its merits; and it would be unfortunate if the ECA, in its zeal for preserving capitalism, should lose sight of its real objective, economic recovery in Europe. What this country wants is a system which assures the fundamental freedoms and yields the optimum efficiency both in production and distribution. But it is a mistake to use the ERP either as a means of imposing a free enterprise system on Europe or to inflate the costs of the ERP in order to strengthen the profit position of American business. For many European countries socialism may well be the more efficient technique, and even if it is not, there are great dangers involved in forcing upon Europe a system of capitalism which her people may not relish. In this country there is altogether too much emphasis on using private channels of trade for ERP purchases, even though the result of doing so may cost the taxpayer billions of dollars, and despite the fact that private enterprise has no special claims to the ERP contracts. And what is more, the support of decadent or derelict industries and firms under the ERP will be anything but a service to the system of private enterprise. A genuine capitalist system in the highest 19th century tradition does not lean on the taxpayer, nor should it corrupt the ERP.

The ERP promises to become too much a businessman's organization. As a recent issue of *Fortune* pointed out, the ERP needs a team of highly talented businessmen, government servants, and other experts. The disgraceful manner in which Congressman Taber scrutinized the "business" qualifications of early appointees is not to be condoned. It is well to recognize the fact that businessmen often have narrow horizons; and they are only too inclined to confuse the interests of business and society. This is not in any sense meant as a reflection upon the two extremely able and public-spirited businessmen selected to run the ERP nor to suggest that businessmen have little to contribute to the ERP.

Seven: The communist opposition. A successful outcome of the ERP will depend upon how communist sabotage is met. Strikes and other forms of interference may hamper Western European progress; and communists are certain to capitalize on any United States "interference" with European policies. In providing an outlet for excess supply, the ERP postpones, at the very least, the inevitable crisis which, in the views of the communist, will destroy capitalism and thus allow communism to make further gains. Brazen Soviet foreign policy, which surely contributed greatly to the ERP and recent military expansion in this country, may then well prove to be a boomerang for the Russians. One of the unresolved questions at the present time is the extent to which economic aid will have to be supplemented by military aid. Much will depend upon how vigorous communist resistance to the ERP proves to be, as well as upon other facets of Russian policy.

Eight: Attitude of other nonparticipating countries. This country expects the other Americas to provide part of the funds and a large proportion of the supplies required under the ERP. In exchange for the latter, they are to receive dollars and to a small extent, IOU's. The burden of the ERP upon this country will depend upon the willingness of the other Americas to make supplies available at reasonable prices, and upon their acquiescence to a policy of deferring use of a substantial part of the dollars received under the ERP. In other words, they are being asked to provide goods under the ERP in exchange for credits or dollars; and the use of these dollars is to be subject to control by the United States.

HIGHLIGHTS

The contribution of the other Americas to the ERP is a matter of vital importance. Here is an area with a population of about 125 millions and a national income roughly estimated at $25 billion. Yet this area, with but one-eighth the national income of the United States, with an average standard of living far below ours, is being asked to export to the participating countries $17.8 billion in the four and a quarter years (compared to $21 billion for the United States), and $4.8 billion of this amount in the first fifteen months. The *excess* of exports of the other Americas to the ERP countries over imports from them is to be $3.1 billion for the first fifteen months, and an annual average of $2.1 billion over the four and a quarter years. For the United States, the latter figure is $2.8 billion. *Whereas the ERP goods to be provided by the United States (excess of exports over imports) is to be about 1⅓ per cent of the income of this country, the burden on the economy of the other Americas is to be about 8 to 9 per cent of their income, or about 6 to 7 times as much as for the United States.* For the first fifteen months the other Americas are to provide an export *surplus* to the ERP countries equal to about 10 per cent of their national income, whereas this country's excess of exports to these countries is to be less than 2 per cent of her income.[6] Insofar as the other Americas are allowed to validate their dollars on the American markets currently, the burden will be reduced.

American experts are undoubtedly optimistic in expecting such a heavy sacrifice from the other Americas. Latin American countries, in particular, will not accept a program which puts this additional strain upon their already highly inflationary economies. They already smart from the unavailability of goods in the war and early postwar years, from the decline in the goods value of dollars accumulated during the war, and from the accumulation of domestic purchasing power associated with the excess of exports over imports. Above all, they will not welcome a pro-

EUROPEAN RECOVERY PROGRAM

gram which will require of them increased exports and further expansion of domestic currency not offset by a corresponding rise of imports. According to an estimate by the Department of Commerce, all non-ERP countries in 1948 will receive only $6.7 billion of United States exports on the assumption of no ERP, and $8.2 billion with an ERP. (In 1947 they received $10 billion — annual rate for first half of 1947.) Against $2.5 billion of excess exports by the other Americas alone, *all* non-ERP countries are to receive only $1.5 billion additional of United States exports.[7] In summary, the American experts are likely to be disappointed in the degree to which the "goods" (and undoubtedly the credit) burden will be accepted by the other Americas.

RECOVERY?

Output and inflation. Europe recovered remarkably well in 1946 and though recovery stalled in 1947, the gains in 1946 and 1947 exceeded those of 1919 and 1920.[8] With the help of the ERP, European economic conditions should continue to improve in 1948 and later years. But much depends on political developments, and the effectiveness with which the ERP assistance is used.

A crucial factor will be monetary and fiscal policy. Open or suppressed inflation prevails everywhere. In 1947 prices continued to rise at an uncomfortable rate in France, Italy, and Greece, in particular, although in the latter part of 1947 there was some improvement; in Western Germany the currency was virtually worthless except in rationed markets. At the Paris meetings of the CEEC, several of the participating countries surveyed the monetary and fiscal positions of their countries and suggested measures to keep prices under control. The proposals varied greatly. France would bring the amount of extraordinary expenditure in line with receipts to be expected from national savings and external assistance, and cover other expenditures out of current budg-

HIGHLIGHTS

etary receipts. The British boasted of a budgetary surplus despite expenditures of £400 million on subsidies, which, however, tended to keep wages down. Sweden would not raise interest rates, but proposed other ways of excluding excessive investments. Greece was able to promise little in view of her very difficult exchange and budgetary problems.[9]

Early in 1948 the Secretary of the Treasury reported on the measures taken by the ERP countries. In December 1947, for example, the Austrian Government introduced a monetary purge and promised a balanced budget. Belgium proposed a budget for 1948 with a deficit indeed, but one without serious inflationary effects. France, late in 1947, introduced a program of tax reform and, despite price rises, substantial cuts in public expenditures. The 1948 budget calls for large rises in taxes, the elimination of subsidies, and other economies. Moreover, in 1947, the government blocked 40 per cent of the investments programmed under the Monnet Plan. Italy announced a courageous anti-inflationary program: a capital levy, forced investments of deposits in government securities, and a reduction of the public deficit from 586 billion lire in 1946–47 to 311 billion lire in 1947–48, the latter an amount corresponding to extraordinary expenditures to be financed by savings and foreign aid. Prices actually began to decline. The Netherlands was unable to eliminate its deficit, in part because of heavy overseas expenditures; but its inflationary effects would be neutralized to some extent by receipts from a capital levy, foreign aid, and other factors. With a moderate surplus for the fiscal year 1948, and savings and foreign aid exceeding extraordinary expenditures, inflation in the United Kingdom was not serious. Special measures were taken, however, to deal with the excess of disposable income and liquid assets in the hands of the public over the supply of consumption goods available.[10]

In the latter part of 1947 and early 1948, ERP countries appar-

EUROPEAN RECOVERY PROGRAM

ently made some progress in their fight against inflation. It would be an exaggeration to say that the disease is under control. And unless it is cured, the effects on output and foreign deficits will continue to be serious. With rising prices and exchanges not allowed to reflect the internal decline in value, the adverse effects of inflation are even greater than usual. Again, the reader should not interpret the last remark as an admission of the great importance of "unrealistic" exchange rates.

The Balance of Payments. Europe, and in particular Western Europe, may achieve an economic recovery with output rising substantially above prewar levels, and yet may continue as a pensioner of the United States. The most difficult problem confronting Europe is not the expansion of output but rather the elimination of the large deficit in her balance of payments.

Europe's deficit (exclusive of that of the USSR) on commodity trade was $1.5 billion in 1938; and the Economic Commission for Europe puts the prewar deficit at $2 billion.[11] In 1947, the trade deficit had risen to close to $7 billion. In 1948 European nations are confronted with the problem of closing a gap of $2 billion in their combined overseas trade accounts, or about $3.3 billion on the basis of 1947 trade reduced to 1938 prices. The explanation of the increased deficit (*on current account*) of $7.5 billion in 1947 over 1938 is first and foremost the rise in prices of imports ($3.6 billion); second, the net change in income from investments and service receipts ($2.7 billion); and third, the net change associated with a rise in imports and a decline in exports ($1.2 billion).[12]

These factors suggest the cures for the European deficit. A reduction in prices of imports would be especially helpful for an area that imports much more than it exports. United States leadership in anti-inflationary policies is especially important here, since this country accounted for about $6 billion, or 30 per cent of Europe's imports in 1947, and 45 per cent of Europe's

[20]

HIGHLIGHTS

overseas imports. Insofar as a reduction in prices would bring economic depression, however, the gains would be substantially offset by reduced exports and lower export prices for Europe.[13]

Very little can be done about the loss of $2.7 billion on invisible account. (For ERP countries the corresponding figure is $2.1 billion.) Perhaps the most serious economic distortion associated with the war is in the loss of foreign investments and earnings on services (part of the latter will be recouped), which made possible Europe's large excess of imports before the war. As exports and imports gradually attain a balance, the losses resulting from higher priced imports will be recouped; but not those associated with the major part of the losses on invisible account.

Obviously the ultimate solution lies in a rise of exports or (and) a reduction of imports. As the Economic Commission for Europe expresses it: "In relation to the 1947 levels of trade (expressed in 1938 prices) the gap is about $3.3 billion and would involve a 114 per cent increase in exports or a 53 per cent contraction in imports." [14]

Since Europe's prewar imports were mainly foods and raw materials, it is not possible to reduce imports substantially below the prewar levels; and in fact Europe will need three to four hundred millions of dollars of additional imports of these products. The temporary bulge in imports for relief and reconstruction may indeed be removed within a few years. The Economic Commission for Europe concludes that main reliance will have to be put in an expansion of production of about $2 billion in heavy industries, the major proportion to be exported and part to provide substitutes for products previously imported. Exports of heavy products will then have to rise by 200 per cent.[15]

This summary fails to touch upon some of the most difficult problems. For example, whereas before the war the United States had an import surplus with non-European countries, in 1947 these countries had an adverse balance with the United

EUROPEAN RECOVERY PROGRAM

States of $4.5 billion; and Europe not only cannot expect these countries to pay part of her debt to the United States as before the war, but, in fact, Europe is covering part of the deficits of overseas countries vis-à-vis the United States. Moreover, in the four and a quarter years under the ERP, the executive branch estimates that the international accounts of ERP countries with other (that is, non-American) participating countries will be roughly in balance. ERP countries will not then be able to pay for the excess of imports from the Americas with cash due from the other nonparticipating countries. In view of the latter's current adverse balance with the United States, it is most unlikely that even should Europe obtain a credit balance with the other nonparticipating countries over the next four years, that they in turn would have dollars available to be used by Europe.[16] (We should not leave out of account the vast blocked sterling balances belonging to overseas countries; for before Europe will be able to obtain dollars from overseas countries, exclusive of help under the ERP, Europe may have to pay back ten to fifteen billion dollars of short-term debt in blocked balances.)

In 1947 Europe's adverse balance of trade with the United States was 70 per cent of the total deficit.[17] It is especially important that measures be taken to reduce this adverse balance. But rise of European exports, particularly manufactured goods, to the United States is not likely to be large; and gains of exports in other markets under present bilateral trading, will not yield corresponding supplies of dollars. Unless great advances are made towards multilateralism, the expansion of exports will not solve the European-United States balance-of-payments problem. Even under rather liberal trade policies in this country, the required expansion of our imports yielding adequate supplies of dollars will probably not be forthcoming.

On this score, it should be noted that the executive branch estimated exports from ERP countries to the United States at

HIGHLIGHTS

$1.80 billion in 1948–49, and $2.76 billion in 1951–52. This is not a large rise in view of the low state of European exports; and it is low in view of the large deficits vis-à-vis the United States. According to the same estimates, over these years exports to ERP countries from the United States are to decline only from $5.6 billion to $4.6 billion. Indeed, the estimated deficit in the balance of payments for ERP countries is to fall from $7.5 billion in 1948–49 to $2.5 billion (average of range) in fiscal 1952.[18] But the gains to the United States will be much smaller than the over-all improvement of $5 billion, should the trade deficit of ERP countries with this country be reduced by only $2 billion — unless a multilateral system is once more introduced. Gains of Europe with other countries will not yield corresponding supplies of dollars to cover deficits with the United States. That countries in an especially weak position — for example, the United Kingdom which accounts for the major part of Europe's losses on invisible account — press aggressively for more exports and cut imports from Europe drastically, should further increase the difficulties of restoring multilateral trade.

We may conclude that the most perplexing problem will be the restoration of Europe's balance of payments to a position of equilibrium. Even if European output rises substantially above prewar levels, if recovery elsewhere speeds ahead, if inflation is controlled, if United States commercial policy continues its liberal trends, and if required adjustments in exchange rates are made, — even then, Europe is not likely to succeed in balancing her international accounts within four years. But if these favoring developments do not take place, the current deficits will rise above anticipated levels, and the attainment of equilibrium will be further postponed.

In one respect, the adjustment should seem easy. Western Europe may well increase her national income by $20 billion from 1947 to 1951 on top of an increase of almost the same

EUROPEAN RECOVERY PROGRAM

amount from 1945 to 1947. Surely an improvement in the balance of payments by about $4 billion ($2 billion in 1938 prices), should not prove to be an impossible hurdle. The sacrifices required would be 20 per cent of the gains over four years, or 10 per cent of those over six years and about 4 per cent of the national income. With the aid of state control of resources, the necessary adjustments may be made more easily than under the "automatic" response of interwar capitalism. But can we be sure of the rise in income, of the control of inflation, of willingness to import on the part of the United States and others and, above all, convertibility of currencies?

IN SUMMARY

The objective in this opening chapter has been to emphasize some vital aspects of the problems confronting the ECA. Properly administered and under favorable political conditions, the ERP may serve as a catalyst, raising Europe's incomes by several times the United States investment. But to achieve this result the ERP should not become a subsidy program for American business and farmers seeking new markets, and the United States Government should support domestic policies (for example, antiinflation control) without which the ERP is doomed to failure. Furthermore, in concentrating on the maximum gains over four years, the government may be greatly increasing the cost of restoring equilibrium conditions in Europe. The responsibilities and sacrifices demanded of this country are greater than have so far been revealed; and in part they are obscured by the excessive paper burden put on the other Americas. Above all, success depends upon the policies of Europe, upon the skill with which we use the ERP to suggest to Europe judicious policies with resulting expansion of output, and, in particular, upon the courage with which Europe confronts its inflationary and fiscal problems. *Even if the desired rise of output is achieved, however, there will*

HIGHLIGHTS

remain serious obstacles to wiping out the major part of the deficit in the balance of payments, and in particular with the United States. Here is the most perplexing problem of all, and it may well not be substantially solved in four or five years, even if the ERP is favored by rising productivity and output and correct fiscal and monetary policies. The next two chapters contain a further elaboration of major issues.

PART ONE
MAJOR ECONOMIC AND POLITICAL ISSUES

Introduction

Chapter 1 deals briefly with major issues generally discussed more fully in Part II. It is not, however, merely an introductory or summary chapter. The busy reader might be content with an examination of this chapter as a substitute — though inadequate — for Part II; but he should not skip it merely because he intends to read Part II. It contains many facts and much important analysis not to be found in later chapters. As Chapter 1 serves as an introduction to Part II, Chapter 2 is preliminary to the whole volume. This volume is concerned primarily with the economic issues; but obviously the ERP is a program for political action and, therefore, a book on the ERP without consideration of political issues would be inadequate. Several important political issues are discussed in Chapter 2. I have also considered the problem of East-West trade in the second chapter though many might consider this more of an economic than a political issue.

1. Economic Crisis in Europe

PASSAGE OF THE FOREIGN ASSISTANCE ACT OF 1948

From June 5, 1947, the day of Secretary Marshall's Harvard address on European economic recovery, to April 3, 1948, the day the Foreign Assistance Act was approved by the President, the issue of European recovery, and this country's contribution to it, had become the most important single political and economic question facing the United States; and it promises to retain a prominent position for years to come.

On the latter day, this country embarked on a program which was to cost more than $5 billion for one year beginning in April 1948; and the government proposed an ERP for four and one-fourth years, but subject to authorizations of subsequent Congresses.[1] Congress appropriated slightly less than $5 billion.

THE DRAIN OVER THE YEARS

In many respects the ERP, expected to cost fifteen to twenty-five billion dollars, is not a complete break with the past; over the years 1914 to early 1948, this country poured around $100 billion of goods and services largely into Europe, for which we received in return, insofar as a *quid pro quo* was offered, IOU's largely of dubious value, and gold. Of approximately $80 billion given away or advanced, little will ever be received in return; and surely few would put any high value upon the goods which we are likely to receive in return for the $20 billion of gold imported. As large as $100 billion seems, it amounted only to about 4 per cent of the total United States income in this period of thirty-three years; and to about 40 per cent of the dollars required to pay for our exports of commodities and services.[2]

EUROPEAN RECOVERY PROGRAM

CATALYST OR RANSOM?

Demands likely to be made upon our economy under the ERP are not large when compared with the 4 per cent of our national income exacted since 1913; for the ERP should not require more than 2 or 3 per cent at a much higher level of income — and the higher the income, the less the sacrifice imposed by the loss of a given percentage of income. What is more important is the significance of the continued demands. Is the egalitarian principle to be stretched across national frontiers? Are the fifteen to twenty-five billion dollars required under the ERP to be another wedge in the share-the-wealth-and-income campaign? The boy who has all the marbles is not very popular. A country that seems to have nine times as much income per capita as the rest of the world is fair game. In our anxiety to stop the spread of communism, we find ourselves in a vulnerable position. *It is important that the ERP become a catalyst for European recovery, not a ransom to be paid to blackmailers who threaten us with communism.*

RECOVERY AND INDUSTRIAL OUTPUT, 1945-46

In many respects Europe's recovery has been very satisfactory. By the last quarter of 1946, fifteen countries, including the three Western Zones of Germany, had increased their output to 83 per cent of the 1938 level; and exclusive of Germany, to 98 per cent. (The countries included were the ten most important ERP countries and Bulgaria, Czechoslavakia, Finland, the three Western Zones of Germany, and Poland; and these accounted for 77 per cent of European industrial output.) In comparison with the recovery after World War I, the record was surprisingly good. As the Economic Commission for Europe observes:

> Nevertheless, the general level of industrial production reached the same relation to the prewar figures in the year 1946 as in 1920, while

the performance in the first three quarters of 1947 has definitely exceeded that of any postwar year up to and including 1923.[3]

In view of the substantial gains achieved, the reader may wonder about the 1947 crisis. He may find evidence of crisis conditions in indexes other than those for industrial output. But even these output figures are not reassuring, first because a 10 per cent rise in population should be considered, and second because the rise definitely flattened out in 1947. Although the output for the fifteen countries excluding Germany from the first to the last quarter of 1946 had increased by 23 per cent, the gain in the first three quarters of 1947 was but 1 per cent. Recovery had definitely reached dead center.[4]

RECOVERY AND NATIONAL OUTPUT

Income is a more comprehensive index of economic well-being than industrial output because it includes agricultural output, private services, and, to some extent, government services. In testifying on behalf of the executive branch of the United States Government, Ambassador Lewis Douglas estimated the national income (dollars of constant purchasing power) of the sixteen participating countries as follows:[5]

In Billions of Dollars

1940	78
1945	55
1947	69

These estimates of national income are to be taken with a grain of salt. As is suggested in Chapter 3, there are serious difficulties in comparing income over time or space. Table 1 suggests that income reduced to 1938 currency values may yield surprising results. (The problem of converting European incomes into dollar values will be discussed later.) This table is based on informa-

EUROPEAN RECOVERY PROGRAM

tion kindly supplied by the Statistical Office of the United Nations. The income estimates in domestic currencies are their contribution; and the cost of living figures by which they are adjusted to 1938 values are obtained from their bulletins. (Calculations are mine.) According to this table, incomes in the United Kingdom rose by about 40 per cent more than prices. Yet few would maintain that British real income in 1947 was even 25 per cent above that of 1938, nor that real income in Denmark rose by an amount approaching 40 per cent. The explanation of this paradox lies largely in the increased proportion of money income in 1946–47 relative to prewar income that does not represent real income: a much larger part of income is not spendable. Furthermore, the rise in the cost of living under controlled conditions is not an ideal variable for deflating the national income.

TABLE 1
INCOME AND COST OF LIVING, VARIOUS COUNTRIES, 1946 AND 1947
($1938 = 100$)

	National Income	Cost of Living
Belgium (1946)	292	318
Denmark (1946)	205	159
France (1947)	934	1040 *
Netherlands (1946)	160	192
Norway (1947)	189	161
Sweden (1947)	189	158
United Kingdom (1947)	187	132

Source: U.N., *Monthly Bulletin of Statistics*, February 1948, pp. 151–159, and letter to the author from Department of Economic Affairs, United Nations, April 23, 1948. (Calculations mine.)
* Foods only.

John J. McCloy, head of the International Bank, put the income in 1946 of the sixteen ERP countries and Western Germany ($11 billion) at $99 billion. These countries, with a population

CRISIS IN EUROPE

of 260 million, or close to twice the United States population, had a total income of but 46 per cent that of the United States. Standard of living, as indicated by income per capita minus expenditures on investments, was roughly four times as high in this country as in the CEEC countries. In Chapter 3, I suggest that the ratio had been 2 to 1 before the war. Switzerland's standard of living of $710 per capita was a maximum in Europe; Greece's, of $100, a minimum. (In the United States, it was $1390.) [6]

European income, especially when expressed in dollars, is suspect. Yet, aside from the imperfect statistical summaries, there are many reasons for suspecting a decline of national income. We shall discuss the problem in terms of income but subject to the reservations stated.

Income in Europe did not rise as much as industrial output. Income for the sixteen countries in 1947, according to the executive branch estimate, was 12 per cent below the prewar amount; but industrial output had rebounded virtually to the prewar level. The first, and most important, explanation of the relatively small recovery of income is the retarded rate of recovery in agriculture, inclusive of the crop failures in 1947. In a comprehensive survey of European agricultural production (exclusive of the USSR), the Economic Commission for Europe estimated output in 1945–46 at 63 per cent of that before the war, and in 1946–47 at 75 per cent. Agricultural output, relative to industrial output, was far below the prewar ratio. Production of bread grains in 1946–47 was only 75 per cent of that from 1934 to 1938; coarse grains, 73 per cent; fats, 63 per cent; meat, 61 per cent. Whereas the CEEC had estimated the output of wheat in 1946–47 for the sixteen countries and Western Germany at 28.4 million tons and in 1947–48 at 21.2 million tons, Secretary of Agriculture estimates were 31.0 and 23.9 million tons, respectively. [7]

EUROPEAN RECOVERY PROGRAM

INCOME AND DISINVESTMENT ABROAD

In analyzing income totals, we should take into account the large net disinvestment abroad, *here defined as sale of foreign assets or (and) use of proceeds of foreign loans.* Ordinarily amounts thus disinvested are deducted from national income. *In other words, the measure of distress should be not the decline in national income, but rather reductions in the total of national income minus resources made available from sale of assets and borrowing abroad.* In fact, grants and gifts which technically should not be considered as part of disinvestment, are also appropriate additions to national income for the purpose of measuring economic well-being.

In this connection let us consider, first, an example from the British, and then European, experience. Disinvestment in the United Kingdom accounted for £380, £675, and £250 million, respectively, in 1946, 1947, and 1948 (estimated). Total resources available for home use were then 4, 8, and 3 per cent in excess of the national income.[8]

Relevant to this discussion are the $15.6 billion made available by this country in 1946 and 1947 to foreign countries in the form of credits and grants, of which the ERP countries received the major part.[9] For example, in the two and a half years ending December 31, 1947, they obtained loans and property credits of $7.7 billion and grants of $4.0 billion, and by December 31, 1947, had utilized almost $10 billion of the total. In addition, in the two years ending December 31, 1947, their gold reserves had been reduced from $5.7 billion to $3.7 billion and their banking funds in this country from $2.1 billion to $1.5 billion.[10]

This survey suggests the following: (1) *Over a period of two and a half years the ERP countries obtained annually about $5 billion, or roughly 5 to 7 per cent of their income in resources not generally included in their income figures. To this extent, the*

CRISIS IN EUROPE

income figures understate the flow of goods and services made available. (2) *These sixteen European countries and Germany, however, suffered an absolute deterioration in their economic position, and, a fortiori, a relative decline vis-à-vis this country.*

Per capita income of the ERP countries seems to be substantially less than that before the war, even when allowance is made for the influx of goods not technically included in income. Ambassador Lewis Douglas, representing the executive branch, put the decline in total income from 1940 to 1947 at 12 per cent, and about 20 per cent on a per capita basis. My analysis on pp. 86–91 yields similar conclusions.

INVESTMENT: FRENCH AND BRITISH EXPERIENCE

Income statistics may, however, be misleading: it is imperative to consider the use to which income is put. Income yields less in current consumption insofar as an increased part goes to government and investment. It is now a commonplace that in the early postwar period European countries, impressed by Russian planning and anxious to recoup losses resulting from the war, embarked on overambitious investment programs. The Monnet Plan in France, for example, *called for* investments in excess of 20 per cent of the national income. Whereas investments were but 14 per cent of consumption in 1938 prices, they *attained* 19½ per cent in 1946. The basic inflationary pressure arises from the shortage of savings relative to investment. In order to exclude inflation, savings should equal investment, that is, equal the sum of (1) government deficit and (2) capital formation at home, minus (3) net imports. Should savings equal less than (1) + (2) − (3), then spending is financed out of created or newly activated money, with inflationary effects. In 1946 the required ratio of savings to consumption in current prices was 33 per cent, an amount far in excess of actual savings. Again, in *current* francs, government expenditure in 1946 was eight times as high as in 1938; but consumption was only five times the 1938 amount.[11] According to the International Bank, the $4.665 billion requested in the CEEC report for equipment would correspond to an investment program of $77 billion over the four years, or 17 per cent of the income of the CEEC countries. This was too much and explains why the Bank cut these requirements by 30 per cent and others by only 6 per cent. Again, in reply to a question from the Senate Committee, the Secretary of the Treasury showed that several European countries were investing more than before the war. Table 2 shows net foreign investments, not to be confused with gross figures discussed above.

Table 3 shows that British consumption was sacrificed to the requirements of investment programs and government needs. Had it not been for the external disinvestment, the decline of consumption would have been greater. (In three other countries, Poland, Hungary, and Czechoslovakia, plans required investment of 20 per cent [gross], 10 per cent [net], and 21 per cent [gross], respectively.) [12]

United Kingdom: Current Expenditures by Percentage

	1938	1947
Personal	72	65
Government	15	22
Gross capital formation at home	14	20
External disinvestment	-1	-7

BRITISH ECONOMISTS ON EXCESSIVE INVESTMENT

Investments in Europe are altogether too large; and investment *programs* even larger; there is scarcely a dissent to that position. Harrod, Hicks, Henderson, Robbins, and Robertson — surely a galaxy of British economists — all agree that investments are excessive. Particularly in 1946–47, the investment industries advanced much more rapidly than others. By investment industries we mean those which produce capital goods rather than goods immediately available for consumers — for example, tools,

TABLE 2

ESTIMATED PER CENT RATIO OF NET INVESTMENT TO NET NATIONAL INCOME (INCLUSIVE OF NET FOREIGN AID)*

	1938	1946	1947	1948
France	4.5	6.0	9.0	8.0–9.0
United Kingdom	6.8	8.5	10.0	10.0
Netherlands	12.0	11.4	12.0	18.1

ERP: Sen. Hear., pp. 418, 1006–1007.

TABLE 3

UNITED KINGDOM: USE OF THE NATIONAL INCOME, 1938, 1947, 1948

	1938 Percentage	1947 * Provisional Percentage	1948 Estimated Percentage
Current Expenditure			
Personal consumption	78	70	69
Government current expenditure	16	24	22
Addition to Assets			
Net capital formation	7	14	12
Less: External disinvestment	−1	−8	−3
National Income	100	100	100

Source: *Economic Survey for 1948*, p. 46.
* The United Nations presents figures for 1938, 1945, and 1946. They allocate *total resources at home*, not national income, thus including *gross* capital formation. In 1946, personal consumption accounted for but 60 per cent of total resources (71 per cent in 1938); government current expenditure, 25 per cent (14 per cent in 1938); and gross capital formation, 14 per cent (15 per cent in 1938). Cf. *Survey of Current Inflationary and Deflationary Tendencies*, p. 25. Cf., also, *National Income and Expenditure of the United Kingdom* (1947) p. 6:

Change in Current Expenditures by Percentage

	1938 to 1947
Personal	−7
Government	+7
Gross capital formation at home	+6
External disinvestment	−6

EUROPEAN RECOVERY PROGRAM

bricks, most chemicals. Output in non-investment industries for ten European countries rose by 19 per cent from the first to the last quarter of 1946 as compared with a 32 per cent increase in the production of important investment goods. In the first three quarters of 1947, there was a slight decline for the former and a further rise of the latter: from 74 per cent of the 1938 output in the first quarter of 1946, major investment-goods industries expanded to 104 per cent by the third quarter of 1947.[13]

With European countries confronted with yawning deficits in their balance of payments, the ambitious investment programs became the target of critics of socialist economic policies. Harrod, for example, pointed out that a rise of British investments by £400 million in 1947 largely explained the deficit in the balance of payments. (Using a method subject to a large margin of error, the British Government estimated gross capital formation at £747, £1221, and £1944 million in 1945, 1946, and 1947, respectively.) Harrod would limit investments to the amounts available from savings plus resources obtained from abroad; and he would cut the annual outlay on investment by £350 million and public expenditures on men and materials by £150 million, or, if these goals were not achieved, he proposed an increase in taxes by an amount equal to the excess of investment over the sum of savings and advances from abroad. Actually in the reversal of investment policy of October 1947, the government proposed to cut the programmed investment for 1948 from £1600 million to £1420 million.[14]

Obviously, *excessive* investment is inflationary because the rise of income associated with investment is not matched by the required increase in the output of consumption goods or, to put it in another way, savings are not equal to investment. Because of the domestic inflationary effects and because of the adverse effects upon the balance of payments, the President's Committee on Foreign Aid urged a radical pruning of European programs. The

CRISIS IN EUROPE

British economist Henderson acknowledged the inflationary effects; but stressing the large backlog of demand he would program for investments beyond the amount of savings; and acknowledging the inevitable inflationary pressures, he would take appropriate action (for example, on the control front?).[15] In other words, though he was prepared to admit the excess of investments, in his view the inflationary test was not the exclusive one. Elsewhere I also point out that in view of the large backlog of required investment resulting from years of disinvestment, the British program was not so injudicious as many economists suggest.[16]

In the next few pages, I comment on the interesting views of British economists on excess investments. Since this is a crucial problem, both because of its relation to inflation and the deficits in the balance of payments, this seems an appropriate place to digress on this vital problem.

In general, the economists of Britain proposed strong medicine and particularly a scaling down of investment outlays. For Robertson, however, the way out was a reduction of communal consumption, a whittling down of ambitious programs, and a rise of taxes.[17] In his view, subsidized consumption is not palatable when a country faces large sacrifices in order to right the balance of payments and recondition plant.

Hicks, Robbins, and Harrod all emphasize the need of relying more on the market mechanism. They seem to be impressed by the disappearance of working capital, which they associate with the absence of price incentives and market governors. Had prices been allowed to rise, dealers would have protected their stocks, and allocation of resources would have improved. Under price control and excess of money, the pressure to cut into reserves of stocks becomes irresistible; and even a rationing or allocation system does not offer adequate protection.[18] In order to replenish working stocks and to improve the distribution of resources,

EUROPEAN RECOVERY PROGRAM

British economists seem disposed to rely increasingly on market incentives, but they are not in complete accord how far or how fast they would move. Robbins, for example, suggests gradual decontrolling and raising of prices; but he sees little advantage in a rise in the rate of interest. Nor does Harrod, faithful to his Keynesian economics, support higher interest rates.[19] Whatever the approach, the verdict generally is a deflation of investment programs.

Investment is not merely a question of amount; it is also a problem of distribution. Inadequate inventories and working capital are a threat to the smooth functioning of any economy. Champernowne pointed out that in Great Britain the number of weeks' stock at consumption rate of current year had declined as shown in Table 4.

TABLE 4

DECLINE OF NUMBER OF WEEKS' STOCK AT CONSUMPTION RATE OF CURRENT YEAR: GREAT BRITAIN

End of Year	Coal	Soft Wood	Hard Wood	Steel	Refined Lead
1942	5.7	24	16	8.9	18.1
1946	2.9	10	12	4.4	5.8

Source: *Oxford University Institute of Statistics Bulletin*, March-April 1947.

American experts stressed the need of (1) concentrating capital formation on crucial industries — for example, coal and food; (2) favoring investments that yielded consumption goods quickly — working capital, not vast programs for expanding iron and steel or electricity capacity; (3) making the most effective use of outlays on fixed capital — improving existing plants, not building new ones. Harrod also has much to say on these issues. To him nothing could be more grotesque than to electrify the Manchester-Sheffield line; and he was not assuaged by the presumed saving of 100,000 tons of coal a year. For it takes only 382 men to pro-

CRISIS IN EUROPE

duce 100,000 tons of coal a year; but this plan would require at least 12,000 man-years of labor spread over four years.[20]

In summary, the side-line economists may be right. On the assumption of full employment, the more that is made available for investment without accompanying reductions in resources at the disposal of government and consumers, the greater the strain on prices, and on the balance of payments. American commentators, with a vested interest to moderate demands on our economy, also view the vast capital programs as a means of bleeding the American economy. In part, imports are used to support the capital program; and in part the latter robs the export markets. Furthermore, higher prices discourage exports and stimulate imports.

Yet the problem may be oversimplified. A capital program which, after six years of heavy disinvestment, accounts for but 10 per cent of Europe's income, say, instead of 20 per cent, will fail to bring plant and housing back to prewar standards for many years and a fortiori fail to improve the capital plant. The result may well be that output will not rise rapidly enough or costs be brought down quickly enough to make Europe substantially less dependent on this country in 1952 than in 1948. The price of a truncated capital program may well be a series of Marshall plans.

INFLATION: SUPPRESSED AND OPEN

Few would deny that there is little chance of a long-lived recovery in Europe unless inflation is checked. Section 115 (a) of the Foreign Assistance Act of 1948 recognizes this fact when it proposes for inclusion, when applicable, in agreements with the ERP countries the following:

> ... taking financial and monetary measures necessary to stabilize its currency, establish or maintain a valid rate of exchange, to balance its governmental budget as soon as practicable, and generally to restore or maintain confidence in its monetary system.

EUROPEAN RECOVERY PROGRAM

In discussing the problem of excessive investment, we touched upon the European inflationary problem. The reader will find further discussion of the problem in Chapter 11. Here it will suffice to run over the main facts.

Europe is divided into two camps, though the boundaries are not clearly marked, namely, countries with *open* inflation and those with *suppressed* inflation. Typical of the former were the hyper-inflation experiences of Hungary and Greece, and the current experiences of Italy where retail prices in May 1947 were about forty-nine times those of 1938, and France, where retail prices in December 1947 were about nine times those of 1938. When inflation is overt, the value of the currency beyond a certain point tends to fall more proportionately than the rise in its amount, with the result that the *real* value of the total circulation tends to fall. For example, in late 1947 the real value of Italian currency outstanding was but 62 per cent of its prewar value, and that of Greek currency outstanding but 48 per cent.

In countries with large amounts of liquid assets, but relatively effective price and other controls, inflation is reflected in the large volume of money relative to prices; and the real value of the outstanding currency tends to rise. In Norway, for example, the real value late in 1947 was 263 per cent of the prewar level; and in the United Kingdom, 184. In countries with open inflation, the incentive to produce may be substantially dulled for various reasons; in those with suppressed inflation, there is a disposition to malinger since additional earnings yield relatively small increments of goods. The disease in the countries suffering large doses of open inflation is mal-allocation of resources, and especially maldistribution.[21]

Open inflation brings about a maldistribution of income which is likely to have serious effects. Even the governments in Italy and France attempt to protect their citizens against the full effects of inflation by providing minimum rations at low prices; and the workers try to raise their wages *pari passu* with rising prices. Yet in Paris, real wage rates were 81 (October 1938 = 100) in October 1945 and 56 in October 1946.[22]

Compare France with another country which has been much more successful in suppressing inflation. Late in 1947 British weekly earnings in manufacturing were 173 (September 1939 = 100) and the cost of living 135 (1937 = 100). This comparison of earnings and the cost of living suggests that British workers have improved their position. Another study yields the interesting result that income of lower-income groups *after* taxes (wages, pay and allowances of the armed forces, and social security benefits and other transfer incomes) rose by 95 per cent from 1938 to 1946, whereas the corresponding income after taxes of middle and upper-income groups increased by but 31 per cent. Clearly those in low-income classes improved their relative position, whether the criterion is the rise of wages relative to that of the cost of living, or their absolute or relative rise of income after taxes. Recent British figures (for 1938 to 1947) are not nearly so clear on the redistribution effected. Wages *after* taxes rose from 39 to 44 per cent of private income; salaries declined from 24 to 20 per cent, and property income and profits from 37 to 36 per cent. (Note, however, that military pay is left out.) The protection offered by an effective rationing and price control system further improved the relative position of low-income groups. With consumption for the nation roughly at the prewar standard (though substantially less, if allowance is made for the unavailability of desired goods), we conclude that the middle and high income classes suffered a large deterioration in their standard of living. Whether this redistribution of real income favoring the workers and other low-income groups against the others contributed more to production than the growing excess of income over goods wanted and obtainable contributed to a decline is not an easy question to answer.[23]

EUROPEAN RECOVERY PROGRAM

SOME ADVERSE EFFECTS OF INFLATION ON GOVERNMENT AND DISTRIBUTION

Several other aspects of the inflation problem should be noted. First, the fiscal aspect. An unbalanced budget contributes to the inflation; but with receipts lagging behind the rise in prices, the advance of prices in turn ultimately reduces the resources made available to the government. In prewar currency values, the expenditures of four out of eleven European governments in 1947-48 were below prewar expenditures: Austria (63), France (98), Italy (60), and Poland (90). Yet government plays an increased role in the life of the community; and deficits in many cases were of the order of 40 to 60 per cent of expenditures.[24] Inflation contributes towards the weakening of governments in a period when their responsibilities are on the increase; and inadequate resources are likely to have serious political consequences.

Second, inflation tends to bring about a maldistribution of food between country and city. Where, as in the Netherlands and Denmark, food prices are held down and inflation is suppressed, the ratio of agricultural to industrial prices tends to fall; and farmers withhold supplies from the city. Where, as in Italy and France, large free markets are allowed to function, the prices of agricultural commodities rise relative to those of factory products, and city dwellers suffer losses in the reduced purchasing power of their products. Price control and rationing covering a limited area, both in commodities selected and proportion of output subject to control, tend to release surplus purchasing power, which is then shunted to agricultural markets, with favorable effects on farm prices.[25]

INFLATION AND LOSS OF COMPETITIVE POSITION

Third, the effects on international trade require further consideration. With exchanges not free to move, the competitive position of countries suffering from open inflation deteriorates;

CRISIS IN EUROPE

for world prices tend to rise as exchanges do not reflect the increase of prices relative to foreign prices. With exchanges free to move, it may be added, the effect might be the maintenance of the competitive position, but a lowering of the terms of trade: poor countries would give too much for imports. In countries with suppressed inflation, the excess of purchasing power, relative to goods at controlled prices, gravitates towards markets where money can be used with relative freedom; and goods available for export decline and, insofar as controls permit, imports rise.

In view of what has been said above, the more rapid rise of prices in European countries relative to prices in the United States *adjusted for exchange movements* is to be expected. In all but five of eighteen European countries, prices in the third quarter of 1947 had risen more than United States prices; in ten out of fourteen countries, *export* prices had risen more than those in the United States. Nevertheless, it might be added, the ratio of European exports (excluding Western Germany) relative to industrial output rose from 61 in the first quarter of 1946 to 86 in the third quarter.[26] That is to say, exports rose more rapidly than industrial output. Large as this rise was, it was not adequate, especially when allowance is made for the low level of exports in early 1946, and the tendency to export excessively to sheltered European markets, yielding relatively small supplies of dollars.

INFLATION: SUMMARY

In short, inflation is a barrier to European recovery, for it brings maldistribution of income; distortions in the economic system, inclusive of mal-allocations; impairs the strength of government; reduces the incentive to produce; and aggravates the deficit in the balance of payments.

EUROPEAN RECOVERY PROGRAM

INTERNATIONAL ECONOMIC ASPECTS

Excessive investment, budgetary deficits, and the like bring inflation; and, as has been noted, the inflation is accompanied by a rising deficit in the balance of payments. In this section we shall discuss briefly aspects of the problem of the international economic position of Europe, and particularly of Western Europe, many of which are discussed more fully in Chapters 4, 5, and 6.

a. *Dollar Scarcity*

Dollar scarcity is the theme of Chapter 4, an important problem, though Harrod and Haberler are inclined to ridicule the concept and to deny its significance.[27] In this introductory chapter the discussion is necessarily brief. As Harrod puts it:

> ... The multilateral system being a more economical method of housekeeping recently urged by father, they say that "the multilateral system will never work so long as there is a dollar famine." They propound this doctrine with all seriousness, as though the dollar famine were some new kind of disease or some new kind of profound and technical disorder that was due to certain subtle workings of our trading or banking system.

In Chapter 4, the author, unlike Harrod, succumbs to the prevailing fad of dollar scarcity.[28] The argument there presented is that the world has been troubled by a scarcity of dollars for more than a generation. Even in the interwar period, dollar scarcity persisted. Prices did not fall adequately in countries losing gold and dollars, nor rise in the others adequately to stop the one-way flow, as is required under the mechanisms of the capitalist system. Cost and price rigidities in countries short of dollars; inadequate demand response, particularly in the United States and France, countries receiving disproportionate supplies of gold, steady relative gains in technology in this country, with attendant gains in its competitive position — all of these are part of the matrix of dollar shortage in the inter-war period. *On balance*, capital movements from the creditor countries were small relative to the favorable balance on current account and the net inflow of gold.[29]

Dollar famine in World War II and after reflects war, production crisis abroad, and many of the other distortions following a great war. Failure of the capitalist mechanism to work is part of the difficulty; but even socialist governments, which might favor export industries directly and discourage imports through exchange restrictions, and which might, in general, through appropriate price and allocation measures, improve the balance of trade, seem unable or unwilling to solve the dollar problem.

Without a doubt, both Harrod and Haberler can, with some justification, point to the tendency of European countries to live beyond their means; and, therefore, they properly emphasize the peculiarly political aspects of the problem. Capitalist countries were not able to solve this problem under relatively favorable conditions in the interwar period. May we not be expecting too much of socialist governments, many of them surviving on a day-to-day basis, should we ask of them the imposition of large sacrifices needed to eliminate the dollar shortage over the next few years? Indeed, the USSR, by scrutinizing imports and largely balancing them with exports inclusive of gold shipments, has substantially solved the dollar problem. And under the pressure of the late summer crisis of 1947, Mr. Cripps proposed a somewhat similar balancing of accounts; but the United States Government, fearful of the effects upon our economy, and for other reasons, instead persisted in its offer of the Marshall Plan. Indeed, a strong socialist government might solve this problem, but the difficulty is that the cure might be worse than the disease. Hence our disposition is to rely upon gradual measures which might help Europe raise her output and reduce her foreign deficit.

b. *Unrealistic Exchange Rates*

Unrealistic exchange rates are frequently suggested as the explanation of the imbalance of Europe's accounts. In the declaration of policy, the Foreign Assistance Act of 1948 asks for "all possible steps to establish and maintain equitable rates of exchange." And after a discussion of overvalued currencies, Hazlitt concludes that "it is hardly surprising, in the face of such regulations, that in most European countries there is a *chronic* excess of imports over exports."[30]

Indeed, as we observed earlier, European currencies are overvalued. But the crucial issue is not that but rather how important this overvaluation is as a factor in disequilibrating the balance of payments. The conclusion in Chapter 5 is that it is not of first-rate importance. In part this is so because of the inelasticity of supplies for export markets, and in particular for dollar markets; when resources in large amounts are not available to service export markets, then the offer of goods at lower prices may not yield more dollars, and may well yield less. In part, the overvaluation is of less than usual importance because both exports and imports are largely subject to direct controls. In economies sensitive to small fluctuations of supply and demand, governments tend to rely less on unpredictable price movements (for example, exchange rates), and more on direct controls. By checking imports and diverting resources to export markets in quantities to yield the largest supply of dollars, given the scanty resources available, governments can neutralize the adverse effects of overvalued currencies. As we shall see in Chapter 5, there are other reasons for preferring overvalued currencies.

One additional point requires emphasis here. Many (for example, the CEEC) count on an improvement in the terms of trade as a means of reducing the adverse balance of payments of Europe. But if the currencies are overvalued, then what is required ultimately is a deterioration in the terms of trade. Europe will have to give more for a given quantity of imports; and therefore, insofar as overvaluation is corrected, so far will Europe's terms of trade deteriorate rather than improve. *The world cannot count on an improvement for Europe resulting both from an improvement in the terms of trade and the correction of overvaluation.*

c. *Terms of Trade and Import Prices*

This is an opportune point to discuss briefly the problem of the terms of trade. In Chapter 6, we observe that the deterioration of Europe's terms of trade is not so clear as has generally been assumed. It is stated there that according to one authority the sixteen ERP countries suffered a worsening of the terms of trade by 20 per cent from the end of the war to 1947. But it is also observed there that in the two years ending September 30, 1947, unit prices of United States exports had risen by 20 per cent and those of imports by 36 per cent. This does not suggest a loss of bargaining terms for the outside world or even for Europe. The European Economic Commission concludes "that, on the average for Europe as a whole, price changes have tended to raise the cost of imports and the cost of exports in about the same proportions." In 1946, the average weighted cost of imports in terms of exports was 85 for thirteen countries on the continent, and in 1947 was 86; for the United Kingdom, the respective figures were 107 and 119 (1938 = 100). Eleven of the countries included are ERP countries. France's 1947 average cost of imports in terms of exports was but 83 in comparison with the British 119. The weighted average of all countries was 97 in 1946 and 102 in 1947.[31]

What is much more important than the terms of trade is the rise of prices, particularly in the United States and the other Americas. Obviously, even with an improvement in the terms of trade, a rise in import prices for countries with large excesses

EUROPEAN RECOVERY PROGRAM

of imports may be very costly. This is especially important for the ERP countries. According to estimates of the United States Government, their *total* exports over fifteen months ending June 30, 1949, will equal only $9.5 billion; their *total* imports, $18.4 billion; and their trade deficits with the *Americas*, $7.8 billion.[32] Whereas in 1936-1938 Europe paid for 57 per cent of her imports from the United States by shipping goods to this country, in the first three quarters of 1947 she thus paid for only about 15 per cent of her imports.[33] *This suggests how important an inflation in this country is for Europe's balance of payments.*

I have found no better discussion of the relative contributions of the effects of rising prices upon the trade deficit of European countries than a study by the *Economic Commission for Europe*, as shown in Table 5.

TABLE 5

EUROPE'S TRADE WITH NON-EUROPEAN COUNTRIES
(*In Millions of Dollars*)

	1938 Current Prices	1946 Current Prices	1946 1938 Prices	1947 Current Prices	1947 1938 Prices
Imports, f.o.b. ..	5,820	9,400	5,350	13,000	6,200
Exports, f.o.b. ..	3,730	4,300	2,300	6,100	2,900
Trade deficit ..	−2,090	−5,100	−3,050	−6,900	−3,300

Source: *EC Europe: Survey*, p. 57.

It is clear that had prices of imports and exports not risen, the adverse balance on trade account from 1938 to 1947 would have increased by but $1.2 billion ($3.3 − $2.1), two-thirds of this being associated with a decline in real exports, and one-third with a rise in *real* imports. Had prices of exports and imports not changed (net) over these years, Europe's overseas trade deficit in 1947 would have been less than one-half as large as it actually was. (See Table 5.) In addition, a serious change in the invisible account

[50]

CRISIS IN EUROPE

occurred. Europe's investment income declined from $1.4 billion to $0.4 billion, and for other current items (for example, shipping, travel, military expenditures) a credit balance of $0.7 billion was converted into a deficit of $1.0 billion. (The net adverse change on *invisible* account for the *sixteen ERP Countries and Western Germany* alone has been estimated at $1.5 billion.)[34]

In summary, Europe's trade deficit in 1947 was $4.8 billion in excess of that in 1938. *Approximately three-quarters of this rise is associated with an increase in the prices of international commodities.* Paying increased prices for imports has proved to be far more costly than the change in the terms of trade. Furthermore, whereas in 1938 the adverse balance was covered by $2.1 billion of earnings on invisible account, against the adverse balance of trade of $6.9 billion in 1947 there were no net earnings on invisible account, but rather a debt of $0.6 billion. *Of Europe's total adverse balance of $7.5 billion in 1947, the rise in trade deficit (in 1938 dollars) accounted for about one-sixth, the rise of international prices for almost one-half, and the losses on invisibles accounted for little more than one-third.*[35]

d. *Financing the Deficit in the Balance of Payments*

A final problem in the balance of payments is financing of deficits. Since this section and section *e* contain detailed statistics, the reader may prefer to skip sections *d* and *e* and read the summary section which follows. In Chapter 6, we shall discuss the extent to which the deficits since the end of the war were financed through the use of resources of the ERP countries and through grants and loans. In the two and one half years ending December 31, 1947, the United States made available about $11.7 billion to Western European countries, of which about $7.7 billion were in the form of loans and property grants and $4.0 billion in grants.[36] With the termination of an active foreign lending program in the middle of 1946, the European countries tended to rely heavily on their own resources in the eighteen months preceding the voting of interim aid. That Europe exported about $2 billion of capital in 1946-47 further impaired her reserve position. In 1946 Europe contributed $1 billion of its own resources towards liquidating a deficit of $5.8 billion; but in 1947 approximately $1.8 billion towards a deficit of $5.5 billion.[37] Obviously, European countries could not long afford to use their foreign resources at the 1947 rate. In Chapter 6, we shall comment also on the adequacy of reserves to meet minimum needs for monetary cover and trade deficits. The excess is small indeed. In the course of the Congressional debate, there were some heated exchanges between executive officials and Congressmen both on the desirability of forcing a thorough-going mobilization of assets in this country belonging to European private interests and on the wisdom of further depleting reserves.[38]

ERP countries are scheduled to import $64 billion of *goods* in the period April 1, 1948 to June 30, 1952, and to export $40 billion. The total adverse balance on *current account* is estimated at roughly $21 billion, or about one-third of the imports. In 1948-49 (fifteen months), the deficit is estimated roughly at $8.5 billion, or 46 per cent of imports, and in fiscal 1951-52 at $2.9 billion or about 19 per cent of imports.[39] Figure 4 indicates that with the passage of time imports will tend to decline and exports to rise. Executive branch estimates of imports were substantially lower than those of the CEEC and their exports substantially higher, and the International Bank was less optimistic than the executive branch.[40]

e. *Variations among Countries*

Over-all figures should not blind us to the large differences among individual countries. Before listing several relevant points, we should comment on Figure 5. The reader should compare the great advance made by the United Kingdom as evidenced in

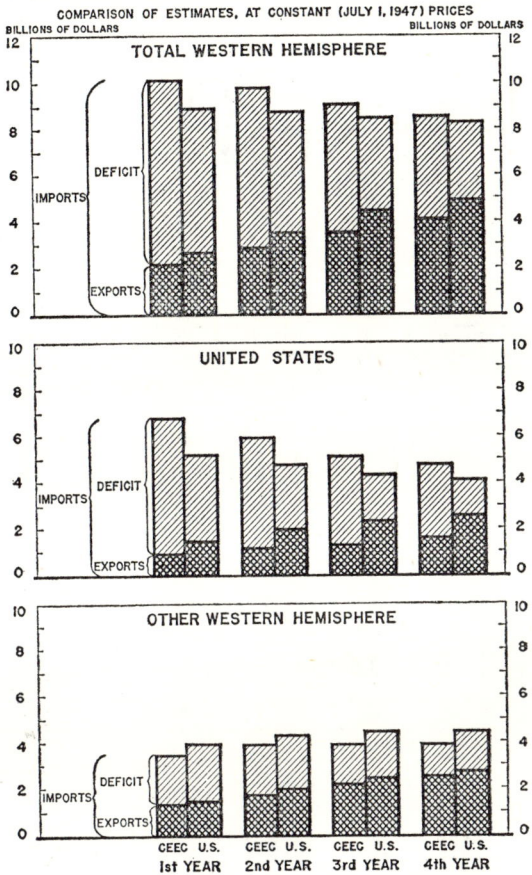

Figure 4

Note — Imports and exports include net debits or net credits respectively, on each of the following accounts: freight, other invisibles, and current account of depencencies.

CEEC estimates relate to calendar years starting with 1948; U. S. experts' estimates relate to fiscal years starting with 1948–49; U. S. estimate for first three-months' period (April–June 1948) is omitted.

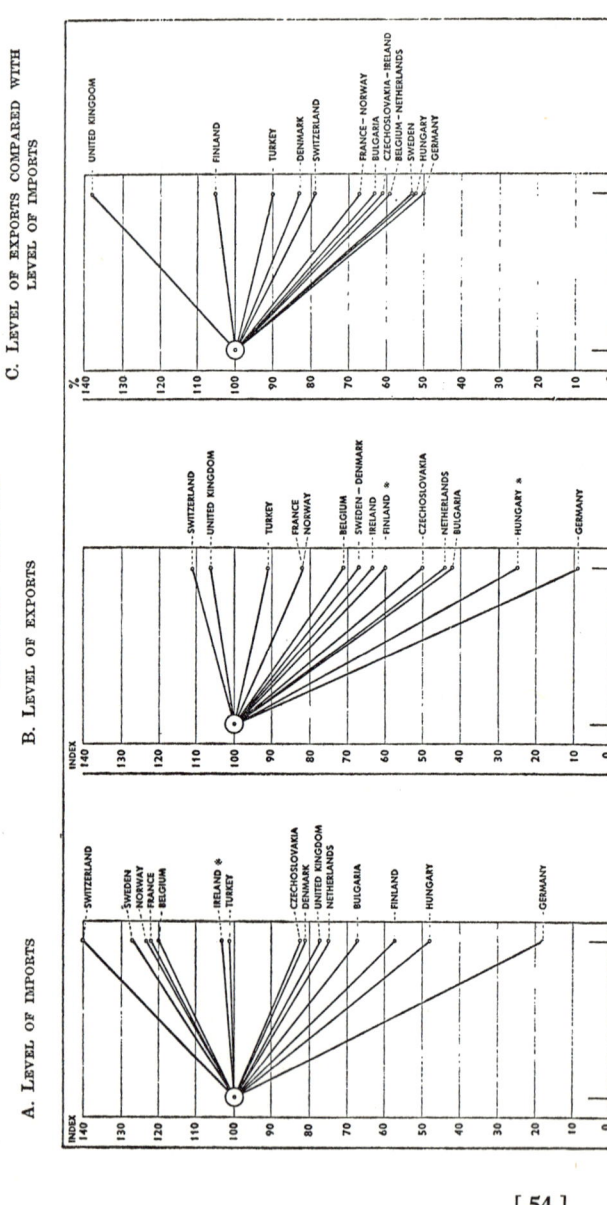

Figure 5

reduced imports and increased exports with the unfortunate position of France, the Scandinavian countries, and Germany. First, we commented above on the improved terms of trade for continental European countries in contrast with a deterioration for the United Kingdom. This contrast is explained largely by the prevailing overvaluation on the continent. Second, consider the importance of imports and the ratio of imports and foreign assistance extended. In 1946 the United Nations listed countries with the following percentage of imports to national income: six with less than 20 per cent; five with 20 to 29 per cent; four with 30 to 40 per cent; and one (Greece) with 70 to 80 per cent. Total aid extended from the end of the war to the third quarter of 1947 as a percentage of imports during 1946 and the first half of 1947 varied as follows: Greece, 147 per cent; Poland, 105 per cent; France, 93 per cent; United Kingdom, 87 per cent; the Netherlands, 60 per cent; Italy, 55 per cent; Norway, 22 per cent; Belgium, 18 per cent; Switzerland, 0.[41]

Third, consider the relative proportion of United States assistance to Western European countries in the form of loans and grants:

Percentage of Loans and Property Credits to Total, July 1945 to December 1947

Norway	99
United Kingdom	93
Netherlands	92
France	85
Belgium and Luxemburg	76
Italy	27
Greece	16
Austria	10
Western Germany	6

EUROPEAN RECOVERY PROGRAM

The variations are undoubtedly largely explained by the differing estimates of capacity to pay and likelihood of repayment.[42]

Fourth, the effects of changing patterns of trade varied from country to country. Thus, the virtual disappearance of Germany as a market affected Denmark, Italy, Sweden, and Switzerland, each with 15 per cent or more of their exports disposed of in Germany in 1938, much more than France, whose exports to Germany had been only 6 per cent of its total exports, and the United Kingdom, with only 5 per cent of its exports having gone to Germany. Bulgaria, Hungary, and Poland were injured even more than many of the ERP countries.[43]

Again, the shift of trade in relation to the United States is of some importance, for the more a country exports to the United States and the less it imports from the United States, the more favorable the effects on its dollar position. Generally, the percentage of imports from the United States was much larger in 1946 than in 1938. (Iron Curtain countries are usually an exception.) Notable rises are: from 12 per cent in 1938 to 55 per cent in 1946 for Italy, 11 to 31 for France, 7 to 23 for Greece, 11 to 25 for the Netherlands, and 11 to 22 for Norway. The rise for Denmark was but 8 per cent to 9, for Sweden 16 to 24, for the United Kingdom but 13 to 17. Heavy reliance on United States imports was likely to be costly in dollars unless total trade declined greatly or large credits were made available.

Shifts in the proportion of exports to the United States were not consistently in the upward direction. Some countries seemed to have much more success in shifting exports to the United States than others, with favorable effects on their dollar position. Significant differences in policies are reflected: from 1938 to 1946 Belgian and Luxemburg exports to the United States rose from 7 to 13 per cent, whereas those from Czechoslovakia declined from 14 to 7; France's percentage remained unchanged at 6; the United Kingdom's fell from 5 to 4; Norway's from 8 to 5; while the

[56]

CRISIS IN EUROPE

Netherlands and Italy showed large rises. Greece expanded her exports to the United States from 17 to 55 per cent.[44]

Finally, we should note that European countries showed varying enthusiasm for the recovery of European markets. In their anxiety to obtain hard currencies, many European countries avoided European markets. In 1938 the credit balances in Europe (excess of exports) for the participating countries were $619 million; in 1946, $908 million; and are estimated to be $673 million for 1948-49. One might contrast the shift from a credit balance of $23 million for Denmark in 1938 to a debit balance of $119 million in 1946, or that for France from + 23 to − 139 million, with Sweden's shift from − 39 to + 76 million dollars, or the United Kingdom's from − 289 to + 553 million dollars. The last could not long continue to finance excess exports to Europe, and in 1947, the British greatly reduced their export surplus.[45]

SUMMARY OF INTERNATIONAL ECONOMIC RELATIONS

By way of summary of the discussion of international economic relations the following should be emphasized: (a) Dollar scarcity is genuine, the explanation being in part economic, in part institutional, and vitally political. (b) The contribution of overvaluation of currencies to this scarcity is not nearly so great as is generally held. (c) Nor is the deterioration in the terms of trade a factor of great significance for Europe as a whole. For the United Kingdom, the rise in prices of imports relative to those of exports may be of substantial importance. Of much greater significance is the rise of prices of imports for countries (inclusive of the United Kingdom) which experience large excesses of imports over exports. (d) Concentration on the over-all European situation obscures differences among countries, as was made clear in the discussion above. We might contrast here British and European experience. The United Kingdom accounted for *one-third* of the

EUROPEAN RECOVERY PROGRAM

European adverse balance of payments in 1947; *only an eighth* of the adverse trade balance: *two-thirds* of the losses since 1938 on invisible account; and about *28 per cent* of the deficit associated with rising prices. It is clear that the British difficulties relative to Continental Europe's are especially to be associated with the change in her invisible position (for example, investment earnings), and her trade figures reflect heroic efforts to make the necessary sacrifices. Compare her improvement in trade from a deficit of £300 million in 1938 to £200 million in 1946 with Metropolitan France's trade deficit of $227 million in 1938 and $1510 million in 1946.[46] (e) Finally, we should add that the burden of financing Europe's excess of imports has largely fallen upon the United States. In fact, the explanation is the low level of imports in this country.

If the average relationship in 1919–20 (5.2 per cent) had prevailed, United States imports would have been almost $12,000,000,000 in 1947, or more than double the actual amount. At the average ratio of 1921 to 1939 (3.4 per cent), they would have been about $7,750,-000,000, or more than $2,000,000,000 larger than the amount actually imported in 1947.[47]

The Economic Commission for Europe thus shows that our imports are low relative to income. In 1929 the percentage of imports to gross national product was 5.7; in 1937, 4.8; in 1947, 3.6 per cent. In part, the explanation of the low level of imports was the *relative* rise of intra-European trade: total exports from twelve major European countries during the first nine months of 1947 amounted to 127 per cent of the 1936–1938 average, while our imports from these countries were but 92 per cent of the same prewar years.[48] Had this diversion not occurred, however, pressure on United States export markets would have been greater. (f) In 1946 and 1947 the United States export surplus to Europe was a smaller part (2.0 per cent) of her gross national product than in 1919 and 1920 (4.4 per cent). In fact, in 1946–47

[58]

CRISIS IN EUROPE

Europe financed a larger part of its imports through exports than in 1919 and 1920. (Trade deficits in both 1919–20 and 1946–47 were equal at $12 billion.) [49]

CONCLUSION

It is not necessary to write a lengthy conclusion since several summaries have been presented earlier in the chapter. Here, however, are the main points once again:

One. Recovery in Europe's industrial output was substantial in late 1945 and 1946; but rather disappointing in 1947. Income did not respond as well as industrial output; but in assessing the relevance of income, we should allow for the exclusion of foreign aid from income figures.

Two. Inflation, both open and suppressed, has had an unfortunate effect on output, on distribution, on the competitive position of the ERP countries, and on the political situation.

Three. Dollar scarcity is genuine, the causes being economic and institutional; the importance of overvaluation of currencies is exaggerated, the most important explanation of the deficit of ERP countries being the rise of import prices and losses on invisible account, not the sluggishness of output or undue allocation of output to domestic uses.

2. Some Political Aspects

THE ERP AND COMMUNISM

This book deals primarily with economic issues, but obviously in a political framework. As the Harriman Committee so well showed, the ERP is a political weapon of first-rate importance. Communism is on the march; communism feeds on distress; and the ERP is an attempt to underwrite recovery in Western Europe, without which Western Europe might easily succumb to communism or some other form of totalitarianism. In a totalitarian world, democratic United States would indeed be vulnerable.

Marxist Eastern Europe awaits the inevitable crisis in the capitalist world, and particularly in the fortress of private enterprise, the United States. Once capitalism flounders and then collapses, the forces of communism will move on irresistibly. Unfortunately for the Marxists, the ERP, in keeping the excess of exports over imports at a high level for several years, will tend to postpone the "inevitable" crisis in the United States; and the rise of military expenditures, induced primarily by Russia's brazen foreign policy, offers further insurance against a depression. By spreading fears in this country, the Russians have been in part responsible for the ERP, and almost exclusively for rearmament; and thus they have unwittingly delayed the "inevitable" crisis which was to run interference for the Russian intelligence and military. Indeed, analysis in 1946 and even 1947, in part based on history, suggested a downturn in 1947 and surely in 1948; but who would predict a serious depression in the next four years with exports at about $14 billion and federal expenditures rising steadily towards $50 billion annually?

A depression seems definitely out. Large public expenditures, in no small part wasted from a broad social viewpoint, are one

SOME POLITICAL ASPECTS

way of averting a collapse. Distress, however, can stem from relatively low consumption in relation to output, and maldistribution. Russia may still achieve her objective unless this country, in the midst of an armament and ERP boom superimposed on an overemployed economy, takes seriously the inflation threat with its accompanying distortions and maldistribution.

IS THE ERP DIRECTED AGAINST COMMUNISM?

A clear-cut answer cannot be given to this question. Surely the ERP would not have had clear sailing had not the communist threat appeared; and it is open to doubt that a generous program would have been approved had Molotov agreed to cooperate in the Paris Conference of July 1947. Had the Italians accepted communism, would they have received aid under the ERP? The answer is undoubtedly no.[1]

In his Harvard address of June 5, 1947, Secretary Marshall apparently offered help to all of Europe:

Any government that is willing to assist in the task of recovery will find full cooperation, I am sure, on the part of the United States Government.

But that he was dubious of Russia's willingness to cooperate was evident from what followed:

Any government which maneuvers to block the recovery of other countries cannot expect help from us. Furthermore, governments, political parties, or groups which seek to perpetuate human misery in order to profit therefrom politically or otherwise will encounter the opposition of the United States.[2]

Undersecretary Acheson sounded a bitter note on Russian interference with recovery in Europe in his June 15, 1947, address at Wesleyan University:

In Eastern Europe, the Soviet Union, over American and British protests, has used its dominant military position to carry on a unilateral policy, contrary to the Yalta Agreements, by which free choice

EUROPEAN RECOVERY PROGRAM

of their destiny has been denied these peoples. Even more important, the minority Communist regimes fastened upon these peoples have acted to cut them off economically from the community of Europe, curtail their productivity, and bind them to exclusive economic relations with the Soviet Union...
As a result, the recovery of Europe has long been delayed — tragically long.[3]

In reporting out the bill on foreign assistance (S. 2202) the Senate Committee on Foreign Relations left the door open to the USSR.

In view of the coöperative nature of the recovery program, the Committee believed the door should be left open for other countries if they choose to enter... Such countries must, however, adhere to a joint program for European recovery.[4]

The House Committee was less diplomatic. After castigating the Russians for draining resources away from European countries which at the same time were being aided by this country, and generally for holding back recovery in Europe, the House Committee in no uncertain terms made clear the main reason for espousal of the ERP.

The Committee has concluded that the program is necessary to prevent the United States from being confronted with a world so unbalanced and hostile as to present almost insuperable burdens to the people of the United States in the future, if Europe is not once more rendered free and adequately strong, both in its political and economic life. The same conclusion has led the Committee to include China as a barrier in the Far East against the further encroachment of communism and the domination of the world by Moscow.[5]

Although the Foreign Assistance Act does not specifically mention Russia, it might be interpreted as leaving the door open to Russia:

The restoration or maintenance in European countries of principles of individual liberty, free institutions, and genuine independence

SOME POLITICAL ASPECTS

rests largely upon the establishment of sound economic conditions, stable international economic relationships and the achievement by the countries of Europe of a healthy economy independent of extraordinary assistance. The accomplishment of these objectives calls for a plan of European recovery open to all such nations which coöperate in such a plan...[6]

But note the following in the declaration of policy in the same Act:

It is further declared to be the policy of the people of the United States to sustain and strengthen the principles of individual liberty, free institutions, and genuine independence in Europe...[7]

REACTION FROM THE USSR

A *Tass* dispatch recorded in the *New York Times* of June 30, 1947 reflected the Russian attitude towards the ERP, a viewpoint which Molotov was then presenting at the Paris Conference of Foreign Ministers.[8] According to the Russian view, the United States had made the largest gains from the war and therefore was in a position to render aid; and besides fearing an impending crisis, this country wanted to extend credits for the purpose of expanding markets. The USSR did approve plans to assess the needs of individual countries and to discover the contribution which the United States might make; but they would not tolerate any infringements of sovereignty involved in an integrated European plan which, *inter alia*, would determine the lines of economic development of each country. At the final meeting of the Paris Conference of Ministers, Molotov reiterated the official Russian view: The USSR could not accept interferences in its internal affairs; opposed domination of Europe by the United States and an ultimate division of Europe into two camps; and they resented the excessive powers arrogated by Great Britain and France to themselves. Why, asked Molotov, should the Russians approve pressure being "put on Poland to produce more coal even

EUROPEAN RECOVERY PROGRAM

though it be at the expense of the other branches of Polish industry because that is in the interest of certain European countries?" [9]

One of the features of the ERP which interested the Russians was the failure to use the United Nations organization for any aid offered. In his defense of our policy, Mr. Austin, before the United Nations, stressed the fact that the U. N. did not have the necessary resources, nor were the other international agencies prepared; and the fifty-five nations in common harness had much pulling power but they were not easy to handle.[10]

Actually, other considerations were also relevant. Experience with the UNRRA had aroused antagonism among many American officials towards disbursements of United States funds by international agencies, for many believed, whether rightly or wrongly, that the money had been used to further political ends not acceptable to the United States. The main reason that a new organization to advance European recovery was set up was undoubtedly the desire to control the use of the resources sweated out of the American economy through taxation or the process of inflation; and there was not complete satisfaction with the results achieved so far either by international or American agencies.

REPERCUSSIONS ON NONPARTICIPATING COUNTRIES

Since the ERP concentrates the major part of our aid upon Western European countries, other areas and countries may well be critical of the new policy. Latin America, Asia, and the Iron Curtain countries particularly are displeased at the proposed distribution of dollars, although China receives additional help under the Foreign Assistance Act of 1948.

That the aid is rendered directly to the sixteen ERP countries and Western Germany does not mean that others will not profit indirectly. As is noted elsewhere, the other Americas may provide close to one-half the exports required under the ERP; and finance

[64]

SOME POLITICAL ASPECTS

perhaps 20 per cent of their excess of exports to ERP countries. Latin America and Canada will then obtain access to the American market with dollars obtained in payment for ERP offshore purchases by the United States. As suppliers of most of the petroleum products required under the ERP, the Middle East will also replenish its dollar reserves.

Actually, the net gains in United States exports to the non-ERP countries receiving dollars for offshore purchases will depend upon the export control policy of this country, and the course of prices over the next few years. Undoubtedly non-ERP countries will have greater access to the United States markets under an ERP program than without it. There is little doubt, however, that the non-ERP countries will suffer an absolute reduction in imports from the United States relative to their 1947 imports, and also a reduction relative to total United States exports. (Against $10 billion annual rate of United States exports in the first half of 1947 to non-ERP countries, the Department of Commerce estimates exports to these countries at $8.2 billion in 1948 on the assumption of an ERP, and $6.7 billion without it.)[11] In short, under the ERP, non-ERP countries will obtain more dollars than without it; but the changed distribution of United States exports will result in a reduction of exports to these countries. *They may well balk at a policy which deprives them of large quantities of goods through offshore purchases under the ERP and is accompanied by a reduction of exports from this country.* With exports up and imports down, inflationary pressures in these countries will rise.

One of the irritants of the ERP is the prices charged by the other Americas for supplies to be financed by the United States. This is part of a larger problem, especially related to Argentina. According to the Herter Committee, the Argentine has refused to cooperate in international allocations of scarce supplies; in December, 1947 she was charging Brazil $4.86 per bushel of wheat, a large part of the excess over the world price being siphoned off by a state trading organization; and yet she was receiving a disproportionate part of scarce items exported from the United States — for example, in six months of 1947, 10.6 per cent of the steel mill products exported and 9.5 per cent of industrial chemicals. The Herter Committee would use export control as a weapon to force the Argentine to cooperate in the ERP program by extending generous credits, selling at reasonable prices, and supporting international schemes for distribution.[12]

Pressed by a Senate Committee, the executive branch submitted a table of prices charged by various countries as of July 1, 1947. Table 6 gives a few examples.

TABLE 6

Prices in Dollars *

	United States	Canada	Other Western Hemisphere
Wheat (bushels)	2.50	2.63	4.85
Rye (bushels)	...	3.72	4.60
Oats (bushels)	1.10	1.25	1.90
Barley (bushels)	1.75	3.10	2.87
Soybean meal (short tons)	88.95	...	104.35

* ERP: Sen. Hear., pp. 215–216.

A somewhat different type of problem is raised by the re-export of products obtained under the ERP. Obviously, it is not easy to draw a precise line between British commodities and ERP commodities exported by the British. Should the British, for example, manufacture and export chemical products out of industrial chemicals sent by this country, would these be exports of ERP commodities? There is strong opposition to the export of commodities imported under ERP, an opposition not always easily explained, since one objective is to strengthen the export position of the ERP countries. Fear of foreign competition still

SOME POLITICAL ASPECTS

rankles American businessmen. Another factor is the fear that the ERP countries will export commodities to Russia which we are anxious the USSR should not receive. But control of re-exports will not be easy. First, because of the difficulty of tracing ERP materials to their ultimate destination. Second and related, a country may be enabled to export many items only because it obtains help under the ERP. Should these be defined as exports of ERP commodities? The distinction between exports of ERP items and those made possible by imports under the ERP is obscure.

Even the Herter Committee seems to share the current fears that the ERP might bring about an improvement in the competitive position of European countries, though this is an important objective of the program; for the Committee writes:

The desirability of studying the export program of the United Kingdom which appears to involve the allocation of the bulk of critical items largely needed by other Western European nations to areas outside the CEEC countries. [Sic] Mining machinery, especially repair parts for equipment made in the United Kingdom, is a case in point. A similar problem is raised by British exports of machinery and equipment to the U.S.S.R. and by re-export of large quantities of steel products expected from the United States. It might appear that the United Kingdom is thus able to select the most advantageous future markets while the bulk of the American exports of similar critical items is channeled into areas of little future value for our export trade.[13]

RELATIONS WITH EASTERN EUROPE

A revival of trade between Western and Eastern Europe was assumed by the CEEC. Although not so optimistic on this score as the CEEC, the executive branch not only was not averse to improvement of trade relations between East and West but even saw large gains in this economic rapprochement; and even would be prepared to support exports from the West which are processed to a minor extent out of materials received under the ERP.[14]

EUROPEAN RECOVERY PROGRAM

Improvement in the East is bound to result from the ERP unless the Eastern countries exclude others from trade with them through exclusive bilateral agreements; for with increased incomes in the West, the East will find profitable markets in Western Europe.[15] The latter will indeed profit, *inter alia*, from the greater availability of coal, grain, and timber from the East.

In 1938, the USSR accounted for but 1.7 per cent of world exports, and other Central and Eastern European countries but 5 per cent; and in 1947, the latter accounted for a little more than 2 per cent. Should these countries reëstablish their prewar position in trade, the results might be important but not decisive.

In general, Eastern Europe's trade and particularly her exports were much lower in 1946-47 than in 1938; and even her imports in real terms declined greatly. Whereas world trade (in dollars) in 1947 was more than 100 per cent above that of 1938, and Europe's imports (exclusive of the USSR) were 73 per cent above those of 1938, Germany's imports were almost 50 per cent lower and for "other Central and Eastern Europe countries" imports were but 22 per cent higher. Export figures are even more at variance: From 1938 to 1947, world exports (dollar value) were up by more than 100 per cent; those of Europe (excluding the USSR) by but 34 per cent; Western European industrial countries by 82 per cent; the United Kingdom by 83 per cent; but Germany's exports declined by 80 per cent and those of other Central and Eastern European countries by 22 per cent.[16]

It is clear that Eastern Europe's trade relative to prewar trade (in stable dollars) and relative to Western European and world trade is down substantially; and the decline is greater for exports than imports. Germany, the bridge to the East, has experienced an especially large loss in exports. There has, of course, also been a redirection of East-West trade in favor of that among Iron Curtain countries.[17]

SOME POLITICAL ASPECTS

Table 7 summarizes the contributions of Eastern and Central Europe to the import trade of important countries and areas:

TABLE 7

IMPORTS FROM EASTERN EUROPE, 1938, 1947

(*By Percentages*)

	From the USSR		From Other Central and Eastern European Countries	
	1938	1947	1938	1947
United Kingdom, etc.	2.9	0.5	3.1	0.7
Western Europe, industrial countries	2.2	0.2	4.7	3.4
Scandinavian countries	1.9	2.6	5.6	4.7
United States	1.2	1.4	2.8	0.7
Other Central and Eastern European countries	0.6	9.9	26.2	14.5
USSR	..	..	4.7	?

Source: *EC Europe: Survey*, pp. 40–43.

These figures suggest the significance of USSR and other Eastern and Central European countries as sources of supplies. Thus, in 1938, 2.9 per cent of the United Kingdom's imports came from Russia; in 1947, only 0.5 per cent.

British exports to the USSR account for a reduced part of total British exports, and yet these exports may account for an increased part of total Russian imports. Thus, whereas exports to other Central and Eastern European countries accounted for 2.9 and 2.7 per cent of British *exports*, in 1938 and 1947, respectively, they accounted for 7.2 and 9.9 per cent of *imports* of these countries in these years. Similar figures for Western European industrial countries vis-à-vis other Central and Eastern European countries give percentages of exports of Western European industrial countries to other Central and Eastern European countries of 4.9 and 5.3 per cent; and percentages of imports of the latter from the former, 11.0 and 17.9 per cent.[18] Obviously an area (A) may

EUROPEAN RECOVERY PROGRAM

obtain an increased part of its imports from another area (B) even though that market (A) may provide a relatively smaller outlet for B's exports — all that is required is that A's imports decline sufficiently.

Trade of the eight Iron Curtain countries in the postwar period reflected large amounts of aid and also reparation payments awarded the Soviet and sales of assets and surpluses by the Soviet. In this manner we can explain the rise in 1946 of Russian imports from Eastern Europe by 14 times over those of 1938 as compared with an expansion of exports to these countries of but 4 times; and we can thus account for the excess of imports over exports for the eight countries during the years 1945–47. It is estimated that these countries received $2.3 billion in foreign aid from May 1945 to the latter part of 1947, of which $1.5 billion were received from the United States; and that in 1946, they paid in cash $102 million for exports of $820 million from the United States and in the first seven months of 1947, $173 million for exports of $326 million from the United States.[19]

A few peculiarities of Eastern European trade should be noted: though the volume of USSR trade with Eastern Europe increased greatly, that among the Eastern countries other than the USSR was much lower in 1946 and the first half of 1947 than in 1938. (Bulgaria was an exception.) In the view of the Herter Committee, the Iron Curtain countries could not export to Western Europe and the United States the equivalent of prewar exports to these areas, unless (with the exception of Czechoslovakia) they greatly increased their *total* export trade relative to prewar trade. This follows from the diversion of trade from the West to the East in 1946–47.[20]

This detailed study of trade structure suggests that Eastern European trade with Western Europe is a matter of importance, and especially to Germany; but of less importance than is sometimes assumed. Both because Eastern Europe's trade has declined

SOME POLITICAL ASPECTS

and because the trade *between* East and West has been sacrificed to the claims of intra-Iron Curtain trade, the East-West trade has suffered greatly. A sudden withdrawal of credits which amounted to more than $2 billion over a period of about two years, would necessarily drastically reduce West-East trade; and in fact unusual transactions (for example, reparations) account for a substantial part of intra-Iron Curtain exports and imports.

Recovery of East-West trade awaits a renewal of credits, which do not promise to be forthcoming under the political conditions of 1947 and 1948; a restoration of normal economic conditions which might allow increased trade on a balancing basis; and more than anything else an improvement in political relations. Without the last, the future of East-West trade is dim.

THE PRESERVATION OF PRIVATE ENTERPRISE

No small part of the support for the ERP derives from a fear of socialism. As a weapon for combating communism and the police state, the ERP is almost universally approved in this country; but its use to combat the spread of socialism introduces a sharp division of views.

In the minds of those who would use the ERP to fight socialism, the emphasis is generally on nationalization. Thus, in its various publications, the House Committee on Foreign Aid devotes considerable space to the British nationalization program, expressing doubts about its wisdom and particularly criticizing the nationalization of the railroads and the anticipated nationalization of the iron and steel industry. Yet at the same time this Committee proposes a super-plan for increasing the efficiency of European industry under United States guidance which would impose standardization, provide for minute allocations of scarce supplies, assure maximum utilization and cooperation among European countries and the United States, and so on. This type of planning, more than nationalization, has become the essence

EUROPEAN RECOVERY PROGRAM

of socialism. On this score, Marx's rating as a prophet suffers. Oddly enough, the witnesses and experts on the Committee seem almost universally to have missed this point. Control over the use of scarce resources will give the state the power to determine what is produced and where, and, therefore, allocation of output among consumption, exports, and investment; and distribution of jobs and man-power. Under these conditions, there is little scope for the private entrepreneur, for profits, for the state will determine the use made of net receipts. Yet the House Committee, expressing itself strongly against socialism nevertheless urges controls which are an important part of socialism; and would not allow petty consideration of sovereignty to exclude the imposed elements of socialism:

> In working toward European unity and the improvement of productive efficiency of Europe, the Administrator will find himself faced with the old cry of interference with national sovereignty . . . Our concern must be with the maintenance of the basic human freedoms — with individual rather than with national sovereignty: For if absolute sovereignty blocks the economic integration which is essential to European recovery, human freedom itself will be lost.[21]

Private enterprise undoubtedly receives favored treatment under the Foreign Assistance Act of 1948. Here are a few examples. In the clash of interests between the foreign owners of concealed assets in this country and the American taxpayer, there was much solicitation for the property rights of the foreigner. The Senate Committee would encourage the liquidation of blocked assets concealed contrary to the law and interests of the countries concerned; but opposed the pledging of foreign-owned assets against loans under the ERP. This would involve seizure and be contrary to the philosophy of the bill.[22]

Second, the Foreign Assistance Act stipulates that the ECA is to "facilitate and maximize the use of private channels of trade. . . ." (Sec. 111 [b]).[23] This particular phrase may well cost

[72]

SOME POLITICAL ASPECTS

the taxpayers billions of dollars. In the tight market conditions of the next few years, the special privileges given to private traders are likely to bring a further mushrooming of export merchants and other middlemen, trafficking in licenses, and similar abuses. Centralized purchasing of the major supplies required under the ERP might well save from 10 to 25 per cent of the total cost. It is well to recall that had the ERP not been approved, exports might have tumbled by four to five billion dollars per year. The additional exports made available under the ERP and paid for by the taxpayer might well be channeled through central purchasing commissions with attendant economies. The war experience with public purchasing commissions is a reminder of what can be done. To Congressman Herter's credit, it may be said that he understood the threat to scarce markets of competition of private or even foreign public purchasing agents.[24]

Third, the ERP was essentially proposed as a businessmen's organization. Throughout the course of passage, it was made clear that the program was to be under the direction of businessmen; and special exemptions are provided for businessmen who aid and retain allegiance to private firms.[25] Obviously, a program controlled by businessmen would be partial to supporting private enterprise. Much is to be said, of course, for efficient management of the ERP, inclusive of protection of the rights of American taxpayers. Experience during the last war suggests that control by the State Department might favor excessive allotments of funds and inadequate safeguards. The diplomat does not usually function effectively as both a diplomat *and* trader.[26]

Yet in setting up a businessmen's organization, Congress may have gone too far in the opposite direction. Businessmen are not broadly enough trained as a rule to view the general interest against that of business. What is good for business is not necessarily good for society, though often the interests are compatible. Again, should the ERP be largely manned by business execu-

EUROPEAN RECOVERY PROGRAM

tives, then the danger of favoring particular private interests at the expense of the public becomes a real threat: Such abuses were serious during World War II. At least it may be said that in appointing Messrs. Hoffman and Harriman to the key positions, the President selected two businessmen with an unusually high sense of the public good. Will they be able to withstand the pressure of thousands of businessmen, well intentioned but ignorant of the larger issues?

Undoubtedly a major issue will be the relation of resources made available under the ERP and the attitude towards nationalization. The Foreign Assistance Act provides for agreements with the participating countries, which are to make "efficient and practical use, within the framework of a joint program for European recovery, of the resources of such participating country, including any commodities, facilities or services furnished under this title..." (Sec. 115 [b], [4]). Obviously, the ECA can withhold aid from a nationalized or to-be-nationalized British iron and steel industry on the grounds that nationalized industries do not operate efficiently. The British, of course, would resent the use of the test of nationalization by the ECA. Many in this country and in Europe believe that the pace of nationalization in England has already been slowed up in deference to United States opinion and a fear that nationalization would be countered by reduced aid.[27]

It is, of course, next to impossible to prove that a nationalized iron and steel industry or coal industry is more efficient than privately owned industries. It is well known that these British industries did not operate efficiently under capitalism; that they were short of capital; and that if the necessary rationalization is to be effected, it can only be done through further public help. Besides, the Labour Government has a mandate from the people to extend nationalization. It is well also for Americans to realize that private enterprise may well be a luxury in countries short of

SOME POLITICAL ASPECTS

capital and almost all vital materials. Planning and nationalization follow, rather than precede, distress.

But there are other relevant considerations. Even if nationalization ultimately brings economies, reduced costs, and higher output, the transitional effects are likely to be serious. The ECA may well ask whether the American taxpayer should pay the price of an experiment of which he does not approve. In short, problems of fundamental political and economic policy, of sovereign rights, arise and are not to be easily resolved; and these may jeopardize the position of the ECA Administrator caught between the British Labour Government (say) intent upon nationalization and the supporters of private enterprise here.

It would probably be preferable to allow the British to make the decisions; but whether the ECA can survive politically if it incurs criticism for subsidizing socialism is another matter. The vital issue is not between socialism and private enterprise, alternative methods of achieving economic ends, and each appropriate to different economic environments, but rather *between the police state and freedom*. It is to be hoped that nationalization and even socialism will bring the British both high standards of living and international equilibrium and, above all, that they will be compatible with human freedom. The last is the vital issue. Effectiveness of private against public ownership depends in part upon the nature of the industry and upon general economic conditions; but it is well to recall that noneconomic issues are also involved.[28]

COOPERATION

In asking for aid, the CEEC countries agreed to put their own houses in order: set up production targets, achieve monetary and fiscal stability, introduce customs unions, make the most efficient use of plant and man-power. In the discussions of the Foreign Assistance Act of 1948, both the House and Senate Committees made it clear that they would hold the European countries to

EUROPEAN RECOVERY PROGRAM

their promises. Secretary Marshall indeed pointed out that we have to respect the sovereignty of these nations, while others suggested that there was no issue of sovereignty; for the countries had promised to cooperate. In the view of the administration, periodic appraisals would be made and the penalty for not adhering to agreements would be loss or reduction of aid.[29]

Section 115 (b) of the Foreign Assistance Act recognized the importance of these agreements. I reproduce below the major provisions:

Such agreement shall provide for the adherence of such country to the purposes of this title and shall, where applicable, make appropriate provision, among others, for —

(1) promoting industrial and agricultural production in order to enable the participating country to become independent of extraordinary outside economic assistance . . .

(2) taking financial and monetary measures necessary to stabilize its currency, establish or maintain a valid rate of exchange, to balance its governmental budget as soon as practicable, and generally to restore or maintain confidence in its monetary system;

(3) cooperating with other participating countries in facilitating and stimulating an increasing interchange of goods and services among the participating countries and with other countries and cooperating to reduce barriers to trade among themselves and with other countries;

(4) making efficient and practical use, within the framework of a joint program for European recovery, of the resources of such participating country, including any commodities, facilities, or services furnished under this title, which use shall include, to the extent practicable, taking measures to locate and identify and put into appropriate use, in furtherance of such program, assets, and earnings therefrom, which belong to the citizens of such country and which are situated within the United States, its Territories and possessions;

(5) facilitating the transfer to the United States by sale, exchange, barter, or otherwise for stock-piling or other purposes, for such period of time as may be agreed to and upon reasonable terms and in reasonable quantities, of materials which are required by the United States as a result of deficiencies or potential deficiencies in its own

SOME POLITICAL ASPECTS

resources, and which may be available in such participating country after due regard for reasonable requirements for domestic use and commercial export of such country;

(6) placing in a special account a deposit in the currency of such country, in commensurate amounts and under such terms and conditions as may be agreed to between such country and the Government of the United States, when any commodity or service is made available through any means authorized under this title, and is furnished to the participating country on a grant basis. Such special account, together with the unencumbered portions of any deposits which may have been made by such country pursuant to section 6 of the joint resolution providing for relief assistance to the people of countries devastated by war (Public Law 84, Eightieth Congress) and section 5 (b) of the Foreign Aid Act of 1947 (Public Law 389, Eightieth Congress), shall be held or used within such country for such purposes as may be agreed to between such country and the Administrator in consultation with the National Advisory Council on International Monetary and Financial Problems, and the Public Advisory Board provided for in section 107 (a) for purposes of internal monetary and financial stabilization, for the stimulation of productive activity and the exploration for and development of new sources of wealth, or for such other expenditures as may be consistent with the purposes of this title, including local currency administrative expenditures of the United States incident to operations under this title, and under agreement that any unencumbered balance remaining in such account on June 30, 1952, shall be disposed of within such country for such purposes as may, subject to approval by Act or joint resolution of the Congress, be agreed to between such country and the Government of the United States . . .

(9) recognizing the principle of equity in respect to the drain upon the natural resources of the United States and of the recipient countries, by agreeing to negotiate (a) a future schedule of minimum availabilities to the United States for future purchase and delivery of a fair share of materials which are required by the United States as a result of deficiencies or potential deficiencies in its own resources at world market prices so as to protect the access of United States industry to an equitable share of such materials either in percentages of production or in absolute quantities from the participating countries, and (b) suitable protection for the right of access for any per-

son as defined in paragraph (iii) of subparagraph (3) of section 111 (b) in the development of such materials on terms of treatment equivalent to those afforded to the nationals of the country concerned, and (c) an agreed schedule of increased production of such materials where practicable in such participating countries and for delivery of an agreed percentage of such increased production to be transferred to the United States on a long-term basis in consideration of assistance furnished by the Administrator to such countries under this title . . .

An examination of these crucial provisions in the act will convince the reader that these agreements and their control will prove to be one of the most vexatious aspects of the ERP. Here are two examples of the problems that may arise. (1) A country may agree to a production program; but its achievement may be jeopardized by strikes engineered by communists. Will the country continue to receive help? Will the United States put pressure on the authorities to settle the strike? (2) Who is to say what is a *valid* rate of exchange and how soon a budget should be balanced under the phrase "as soon as practicable"? American experts may seem unconvincing when they urge correct budgetary and anti-inflationary measures in view of the shortcomings of United States policy in these areas. In the recent controversy with France on her devaluation policy, the United States, strengthened in her bargaining position by the largess promised under the ERP, was unable to prevent France from adopting an exchange policy incompatible with the principles promulgated by the CEEC several months earlier.[30] Should the ECA deem current exchange rates a burden on the balance of payments, the matter will be referred to the International Monetary Fund.[31]

Clearly since the summer of 1947 some progress has been made in providing machinery for customs unions and even for unions with broader political and military objectives. Yet it is also evident that the major advances are still on the lines of bilateral agreements, and largely on a balancing basis. The sixteen

SOME POLITICAL ASPECTS

European countries have made only infinitesimal progress towards the goal of multilateralism.[32] American administrators will not find it easy to accelerate the rate of progress, and particularly when their efforts are thwarted by an unsympathetic Ways and Means Committee which at the beginning of negotiations under the Foreign Assistance Act of 1948 (May, 1948) reported an unfortunate bill on the Extension of Reciprocal Trade Agreements. This bill as passed by the House in this crucial month may be interpreted as an announcement that the program to increase trade and particularly United States imports, a condition for success of the ERP, does not interest the lower House. Even the final act was unsatisfactory.

The participating countries are under obligation to provide materials to replenish this country's stock piles and also to give the United States fair access to materials obtainable from them which are short here. Stock piles are to be made available, however, only "after due regard for reasonable requirements for domestic use and commerial exports of such country." Again, it will not be easy to determine the surpluses thus defined nor the manner of payment, if any. United States officials may well have been over-optimistic concerning the amounts to be made available under the proposed stock-piling programs; and they may be correspondingly disappointed by the results.[33]

Let us return once more to the problem of local currencies obtained for grants of commodities or services under the ERP. This is one of the most difficult areas for cooperation, and disagreements may have serious political consequences. Under item 6 of the agreements quoted above, it will be noticed that the currency may be used for purposes of internal stabilization or for the stimulation of productive activity. Impressed by the need of internal investment and the unavailability of domestic currency from non-inflationary sources, the Herter Committee urged the use of domestic currency thus obtained for stimulating investment.³⁴ In the committee's view, the use of money thus obtained would not be inflationary. This assumes, however, that it is possible to control inflation without destroying purchasing power. In some of the European economies, the only way of dealing with inflation is to reduce the amount of money outstanding. Even repayment of debt held by the public with currency received in payment for ERP commodities may be inflationary; and use of this currency to increase domestic investment may be even more inflationary. When total purchasing power is large relative to supplies available for purchase at constant prices, diversion of money from one use to another is not adequately anti-inflationary. Also, the view held by the Herter Committee assumes that the expansion of investment at the expense of consumption is merely a matter of providing non-inflationary finance. This policy raises broader issues of allocation of resources between consumption and investment.³⁵

Cooperation will pose many additional difficult problems for the ECA. When the objectives of the ERP may profit thereby, participating countries are required, irrespective of previous commitments, to yield on German reparations and dismantling of plant from the Western Zone (Sec. 115 f). This policy was incorporated into the Foreign Assistance Act despite the assurances of the State Department that Germany was in no position to put this plant into effective use for years.³⁶ We might also mention other obstacles. Can we expect cooperation if the United States uses the ERP as a dumping device?

BRIEF NOTE ON ADMINISTRATION

Administration of the program is, indeed, an important issue, for costs will be affected by the kind of administration that is had; but this problem will not be discussed in detail here. It will be the task of the administration, within broad limits laid down by Congress, to determine the distribution of aid among countries,

SOME POLITICAL ASPECTS

the form in which it is to be given (for example, capital or consumption goods, loans or grants), the use to be made of domestic currencies received abroad for goods under the program, the compliance with the terms of the agreements, and so on.

In the course of passage, all kinds of administrative problems emerged. Should the tasks both at home and abroad be performed by existing agencies, or should a new agency be set up? If the decision was to be in favor of a new agency, should it control existing agencies in the performance of functions in which the ERP has a dominant interest? What should the relation of the new agency be to the State Department? Three major proposals were made. Clearly the Budget-State Department proposal for an agency operating under the State Department had the advantage of promising integration of the ERP with foreign policy generally; but it had a weakness resulting from the inability of the State Department officials to operate efficiently as traders and negotiators — many will recall the failures of the State Department during the war. Few outstanding men would be ready to run the ERP under State Department rule. Proposals by the Herter Committee to establish a corporation to operate the program also had certain advantages, and particularly that it might operate in the efficient manner expected of an enterprise run along business principles; and another advantage was a degree of independence from the tyranny of the appropriations committees headed by Senator Bridges and Congressman Taber. (These committees are altogether too powerful, for they are in a position to nullify the policies supported by Congress as a whole.) Finally, there was the Vandenberg-Brookings proposal, the favored and enacted one, that a director, of virtually cabinet rank, operate the ERP, with provisions for integrating his work with that of the State Department and other agencies with relevant authority. In this manner, the government might enlist first-rate administrators and apply business principles; but there is also the danger of

EUROPEAN RECOVERY PROGRAM

failure (1) to obtain consistent policies among ERP, State Department, and other agencies, and (2) to weigh properly noneconomic against business or economic considerations. The unfortunate disagreements during the last war among the State Department and the Board of Economic Warfare (later the Foreign Economic Administration) and the RFC, all operating abroad, will be recalled, and are a warning to both State Department and ECA of the difficulties in the years to come.[37] Under the Foreign Assistance Act of 1948, the President is instructed to arbitrate residual differences between the European Cooperation Administration (ECA) and the State Department.

CONCLUSION

In the minds of its supporters, the ERP is a major undertaking to bring about economic recovery in Western Europe; and indirectly hasten reconstruction elsewhere. It is also anticipated that economic recovery will make it possible for Western European countries to bolster their military strength, thus enabling them to withstand further encroachments by Russia. Whether ERP will have to be supplemented by military aid (for example, Lend-Lease) depends upon the rate of recovery and future Russian policy. As is suggested in this chapter, the successful outcome of the ERP will depend upon the fulfillment of the conditions under which Europe accepts assistance; upon political developments; upon the cooperation of nonparticipating countries; upon the skill with which the ECA uses its persuasive powers over European governments; and upon many other factors.[38]

PART TWO
EUROPE AND HER BALANCE OF PAYMENTS

Introduction

As has been noted, Chapter 1 serves as an introduction to Part II. There the major issues were discussed briefly. The object of this brief introduction is to indicate the contents of Chapters 3 to 6, that is, of Part II. In the opening Chapter (3) the reader will find mainly a statistical summary of the production and income crises in Europe and a comparison of the developments among European countries, and of Europe and the United States. Because statistics are dull, many may be satisfied with a reading of the concluding section. Besides, a discussion of similar issues was presented in Chapter 1. Chapters 4 to 6 are more important. In the first of these chapters, we deal systematically with dollar shortage, the nub of the European crises; and conclude with estimates of United States assistance to Europe in the years 1914 to 1947. Then in Chapter 5, we turn to a consideration of exchange rates. This is important, because it is widely held that the problem of international disequilibrium or dollar shortage could be solved if realistic exchange rates were established in Europe. Related problems (for example, the terms of trade) are also considered here. The final chapter (6) serves to integrate the materials in this part (see especially the concluding section). Three problems consume most of the space in this chapter: the causes of Europe's (and particularly Western Europe's) adverse balance of payments in the postwar world; the manner of financing the deficit; and the varying estimates of the balance of payments.

3. Deterioration in Europe

THE 1947 CRISIS

The year 1947 was a crisis year for Europe. Ever since 1914 Europe had experienced one crisis after another; but the 1947 crisis was unique. The turning point in economic affairs was the result of many years of unfavorable developments: the excessive diversion of resources to preparation for war and other wasteful purposes, two major wars and their aftermath, the emergence of newly industrialized countries, and the accompanying world-wide penchant for trade restrictions, political instability — these are the more important causes of Europe's economic decline. The year 1947 brought serious crop failures, continued inflationary pressures, a growing deficit in the balance of payments and dwindling reserves and, related to these, unfavorable political developments.

Each important country in the interwar period conformed to the general pattern and yet deviated from it. For Great Britain, special difficulties stemmed from the growing protectionism elsewhere, the increased competition of newly industrialized countries, failure to keep pace with technological developments in the most advanced countries, and, at times, a disposition to hamstring her economy with injudicious monetary and exchange policies. Germany in the twenties suffered from a costly inflation which virtually wiped out the middle classes, the threat of reparations and the wasteful use of capital, and, under Hitler, from the unfortunate diversion of resources to preparation for war, and the harmful resurgence of economic nationalism. Victimized by a monetary policy which made profitable enterprises all but impossible and which spread dissension and spawned communists, and weakened by a party system which denied political stability to the country, France, in the interwar period, suffered from a steady succession of crises. Again, small countries in Eastern Europe, concentrating on agriculture and without the resources to industrialize, became the victims of the petty protectionism of the period which required each country to become as self-sufficient as possible, irrespective of the cost in additional work and reduced standards of living. Russia, indeed, once she was able to emerge from the chaos of revolution and war, introduced a series of Five-Year Plans which raised her economy to new heights: in the thirties, she was able to insulate her economy from the effects of the world-wide depression. Fearful of an attack and determined to industrialize as rapidly as possible, the government planned large increases in the number of workers and hours of work but denied workers any large share of the additional output.

PREWAR AND POSTWAR INCOME IN THE UNITED STATES AND EUROPE

It is no secret that the income of the United States now accounts for (very roughly) 40 per cent of the world's total, although her population makes up but 7 per cent; and the rest of the world 93 per cent of the population and 60 per cent of the income. Hence the ratio of income to population in 1946 was about nine times as large in this country as in the rest of the world.[1] The economic advantages of the United States in part explain the disposition to seek aid in this country; and the fact that the relative superiority here has increased greatly since 1939 further strengthens the movement to achieve an international redistribution of goods.

Europe's per capita income is substantially higher than that of most countries other than the United States and a number of rich agricultural countries; but the large declines since 1939, and the emergence of a political and economic crisis in 1947 suggest to American authorities the need of aid to Europe even though,

DETERIORATION IN EUROPE

on *international* standards, Europe is still moderately well off. It is well to compare Europe's per capita national income with that of the United States.[2] The latter is presented here, and incomes for Europe in Table 8.

Per Capita Income, U. S.

1939	$ 554
1946	1262
1947	1410

In the table that follows, national income, per capita income and the ratio of taxes to income are given for the sixteen cooperating countries under the ERP and a few others, both for 1939 and 1946. (For purposes of comparison, I have included some figures for 1935-1938.) Figures are not available for three of the participating countries (Eire, Portugal, and Turkey), and I have omitted those for the relatively unimportant countries, Iceland and Luxemburg.

These figures should, of course, be used with extreme caution. National income figures even in this country are subject to a substantial margin of error; and the magnitudes attained depend to some extent on the philosophy of the statistician — for example, should all expenditures of government, inclusive of those going into wasteful channels, be included? In many European countries, the basic data are lacking, and statistical techniques are not adequately developed. In Chapter 1 we discussed another related issue: the relevance of foreign aid and the allocation of income as determinants of standards of living.[3]

In Table 8 national income figures of many countries are compared. Particularly in a world full of controls such comparisons are of limited values. In one country (for example, the United States) almost complete freedom prevailed in the disbursement of income. In another (such as the United Kingdom) controls

EUROPEAN RECOVERY PROGRAM

TABLE 8

National Income Per Capita and Ratio of Taxes to Income, European Countries, 1935–38, 1939, and 1946 *

	Real Income Per Capita in International Units, 1935–38 (1)	National Income Per Capita in Dollars		Ratio of Taxes to Income 1946 (4)	National Income in Billions of Dollars, 1946 (5)
		1939 (2)	1946 (3)		
Austria	...	166	88	1:3.5	1.5
Belgium	315 †	261	517	1:3.3	3.9
Czechoslovakia ‡	161	134	232	1:3.6	..
Denmark	347 §	338	562	1:8.4	2.0
France	358	283	214	1:1.7	18.0
Germany ‡	343 ‖	520	...	....	11.0 ¶
Greece	...	136	...	....	0.8
Hungary ‡	161	125	109	1:3.6	..
Italy	158	140	94	1:6.3	10.2
Netherlands	335	338	321	1:2.4	4.2
Norway	279	279	505	1:5.5	1.4
Poland ‡	117	95	70	1:2.7	..
Sweden	367	436	635	1:5.1	5.0
Switzerland	455	445	...	....	3.4
United Kingdom **	584	468	653	1:2.3	32.0
USSR‡	108	509	...	....	..
Yugoslavia ‡	...	96	...	....	..

* All but Columns 1 and 5 based on *NAC*, p. 131. Column 1 from C. Clark, *The Economics of 1960*, 1944, Appendix. Column 5 from *ERP: Sen. Hear.*, III, p. 1005.
† Belgium and Luxemburg.
‡ Not a participating country.
§ Denmark and Iceland.
‖ Germany and Austria.
¶ Western Germany.
** Great Britain and Northern Ireland.

were widespread, with the result that a large part of income received had only a theoretical purchasing power. For reasons of this sort, a dollar of income in the United Kingdom was clearly worth more than a dollar in Poland, where controls were more prevalent than in the former, but considerably less than in the United States.

DETERIORATION IN EUROPE

Another difficulty originates in the conversion rates. National incomes are expressed in domestic currencies and are converted into dollar equivalents on the basis of exchange rates. Unfortunately, these rates do not closely reflect relative purchasing power. In general, European currencies are overvalued. Converting the franc income at 119 francs = 1 dollar in 1946-47 in order to obtain the dollar equivalent, gives an exaggerated figure for the dollar income of France since the real value of the franc was nearer to 200 than to 119 francs for a dollar. The absurd results obtainable are well illustrated by the dollar income figures for the USSR: in 1939 the ruble was so overvalued that national income figures (for this and other reasons) yielded a per capita income figure almost as large as that of the United States.[4]

Keeping these reservations in mind, we draw the following conclusions from an examination of Columns 2 and 3. (The reader is reminded that in 1946 prices in this country were up more than three-fifths above prewar prices, and it, therefore, required an increase of more than 60 per cent in dollar per capita income in 1946 to yield the same standard of living as in 1939.)

(a) *An unweighted mean of European income (expressed in dollars) yields a little more than one-half of United States per capita income in 1939; and — despite the large overvaluation of most European currencies with a resulting overestimation of dollar incomes of European countries, and the artificially high incomes relative to spendable income in 1946 — the ratio of European per capita income to United States income in the latter year was little more than one-quarter.* Clearly, the United States had gained substantially on an absolute, and even more on a relative scale.[5]

(b) Of the European countries for which information is available, Belgium alone increased its per capita income as much as dollar prices had risen, that is to say, the Belgian per capita real income (again subject to the reservations noted) in 1946 was

EUROPEAN RECOVERY PROGRAM

above that of 1939. Increases of dollar incomes in Denmark, Czechoslovakia, and Norway roughly corresponded to the rise in prices expressed in dollars.[6] In view of the large restrictions on spending in these countries and especially in Czechoslovakia, it should *not* be assumed that equal dollar incomes corrected for price changes yield equivalent standards of living. Sweden and the United Kingdom suffered a substantial decline in real per capita income, and Austria, France, Hungary, Italy, and Poland, very large declines: even the dollar per capita income was down for the last five countries. With limitations on spending inclusive of much heavier direct taxes, the reduction in real income is not given merely by a comparison of the rise in per capita income and the cost of living. The USSR and Germany also suffered large losses. The reader should also refer to the discussion in Chapter 1, where indices of national income and cost of living in domestic currencies, 1938 to 1946–47 are compared.[7] There the reader will find that the comparisons yield absurdly high real incomes.

(c) In column 1, the reader will find Colin Clark's estimate (in international units) of per capita incomes for the years 1935-1938. These estimates to some extent serve as a check for those in Column 2, although these, also, are based to some extent on Clark. The latter's figures relate to 1935-1938, not 1939, and the geographical area covered is not always identical. The significant differences are: (1) *The USSR* — Clark's estimate of $108 in comparison with the absurdly high $509 in Column 2. (2) *Germany* — Again Clark's estimate is lower — namely $343 in comparison with $520. (3) *United Kingdom* — Clark's estimate is about one-quarter higher than that in Column 2.

(d) A word about taxes. They were not uniformly high in relation to income — note the ratios for Denmark, Italy, Norway, and Sweden. For the United Kingdom and France, with the ratio of per capita tax burden to income equal to 1:2.3 and 1:1.7

DETERIORATION IN EUROPE

respectively, the burden was indeed onerous. (The United States ratio in 1947 was about 1:4.) These comparisons should be considered in the light of the heavy burdens assumed by governments in European countries, for many of which private enterprise and consumers assume responsibility in this country. These figures are of limited value for other reasons also. In part, comparisons are vitiated by the varying manner in which taxes are included in income figures.

PRODUCTION FIGURES

Available industrial production indexes should be examined in the light of the results of our income table. Chapter 1 includes a brief summary of output figures.[8] Income, of course, is a much more comprehensive variable than industrial production, as it includes government, services generally, and agricultural output. Statistical difficulties of varying degree arise in the compilation of both income and production figures. The reader will recall especially the discussion on pp. 31–35 where the relevance of aid from abroad is considered and brief comparisons are made between income and less comprehensive indexes. Note the following:[9]

(a) Results vary as Figure 6 shows (1938 = 100).

(b) Italy, with an index of industrial output of 47 in 1946 seems to have suffered a decline in industrial production in 1946 equal to that in income.

(c) Industrial output in France, however, attained a peak of 102 in April–May 1947, but in 1946 output was 79 per cent of the 1937 output. The latter compares with a *decline* of income in *stable* dollars of more than 50 per cent. The difference is to be explained by (1) a substantial reduction in agricultural output, which is part of income; (2) controls of incomes, and notably wages; (3) a possible movement to tertiary, for example, service

EUROPEAN RECOVERY PROGRAM

INDUSTRIAL OUTPUT IN EUROPE BY GROUPS OF COUNTRIES
Index Numbers — 1938 = 100
(Logarithmic scale)

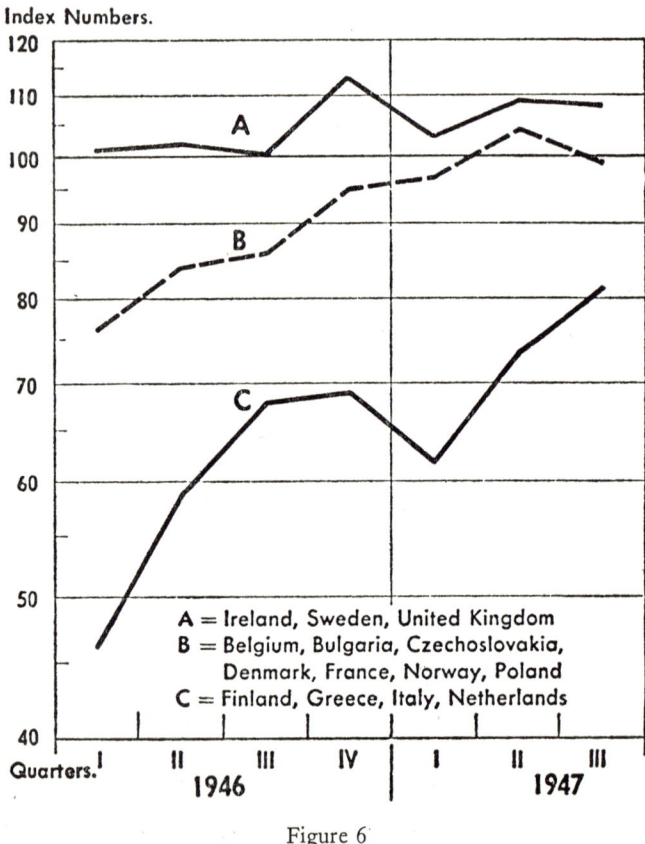

Figure 6

and selling, or (and) the low level of pay in these industries; (4) statistical deficiencies.

(d) Germany's industrial output in 1947 reached a high of 51 in the American Zone and 40 in the British Zone (1937 = 100).

DETERIORATION IN EUROPE

(e) Belgium's industrial index of 72 in 1946 (and peak of 87 for the first nine months of 1947) was rather low compared with a substantial rise in *real* income. Perhaps the overvaluation of the franc (conversion rate for income) explains the proportionately large rise in income.

(f) For Denmark (1946 = 101 and peak in 1947 = 120), Norway (1946 = 100 and peak in 1947 = 124), Sweden (peak = 109 in 1947), United Kingdom (109–110 in 2nd and 3rd quarter of 1947), the differences in movement from prewar values to 1946–47 for the two series were not substantial.

(g) The Netherlands figure for industrial output (1946 = 74) is large relative to a 5 per cent decline in dollar income and about 40 per cent in real income.

Perhaps a word should be added concerning 1947. On the whole, further progress was made, the industrial index for eight of the ERP countries rising from 90 in December, 1946 to a peak (average of peak months) of 102 in 1947, and 98½ in the last month (generally in last quarter) for which figures were available.[10]

CONCLUSION

In summary, the economic condition of this country, as expressed in employment and growth of income, has greatly improved since 1939. In fact, advances that might ordinarily require a generation to achieve were telescoped within a period of only 7 years. It remains to be seen whether or not these gains can be maintained. Europe, on the other hand, has lost ground absolutely and a fortiori relatively. Although income and production figures do not always check, they point to the general conclusion that national income on a per capita basis in Europe has fallen from one-half the United States level in 1939 to one-quarter in 1946. Losses reflect both gains in the latter, and declines in the former. Unfortunately, the European losses were even greater than is

EUROPEAN RECOVERY PROGRAM

suggested by these fractions. With the European currencies generally overvalued, reconversion into dollars of income expressed in local currencies tends to overstate the dollar incomes; and the average dollar of income in a European country flooded with controls, inclusive of restrictions on spending, is not worth as much as a dollar in this country. That the distribution of losses is very uneven further accentuates Europe's difficulties: Germany, Italy, Austria, and Eastern Europe are producing far below prewar levels, while the Scandinavian countries and the United Kingdom are once more producing at or above prewar levels. France and the Netherlands fall in between the two groups.

4. Dollar Shortage and Foreign Aid

INTRODUCTION

The theme of the last chapter was that Europe, after a serious deterioration relative to prewar conditions, experienced a unique crisis in 1947. Our next problem is that of the balance of payments. A production crisis does not necessarily generate a deficit in the balance of payments: in fact, deficits in the balance more generally accompany large economic advances. In order to understand the problem, we discuss in turn (1) the problem of dollar shortage, (2) exchange rates, (3) terms of trade, and then (4) the balance of payments.

One introductory remark is in order. Payments under the ERP may be assumed to be 5 to 6 per cent of the income of the cooperating countries,[1] and *total* imports, 15 to 20 per cent. Why, it may be asked, can these countries not cover the small deficit which is but (say) 5 per cent of their income and 30 per cent of *all* their imports? Against the large expenditures for war and the recovery of income since the war, the amounts involved seem small indeed. Surely, it might be said, Europe can reduce its imports and increase its exports each by 2 per cent of her income. These statistics raise the fundamental question of the need of a recovery program for Europe.

Overall analysis does not, however, give all the answers. In the process of revitalizing her industries and agriculture and of offsetting deficiencies resulting from crop failures and the breakdown of trade with other parts of Europe and Asia, the participating countries are confronted with yawning deficits in particular items. For example, numerous European countries even before the war were far from self-sufficient in food: the percentage of production to requirements was 32 for the United Kingdom, 47 for Switzerland and Norway, 62 for the Netherlands, 75 for Austria, and 83 for France. It is quite clear that countries normally dependent on foreign sources of food supplies are greatly injured by a reduction in cereal output by 14 per cent (1946–47 as compared to prewar output) and in several important foods, by even larger percentages, and these same countries, confronted with population increases of about 10 per cent over prewar levels, will indeed require additional help from abroad. Reduction in the caloric intake below the 1947 level might be very costly: food supplies yielded about 2500 calories daily in the principal countries of Western Europe or only about 85 per cent of prewar consumption, with urban consumers receiving substantially less. Approximately 2000 calories are required by a worker just to maintain himself; and the average American receives 3450 calories.[2]

Undoubtedly, European countries might make greater sacrifices. But the effects on output might greatly exceed the savings. Without adequate food and incentives, production and exports will suffer. No democratic European government is likely to survive which would impose the sacrifices in consumption standards (for example, a reduction of the daily caloric intake by 20 per cent or more)[3] involved in raising exports and reducing imports over the next four years to the extent of fifteen to twenty billion dollars, the assumed requirements under the ERP. This issue is discussed further elsewhere. Now we return to the problem of dollar scarcity, which is central for the problem of the balance of payments, and then to the related problem of loans and gifts to foreign countries, a manifestation of the dollar shortage.

DOLLAR SCARCITY: MYTH OR REALITY?[4]

One of the phenomena of recent economic history has been the so-called scarcity or famine of dollars. Foreign countries gener-

DOLLAR SHORTAGE

ally, not Europe alone, have been short of dollars. As will be shown presently, the persistent shortage of dollars is not to be explained by orthodox economics. The need of an ERP stems in part from a shortage of dollars. Europeans, without access to the printing press for the creation of dollars, are dependent upon sales of goods and services to this country and to a few other countries with convertible currencies, and upon loans and gifts from the United States, the almost exclusive source of dollars. Ever since World War I there has been a shortage of dollars, which was made up by shipments of gold and borrowing, and which was aggravated in the thirties by a flight of capital to this country.

Europe's need for aid rests in part upon the persistence of this dollar shortage; and for this reason we discuss it in some detail. There are economists who contend that the dollar shortage is a mirage. Obviously, had Europe not indulged in the luxury of two major wars, there well might have been no shortage of dollars, and certainly not one of large proportions. Again, it has been argued brilliantly by Roy Harrod that the British shortage results in no small part from ill-advised policies, and in particular from excessive capital investments inclusive of housing.[5] Obviously, a shortage may persist if a country insists upon living beyond its means, putting the resulting adverse balance of payments down as dollar shortage. Harrod shows, for example, that the British capital program was raised from £700 million in 1946 to £1100 million in 1947 — and with disastrous results. Undoubtedly, when dollars are made available too freely, there may be a disposition, as he suggests, for European countries to assume a mendicant attitude. On this score, it is well to recall that the Harriman Committee and the executive branch both reviewed the programs of capital expansion of the participating countries, suggesting a substantial scaling down.[6] In their determination to rebuild and to improve their economies, and in their nascent en-

EUROPEAN RECOVERY PROGRAM

thusiasm for planning, the European countries embarked on 2, 3, 4, and 5 year plans which involved them in excessive capital building. Unmindful of the adverse effect on the balance of payments — less exports are made available and more imports are required — and unprepared to squeeze consumers *pari passu* with the expansion of the capital program, the European countries soon faced a serious shortage of dollars.

This much I grant. But I do not go all the way with the disbelievers. In any reasonable and practical program of allocation of economic resources — under a free or controlled economy — and on the assumptions of two wars and political instability, I insist that a serious dollar shortage would have prevailed in 1914–1945, and would have become a fully grown crisis in 1947. Cautious policies, not hampered by reckless investment programs, would *generally* merely have reduced the demands on this country.

Of course, one may contend that dollar famine need not occur if the countries tending to be in short supply cut their garments according to the cloth. Russia, with a relatively low standard of living, gives little indication of a shortage of dollars. The totally planned economy might indeed solve its dollar problem by comprehensive control of the exchange market and foreign sales and purchases, and by meshing export and import policies with domestic consumption and capital policies. Undoubtedly many European countries, embarking on a fully planned economy but inexperienced in planning, and others, satisfied with semi-planned economies, would not have suffered from dollar shortage in the technical sense (see below) had they done an adequate planning job. Yet this may be conceding too much. Russia's dollar shortage is genuine even though she no longer obtains dollar advances or gifts. She pays the price of restricted imports in more work and a reduced standard of living. Other countries prefer not to pay this price for a pay-as-you-go dollar policy.

DOLLAR SHORTAGE

The discussion that follows largely relates to the economies which still depend significantly on price movements to achieve equilibrium; their dollar shortage can be explained in large part by the defective operation of the price mechanism. Whereas these economies depend substantially on price and exchange movements to achieve equilibrium, the planned economy relies primarily on controls.

WHAT IS DOLLAR SCARCITY? [7]

In recent years American economists have stressed the apparent scarcity of dollars on exchange markets as an argument in support of a generous program of loans to foreign countries, and liberal trade policies in this country. Their position has been that so long as the dollar scarcity persists international equilibrium will not be achieved; and without an approach to equilibrium economic warfare becomes more intense.

By a "dollar scarcity" I mean an excess of dollars used over dollars supplied, the difference being made up by borrowing on short-term account from the United States and (or) shipping gold to the United States. By lending on long-term account the United States of course made dollars much less scarce in the twenties than they would otherwise have been; but by importing capital in the thirties the scarcity was aggravated. During the war the United States Government treated the problem of scarcity through public loans. Dollar shortage reflects a weakness in the balance of payments. Emphasis is put upon dollar shortage, because dollars are freely convertible into foreign currencies and goods. The dollar is, therefore, a highly desirable currency. One of the problems confronting many countries is the tendency to accumulate soft currencies inconvertible into dollars: there is, therefore, a disposition to sell for hard (for example, dollar) currencies and buy for soft currencies.

"Dollar scarcity" is not exactly a respectable term among economists. Yet it dramatizes a persistent disequilibrium in the balance of payments of the United States vis-à-vis the rest of the world over a generation. It will be noted below that over the years 1919–1939 the supply of dollars used over the supply offered was no less than $10 billion (balance of all current transactions minus net outward movement of long term capital movements).

TABLE 9

ITEMS IN THE BALANCE OF PAYMENTS OF THE UNITED STATES, 1919–1939, INCLUSIVE

	Millions of Dollars Plus	Millions of Dollars Minus	Billions of Dollars Net
Balance of merchandise trade	19,270	...	+19.3
Balance, all current transactions (includes merchandise trade)	14,858	405	+14.5
Balance, all other current transactions (excludes merchandise trade)	316	5,113	−4.8
Gold movements, net	1,091	11,904	−10.8
Balance on long-term capital movements	2,554	7,124	−4.6 *
Balance on short-term capital movements	5,018	2,472	+2.5 †
Balance, all capital transactions	5,953	7,977	−2.0
Unexplained items	3,357	4,973	−1.6
Excess of dollars used over dollars supplied	10,644	761	+9.9

Source: Calculated from Department of Commerce, *The United States in the World Economy* (1943), Tables I and II.
* The long-term figures for 1933 and 1934 include some figures representing net transfer of funds in security arbitrage operations, which cannot be divided into domestic and foreign security transactions.
† Balance on short-term capital movements for the years before 1923 not available.

Over this period of twenty-one years the excess of exports was no less than $19 billion. It should be stressed that capital movements over the period were *outward* — $2 billion. Approximately one-quarter of the favorable balance of trade on commodity ac-

DOLLAR SHORTAGE

count was offset by an unfavorable balance on current transactions other than merchandise trade. The continued inflow of gold, accounting for about 75 per cent of the net balance on current account, is evidence of the scarcity of dollars.[8]

In an important sense, the persistence of dollar scarcity is inconsistent with the classical theory of international trade adjustments. An excess of credits on current account should not persistently prevail: the inflow of gold or appreciation of the exchanges should raise costs and prices for the United States, and the loss of gold or depreciation of exchanges reduce costs and prices *on world markets* for the rest of the world to a degree which would once more reëstablish equilibrium. Unfortunately, the required adjustments in wages, other costs and prices were not forthcoming; and, besides, elasticity of demand was not so great as was assumed in classical theory (Marshall, for example), and (or) through the introduction of trade restrictions the significance of elasticity of demand was reduced: prices of foreign goods were not allowed to fall on the American market *pari passu* with the fall in costs. Since the adjustments required and the elasticity assumed did not prevail, classical theory was not very helpful in explaining the actual state of affairs — as Keynes so eloquently and so often argued in the interwar period.[9]

THEORY AND PRACTICE

Unfortunately, the conditions assumed under the classical theory are not in fact realized. In the years 1914–1939 the United States gold stock rose from $1.5 to $17.6 billion. Domestic production of gold accounted for less than $2 billion of the net gain. Gold flowed in eighteen years, and out only eight years (1914, 1919, 1920, 1925, 1927, 1928, 1931, and 1933).[10] The United States share of the gold reserve of central banks and governments increased from 22 per cent in December 1914 to 34 per cent early in 1934. From December 1928 to September 1944 the proportion of central gold reserves

EUROPEAN RECOVERY PROGRAM

held by the United States rose from 37 per cent to 59 per cent.[11]

In the years following World War I there was much criticism of United States policy, on the grounds that this country was not playing the game of the gold standard: the country was receiving gold and yet not putting it to use.[12]

Yet the statistical history of this period reveals neither that gold was sterilized, nor that the United States was not experiencing a serious inflation. Total bank deposits rose from $17.4 billion in 1914 to $36.1 in 1920, and by 1929 they were no less than $51.0 billion.[13] Though in the years 1922–29 wholesale prices and the cost of living were relatively stable — the former declined by 1 to 2 per cent and the latter rose by 2 per cent — stock-market prices rose by about 220 per cent from December 1922 to September 1929.[14] What is even more significant, the country was undergoing what Keynes in his *Treatise* had called a profit inflation. Very large technological advances were evident in a rise in man-hour output in manufacturing of 32 per cent from 1923 to 1929. Yet hourly wages in manufacturing corrected for changes in the cost of living rose by only 8 per cent.[15] Had business passed on to consumers the gains in productivity not reflected in higher wages, prices would have been lower than they actually were. In this sense, monetary policy was inflationary.

In short, the United States experienced a significant monetary, security, and profit inflation: its domestic policies were inflationary when viewed from the requirements of the internal situation; but its policy was not inflationary enough when viewed from the requirements of international equilibrium. Despite net investments abroad of $9.3 billion in the period 1919–1930 — long and short-term investments of $12.6 billion offset by amortizations and retirements of $3.3 billion — the dollar remained scarce. With net investments averaging close to $800 million yearly, the gold inflow was kept down to approximately $1.2 billion for the twelve-year period.[16]

DOLLAR SHORTAGE

In the thirties the scarcity continued. In this period the net inflow of gold was much larger than in the twenties; but whereas capital moved out in the twenties, it moved in in the thirties. The net inward movement was almost $5 billion exclusive of unrecorded items; and in the years 1934–1939 the inflow was almost $6 billion.[17] In the latter part of the thirties, also, preparations for war and prosperity induced by war expenditures contributed to the large rise of United States exports. Although the inflow of gold averaged $1070 million in the years 1931–1939 and averaged only $110 million in the years 1919–1930, the weakness of foreign currencies and the strength of the dollar might well be held to reflect not so much a strong American position, but rather uncertain political prospects abroad.

SCARCITY, EPHEMERAL OR LONG-RUN?

This brings me to the main theme. Is scarcity of the dollar an ephemeral phenomenon or are there long-run forces that tend to make dollars scarce? In his stimulating article in the June 1946 issue of the *Economic Journal*, Lord Keynes seemed dubious of the theory of dollar scarcity, and expressed the view that dollars in the coming years would be plentiful and, therefore, that gold might flow out of the United States rather than in.

At the outset we should draw some conclusions from the experience in the twenty-five years 1914–1939. Adjustments as assumed in classical economics did not take place. *Changes in underlying economic and political conditions tended to prevent the required adjustments in wages, prices, and so on from occurring.* Apparently the rapid relative reduction of costs and the steady gains in rate of offer of new American products greatly in demand tended to give strength to the dollar, and despite monopolistic pricing in many markets and despite the pressure of inward movements of gold and expansion of deposits on prices here, the competitive position of the United States tended to im-

EUROPEAN RECOVERY PROGRAM

prove. On top of this, demand for United States products improved because of the shortages engendered abroad by one major war and preparation for another. So long as the gains in the competitive position of the United States (for example, reduced relative costs and prices, offer of new products) continue at a rate rapid enough more than to offset the corrective effects of gold or exchange movements, so long will the dollar remain scarce. As long as the political situation deteriorates abroad, and as long, therefore, as capital moves into this country or the outflow is discouraged, the dollar will tend to be strong.[18]

CREDITS AND GRANTS, 1914 TO 1947

It is by now clear that the dollar was generally strong over the years 1914 to 1939. Credits and grants over the years 1940–1947 were on a much larger scale than over the period 1914–1939, suggesting that foreign currencies would have taken a tailspin had it not been for the vast supply of dollars put at the disposal of the world through loans and grants in the entire period, and especially 1940–1947 — and primarily for the use of Europe. Table 10 shows the main facts.

This table suggests some interesting conclusions:

(a) The loans of over $10 billion made in World War I and shortly thereafter were relatively small — about $7 billion in 1917 and 1918, and $3 billion after the Armistice. Credits and other financial assistance of about $63 billion over five and a half years, January 1942 to June 30, 1947, averaged three to four times as much per year as in the World War I period. Even in the first two postwar years, the credits and other financial assistance by the Government averaged seven to eight billion dollars a year, an annual rate more than twice as high as in World War I and immediately afterwards, and one-half the rate *during* World War II.

(b) In relation to income the recent burden relative to that

DOLLAR SHORTAGE

TABLE 10

CREDITS AND OTHER FINANCIAL ASSISTANCE, 1914 TO JUNE 30, 1947 *

(*In Millions of Dollars*)

	Credits Utilized	Unutilized Balances
1914 to 1933	10,350	....
1934 to June 30, 1947		
Loans, property credits, and commodity programs	7,191 †	3,127 †
July 1, 1945 to June 30, 1947	6,179	....
Short-term advances	994	15
Other financial assistance	55,583 ‡	2,236 §
July 1, 1945 to June 30, 1947	5,364	....

* Based on *NAC*, pp. 4, 5, 168.
† On September 30, 1947, the amount outstanding was $7,862 million, and the unutilized balance on October 1 was $1,807 million.
‡ Authorization to June 30, 1947.
§ Committed but not appropriated.

in World War I does not seem so onerous as the absolute figures suggest. This is evident from Table 11. More recently the Economic Commission for Europe showed that whereas the United States export surplus to Europe had been 4.4 per cent of the gross national product in 1919 and 1920, it was but 2 per cent in 1946 and 1947. In relation to all countries, the respective percentages were 3.9 and 3.4 per cent respectively.[19] It should be observed, however, that in World War I the theory was that the Allies would repay. In World War II and after the war, only about ten to eleven billion dollars had been advanced as loans, the major part in the postwar years.

(c) Perhaps a word should be said concerning recent *United States* (public and private) long-term capital movements and unilateral *transfers*. In the two years ending June 30, 1947, the amounts involved were $15.6 billion. Approximately $7.9 billion were *loans and other investments*, of which $1.5 billion, or less

EUROPEAN RECOVERY PROGRAM

TABLE 11
PERCENTAGE OF UNITED STATES GOVERNMENT LOANS AND GRANTS OF THE NATIONAL INCOME

Years	Percentage
1917–1919	5½
January 1942–June 1947	7½
June 1945–June 1947	4

Source: Based on materials in *NAC* and National Industrial Conference Board, *The Economic Almanac for 1945–46.*

than 20 per cent, were private. Gifts and grants in aid amounted to $7.8 billion, the private contribution again being about 20 per cent. In two half years over these two years the total amounts were somewhat in excess of $4 billion, but in the others the amount was somewhat less than $4 billion. Over the period as a whole, the proportion of government loans to the total amount of government transfers tended to rise. Thus, in the second half of 1945, government loans and investments were about one-quarter the total for public gifts and grants-in-aid; but in the first half of 1947, they were close to three-quarters of the total.[20]

CONCLUSIONS ON THE DOLLAR SCARCITY

In order to understand the problem adequately, we shall have to discuss exchange rates and the terms of trade, problems deferred to later chapters. Obviously, failure to adhere to a reasonable rate of exchange or (and) a disposition to sell too cheaply or too expensively may aggravate the balance of payments difficulties.

It is safe to conclude that wars, political disturbance abroad, rapid gains by the United States, failure of costs and prices and demand to adjust as assumed under classical theory — all of these help explain the persistence of the dollar shortage. *Undoubtedly, however, the fumblings of planners in unaccustomed occupations, as evident, for example, in visionary plans for investment, and a disposition for moral standards to crack to some extent under*

DOLLAR SHORTAGE

the pressure of war and fascism, with a resulting tendency to seek aid abroad instead of putting one's own house in order — these in part account for dollar shortage.

Over a period of thirty-three years (through 1947) this country has advanced or given away about $80 billion, and accepted more than $20 billion in gold ($35 = 1 ounce). *We have used net about $100 billion of our resources to make these transfers and pay for the gold.* It cannot in general be held that the goods exported were obtained out of resources that otherwise would have been unemployed, for most of the transfers were made in periods of high employment and inflation — the thirties are an exception. *Americans paid for these loans, gifts, and the outflow of goods primarily by cutting down on their consumption and domestic investments.* The cost of importing $20 billion of gold or more was about as high as loans and gifts of an equivalent amount. (Possibly some part of the loans will be repaid, however, in goods or services.)

Despite the large amounts involved, the dollar continues to be scarce. Vast amounts of aid and imports of gold reflect the dollar shortage. The contributions made by the $100 billion calculated above are the more readily understood if this sum is put against the $257 billion of receipts from goods and services sold to foreigners in the thirty-three years ending June 30, 1947: approximately 40 per cent of the dollars required to pay for our exports and services were had from loans, gifts, and imports of gold. Against the nation's income, however, the amounts involved do not seem so large. These 100 billions amount to about 4 per cent of the $2660 billion of income for these thirty-three years. Against this background we should consider the $20 billion required under the ERP.

In wartime and postwar periods, the world has been short of dollars. When the United States Government stopped making dollars available private capital embarked on a large lending pro-

[107]

EUROPEAN RECOVERY PROGRAM

gram in the twenties; and when this source dried up in the thirties, the shortage was corrected by large exports of gold to the United States. Then came the war with sales of capital assets by foreign countries, and Lend-Lease; and the postwar with UNRRA, Civilian Supply, Aid to Greece and Turkey, loans by the Export-Import Bank, and the Anglo-American Financial Agreement. The ERP is the next link in the long historical chain of loans and gifts. In one respect this link is unique: if the European economy is really rehabilitated and put on a self-sufficing basis, it may be the end link. Political stability is, of course, a necessary condition.

5. Exchange Rates and Related Problems

INTRODUCTION

From dollar shortage and United States aid, it is an easy transition to exchange rates, for out-of-line rates are frequently held to be the cause of disequilibrium and dollar shortage.[1] This chapter deals, then, with exchange rates, terms of trade, the French devaluation of January 1948 as a case study of the issues involved, and the relation of external and internal stabilization.

In the discussions of the ERP, there was much comment on the need of establishing realistic exchange rates; and the final legislation deals with the problem. Moreover, in May, 1948 the powerful National Advisory Council, reporting on two years of control over international monetary policies here, stressed the responsibilities of ERP countries to revalue currencies. The presumption is that the failure to allow exchange rates to fall to their equilibrium (?) level results in abnormally low exports and excessive imports: the former become too expensive, and the latter too cheap. Obviously high or overvalued exchange rates will not explain the shortage of dollars over thirty-three years, though they may be one cause of recent difficulties. Failure to adjust exchange rates to the value appropriate to relative purchasing power and other relevant variables may result in large losses of reserves and excessive need for foreign loans. Good French wines and perfumes were too expensive in 1946–47 with the franc-dollar exchange at 119 francs = \$1. In 1946–47, it was widely held that European exchange rates were overvalued, and that exchange rates established by the International Monetary Fund should take cognizance of this fact. Actually, there was little disposition on the part of European countries to reduce the foreign value of their currencies; and going rates were generally accepted by the Fund.[2] It is well to consider the disposition to keep rates high, and the relation of exchange rates to the demands to be made under the ERP.

OVERVALUATION OF CURRENCIES

Estimates based on materials supplied by the Fund suggest that in the second quarter of 1947 25 non-British countries had an average overvaluation of their currencies in relation to the dollar of 25 per cent. An excellent example of overvaluation may be had from an examination of French statistics given in Table 12.

TABLE 12

Prices and Exchange Rates, France and the United States, 1938, 1944, 1947

	1938	1944	1947
1. Francs per dollar	39.95	49.72	119.30
2. Wholesale prices — France	100	265	1204 (Nov.)
3. Wholesale prices — U. S.	100	132	202 (Nov.)
4. Index, francs per dollar	100	125	298
5. Index of $\frac{\text{French Prices}}{\text{U. S. Prices}}$	100	201	594

Source: Calculated from IMF, *Statistics* and *FRB*.

Rows 4 and 5 of Table 12 give the essential comparison. By November 1947, the franc price of dollars was up by 198 per cent; but the French price level relative to the price level in the United States had risen by 494 per cent. On the basis of these prices, the franc was overvalued by about 100 per cent. American goods, therefore, seemed cheap to Frenchmen and French goods expensive to Americans. The French, therefore, tended to buy too much here and sell too little abroad.

It is a mistake, however, to assume that the overvaluation of the franc or other European currencies is the primary explanation of

EXCHANGE RATES

weakness in their balance of payments and of the reduction of reserves.[3] Indeed, gold holdings of the Bank of France declined from $2761 million in 1938 to $1996 million in 1944 and $463 million late in 1947. Yet I am prepared to argue that at any practical exchange rate the French would have suffered large losses in reserves and experienced great pressure on their balance of payments. In the present (1948) situation, there is no equilibrium rate in the absence of substantial foreign aid, which would establish an equality in the balance of payments. Even the devaluation of early 1948 did not seem to improve the French balance.

One might inquire at this point the source of the recently acquired enthusiasm for overvalued currencies. Surely one explanation is the success in the thirties of various countries (for example, Germany) with overvalued currencies. With an overvalued currency, the purchase of foreign goods is encouraged and the sale of goods abroad discouraged. For countries dangerously short of supplies, it is especially important to increase supplies available to the domestic economy; and the cheapness of imports and the high price of exports are means of achieving this objective.

A second and related point is the contribution of an overvalued currency towards solving the inflation problem which hangs over Europe. At high rates of exchange, export and import prices in *domestic* currencies are low, and, therefore, the inflationary pressures originating in international markets are reduced. Moreover, since high exchange rates tend to depress the volume of exports and stimulate imports, high exchange rates tend to increase the supply of goods available in a country and thus contribute towards reducing inflationary pressures.

A third factor of importance is that in the controlled and deficient economies of postwar Europe exchange rates are of less importance than usual. What is exported or imported is determined, not primarily by exchange rates or prices generally, but rather by

EUROPEAN RECOVERY PROGRAM

decisions concerning the allocation of resources: in the deficient economies of Europe, a price concession to foreign purchasers introduced through a reduction of exchange rates is not likely to be of great importance, for resources available for exports are abnormally low.

ESTABLISH NEW PARITIES?

In searching for realistic exchange rates, the critics of postwar exchange policies seek not only a depreciation in relation to the dollar, but also a determination of *equilibrium* rates, not restricted to the relation of currencies with the dollar. Trade of European countries is still primarily with other European countries, and not with the United States. From that viewpoint, overvaluation vis-à-vis the dollar is of secondary importance, though in view of the dollar shortage, a rise in exports to the United States and other hard-currency areas and a diversion of imports to soft-currency countries would help. One reason for the overvaluation in relation to the dollar, though not one of the most important ones, is the strong pull of trade among European countries: shortages are so serious in Europe that these countries bid higher than the United States for Europe's commodities. Sellers then obtain European currencies, not dollars. The competition is not only with other European countries, but also with the purchasers *within* each country: domestic sales on black markets are highly profitable.

By insisting upon an early stabilization of rates and the determination of definitive parities now, sponsors of the ERP may not be furthering their objective of obtaining "realistic" rates.[4] First, present prices are frequently out of line with the supply of money: suppressed inflation may become overt and prices adapt themselves to the bloated monetary supplies (as may happen in Great Britain) or, as has happened, the supply of money may be accommodated to the low official prices (as in Belgium). Hence,

EXCHANGE RATES

should suppressed inflation later become open, current adjustment of exchange rates to prices of 1948 would be unfortunate; and should exchanges be adjusted to prices suggested by current supplies of money but actually not realized, again the rate would prove to be a disequilibrium one. Second, and related to this, the current high level of import and export prices *may* not persist. Sterling, for example, may be too high when wheat is three dollars a bushel; but present rates would be more nearly appropriate once prices of agricultural commodities decline substantially from their present high peak and British productivity rises.

Third, so long as controls play a significant part — and they are likely to do so for many years — relative prices are of less significance than normally. Appropriate exchange rates based on relative purchasing power for a free economy may be way out of line in a controlled economy. In such an economy, the government may divert resources to export markets, impose monopolistic discrimination (for example, charging what the traffic will bear in each market), channel exports into hard-currency markets, scrutinize imports — each of these measures may raise the rate of exchange at which the balance of payments will be even. In short, price movements become of less importance as the determinant of exchange rates.

Fourth, the level of equilibrium rates also depends upon noncommodity transactions. Substantial reductions in governmental expenditures abroad and help under the ERP will, for example, make it possible to maintain a higher pound sterling rate than now seems possible. A moderation of the rate of capital expansion in Britain would also tend to reduce upward pressure on prices and contribute towards the maintenance of sterling at £1 = \$4.

Finally, changes in exchange rates depend not only upon price movements associated with monetary developments, but also upon shifts in the fundamental position, that is, in normal price relationships. It is too early to know much about the semi-permanent movements in real costs, in demand, in the effects of postwar patterns of trade restrictions, in the growing industrialization — all factors related to exchange rates. Until the postwar mold emerges clearly, it will not be easy to discover equilibrium exchange rates. *In summary, the time has not yet come for establishing postwar parity rates.*

THE FRENCH DEVALUATION OF JANUARY 1948

An examination of recent French experience will highlight some of the issues. Although the French have received much support and even pressure from this country to revalue their franc, the responsibility should not be put exclusively or even primarily on American authorities or on the supporters of the ERP. A strong case could certainly be made out for a devaluation of the franc: price movements in relation to exchanges, as well as the rapid loss of reserves suggested the need of radical measures. Adverse balances on 15 of 20 clearing and payment agreements in early 1948 also point to the need of corrective measures: the franc was apparently overvalued not only in relation to the dollar but also in relation to most other currencies. Under these conditions, the French in late January 1948 announced a reduction of parity from 119 to 214 francs per dollar and the special privilege to exporters to convert one-half of export proceeds in dollars (and escudos) at the free market rate (about 300 francs per dollar). The French were determined to stimulate exports to the United States, not to the United Kingdom. Hence their unwillingness to introduce an across-the-board *equal* decline in the franc.

This policy might be effective if exports to the United States (and perhaps *ultimately* to Switzerland) were substantial. Actually, French exports to these countries in 1947 were a small part of total exports. Since this privilege of favorable prices for French

EXCHANGE RATES

exports was denied to buyers in other countries, the effect might indeed be a divergence of exports to the United States and (ultimately) to Switzerland. Such shifts take time, however, and there are limits imposed by the character of exports sent to different markets. Besides, since the French were *generally* short of foreign exchange, there was little justification for discriminating only in favor of the dollar, and possibly the Swiss franc. The large reduction in the dollar value of the franc for export purposes will prove to be effective only if large resources can be released for export, and substantial diversions can be made from other markets to the United States (and similarly for Switzerland). It still remains to be seen whether the time is propitious for these adjustments; and also germane is the moral issue of despoiling other creditors (for example, those with which France was in debt on clearing or payment agreements) through shifts of exports to this country at their expense.

French decisions in January 1948 are subject to criticism not because of the devaluation invoked, but because they introduce a large element of discrimination and encourage the use of multiple currencies, which are contrary to the principles of the Fund, and ultimately will make more difficult the stabilization of currencies and multilateral trade, both essential elements of the ERP. It is not easy to understand why the American authorities did not prevent the French from taking this unilateral action. Clearly, with the leverage of aid under the Export-Import Bank, they might well have stopped the French from pursuing a policy contrary to the spirit of the evolving ERP. That they did not do so, *may* be explained in part by the determination of the American Government or their spokesmen to urge European countries to terminate controls. (The French devaluation was a substitute for a greater degree of control.)

Indeed, without recourse to multiple currencies and discriminatory practices, the French might have achieved their objective of

EUROPEAN RECOVERY PROGRAM

diverting exports to dollar areas and relying more on imports from areas in which they had surplus balances (for example, the United Kingdom). Through controls of exports and imports, they could have shifted exports *to* the dollar markets and raised imports *from* the soft-currency markets. Should this policy have proved ineffective, they might have offered special premiums to exporters dispatching goods to any country in relation to which the French were in debt on current account. This would have been discriminatory, but less objectionable than the system introduced. Under the program actually evolved, the British and other countries will be forced to impose controls on exports in order to prevent the French from buying British goods for pounds sterling (at 856 francs = £1), selling in the American market (at $4 = £1), and repatriating the proceeds ($4) at the price available to French exporters of about 1180 francs = $4. In this manner, the British obtain francs for their goods (or pounds sterling) and the French receive the dollars. To counteract the French measures, the British either will be required to sell goods likely to be re-exported to the French for dollars, or restrict exports to France sufficiently so that the price in francs will rise to a level consistent with the dollar to pound, pound to franc, and dollar to franc (for exporters) cross rates. In other words, the franc price of relevant British goods sold to France should rise about 40 per cent (minus extra transportation and similar charges involved in importing via France to the United States), over the cost of exporting directly from the United Kingdom to the United States.

EXCHANGE RATES AND TERMS OF TRADE

In the years since 1938, the prices of agricultural commodities rose more than those of industrial products. This is not the only explanation of the *assumed* deterioration in the terms of trade of European countries. The CEEC observes that highly indus-

EXCHANGE RATES

trialized countries pay 20 per cent more for imports in relation to prices they receive for their exports than in 1938:

This arises partly from the distortion of world production which forces countries into high-cost sources instead of traditional low-cost sources; partly from artificial price structures in some parts of the world; and partly from a general world upward swing of prices of primary products in terms of manufactured goods.[5]

As we emphasized earlier [6] the deterioration in Europe's terms of trade is not so clear as is assumed by the CEEC. Europe's large adverse balance of payments is associated primarily with the *rise* in the price of imports from overseas, not in a deterioration in the terms of trade; and secondarily in the losses on invisible account — for example, returns on capital invested abroad and shipping earnings.[7] Even with no deterioration in the terms of trade, a country or an area with large excesses of imports will experience increased deficits as a result of increased prices of imports.[8] I repeat also what I said in Chapter 1, that the worsening in the terms of trade is anything but clear for Europe though there is evidence of significant loss in the bargaining position of the United Kingdom. When, therefore, the executive branch estimates that the ERP countries have to export 30 per cent more goods in order to obtain the prewar volume of imports, they surely must have in mind primarily the losses on invisible account.[9]

On the theory that adverse terms of trade assumed by the CEEC will not continue, the CEEC assumes that export prices of the sixteen countries will remain unchanged, while import prices as compared with prices of July 1, 1947, will fall by $7\frac{1}{2}$ per cent in 1949, by 10 per cent in 1950, and by $12\frac{1}{2}$ per cent in 1951.[10] Both the Harriman Committee and the executive branch conclude that the CEEC was too optimistic in its forecasts of improved terms of trade for Europe. First, the decline would be concentrated largely on raw materials and food, which constitute one-third of the imports from the United States under the ERP proposal, and one-half of the imports from all sources. (In the view of the Harriman Committee, prices of industrial products would remain relatively stable.) In the light of continuing scarcities in food and raw materials, aggravated by the depletion of resources and the tendency to restrict output and raise prices in agricultural countries, the assumed decline in prices is excessive.

Second, even by the end of 1947, export prices from the Americas had risen more than 7½ per cent above the July 1947 level.[11] Both the Harriman Committee and the executive branch were unwilling to accept the price estimates made by the CEEC. It makes a difference of two to two and a half billion dollars in the cost of ERP for the four and a quarter years whether prices move as suggested by the CEEC, or as suggested under more reasonable assumptions by the Harriman Committee. In the executive branch study, the range of prices for imports from the United States for 1951–52 was given as 85 to 107.8 (July 1, 1947 = 100) and of prices of exports to the United States from 90 to 105. The range of import prices was 27 per cent and of export prices, 17 per cent; and the range between lowest import prices and highest export prices was more than 20 per cent.[12]

The problems are somewhat more complex than has so far been indicated. It is not easy to forecast export and import prices in the next three to four years, nor their relationships. Much depends upon exchange rate policy. European countries would have suffered a serious deterioration in their terms of trade had they not generally maintained both controls and overvalued currencies and especially since they were confronted with strong demands for raw materials, foods, and machinery from overseas and were selling relatively dispensable products to overseas. Should other European countries follow the example of Italy and France in depressing their exchanges and relying less on direct controls of trade, the terms of trade will move against them. In reducing the

EXCHANGE RATES

foreign value of their currencies, France and Italy are supporting policies of quantity sales and low prices.

Vital also are economic conditions in the United States and economically satellite countries. Should the inflation balloon burst in the course of these four years, then undoubtedly the CEEC's optimistic forecasts may prove to be correct. With price supports and public underwriting of general demand, however, the depression may well be contained. With depressed conditions here, Europe might indeed gain in cheaper food and raw materials; but she would also probably find appropriations under the ERP cut. Gladstonian principles of finance might well prevail in this country which might prevent the ERP from contributing to the support of demand. Surely, in the middle of 1948, neither the prospects of stopping the inflation nor the probability of a substantial depression is great.

STABILIZATION

In the discussion of exchange parity we commented on the problem of timing revisions of rates. Definite parities are not in order until conditions are more nearly normal. A similar generalization applies to stabilization loans: these are likely to be dissipated if offered before internal conditions are stabilized and the balance of payments promises to be in equilibrium. So long as inflation is on the march, establishment of definitive parities is out of the question. For these reasons, the Harriman Committee and the executive branch urge that stabilization loans of $3 billion as proposed by the CEEC be denied until conditions are more propitious. The former proposes application to the International Monetary Fund, and the latter to the United States Stabilization Fund.[13]

Yet even this position is vulnerable to some extent. Chaotic monetary conditions at home jeopardize external stabilization; and the failure to achieve the latter also interferes with internal stability. With exchange rates unstable or under rigid controls, domestic markets are deprived of essential goods or are refurbished at high prices. It is, therefore, not easy to defend the Harriman Committee proposals (1) to make stabilization of internal monetary and fiscal conditions precede recovery of production, and yet (2) to deny Europe external stabilization aid. For in order to achieve internal stability, it will be necessary to increase production and then trade by gradually relinquishing exchange controls and stabilizing the exchanges. But decontrols and relative exchange stability require adequate foreign reserves. As output and trade expand, domestic conditions will become more stable; and then stabilization loans may be required in order to protect domestic stability from external disequilibrating factors. *The big if is, can there be an adequate recovery in output without restoration of fairly stable monetary conditions, and can the latter be achieved without prior replenishment of reserves of the ERP countries?*

IN CONCLUSION

Undoubtedly exchange rates in effect in 1946, 1947, and even 1948 are far from equilibrium rates. Yet American authorities may be doing Europe and this country a disservice in putting pressure upon European countries to establish "realistic" or equilibrium rates at this time. Proponents of this view should be reminded that, under current chaotic conditions, the discovery of equilibrium rates would be a miracle; that once a more normal relation between money and prices is established, equilibrium rates under present abnormal conditions in commodity markets are not likely to be germane; and with inelastic supplies, disordered markets, and the widespread use of controls, exchange rates are considerably less important than many American observers seem to think. Surely, the determination of definite parities awaits the assessment of the structural changes in supply and

EXCHANGE RATES

demand resulting from the war, inclusive of the new position of trade and capital movements in the economy.

A general downward revision of rates may well result in less favorable terms of trade for European countries and, with supplies inadequate, this may result in reduced dollar receipts and increased costs of the ERP; and the sale in large quantities at low prices is scarcely the appropriate policy for impoverished Europe. French experimentation with lowered exchange rates early in 1948 is scarcely reassuring. Insofar as the bait of the ERP contributed to this premature and clumsy attempt to stabilize the exchange at realistic rates, American authorities have little cause for pride. There is no evidence that the franc was depressed appropriately even in the dollar market, and surely not in other markets where francs are in oversupply; or, for that matter, that any conceivable exchange rate would have established equilibrium. It does not help matters that the French indulged in the luxury of multiple and discriminatory rate practices and failed to deal fairly with numerous creditors other than the United States, and that they transferred the burden of controls to others.

6. Balance of Payments of the Participating Countries

INTRODUCTION

In the two preceding chapters, the subject matter related to factors that might explain an adverse balance of payments. Dollar shortage indeed is a term merely describing the adverse balance of payments; but an investigation of the causes of its persistence clarifies the causes of disequilibrium.[1] In assessing the overvaluation of Europe's currencies and its contribution to disequilibrium, we concluded that this was probably not a factor of prime importance. Our next problem is that of the adverse balance of payments of the sixteen ERP countries and Western Germany. The origin of the deficits, the evolution of the estimates, the manner of financing them, the real cost to the United States and the other Americas, the attempts to reduce the sacrifices imposed on this country — these are the main problems. Unfortunately, the detailed estimates do not make for interesting reading. The busy or the impatient reader might well skip a large part of this chapter, for much of it is devoted to necessarily detailed statistics.[2]

CAUSES OF THE ADVERSE BALANCE

The more important causes of the large deficits in the balance of payments of the ERP countries are presented below. However, the reader should be reminded that conditions vary from country to country, as was pointed out in Chapter 1.[3]

In 1938 the sixteen participating countries and Germany had incurred a deficit of $500 million in their balance of payments with nonparticipating countries. Against $6600 million of pay-

BALANCE OF PAYMENTS

ments, their receipts from exports were $4600 million, and investment income and other invisibles, inclusive of shipping, amounted to $1500 million. As a result of the war these countries lost $1500 million of income from shipping and investments. (This amount roughly corresponded to the deficit on visible trade with the American Continent in 1938 of $1450 million.) Actually, in 1947, their invisible account was $500 million in the red.[4]

Another relevant factor is the terms of trade of the Western European countries. In earlier chapters,[5] we dealt with this problem, concluding that a clear case for a deterioration of Europe's terms of trade had not been established by the CEEC. For 1947 the Economic Commission for Europe (ECE), for example, estimated the average cost of imports in terms of exports for Europe at 102 (1938 = 100). These over-all results scarcely suggest a serious deterioration. Also of some significance, the Department of Commerce figures point to a deterioration of the terms of trade of the *United States* of more than 10 per cent from 1938 to 1947. By insisting upon, for the ERP countries, a 20 per cent deterioration of the terms of trade since the end of the war, the executive branch seems to be supporting the position of the CEEC. It is, however, important to distinguish the change since before the war emphasized by the CEEC, and the worsening in the last two years. The Council of Economic Advisors (CEA) shows that in the two years ending in the third quarter of 1947, unit prices of United States imports rose by 35 per cent and of exports by only 20 per cent. Although these indexes for the United States trade should not be compared with those for Europe's trade, nevertheless the dominant position of the United States in Europe's trade suggests a relevance of the CEA's figures for the problem under consideration. It might also be observed that the ECE found a deterioration in Europe's terms of trade of but 5 per cent from 1946 to 1947. *In short, Europe's terms of trade do not seem to be significantly worse in 1947 than in 1938, though*

EUROPEAN RECOVERY PROGRAM

they may have deteriorated moderately in 1946 and 1947. A rise in the prices of imports relative to exports over the years 1938 to 1947, therefore, did not contribute greatly to Western Europe's deficits on international account. As we emphasized before, however, the rise in the prices of imports for an area that imports much more than she exports is another matter. *The rise of import prices was a factor of first-rate importance.* In 1938 Europe's imports were $5.8 billion; her exports, $3.7 billion. In 1947 the adverse balance was much larger: her exports in 1938 prices were 78 per cent of the 1938 amount and her imports, 102 per cent.[6]

Another cause for Europe's deficiency of dollars is the failure to obtain hard currencies (that is, dollars or currencies convertible into dollars) for her exports. In part this may be ascribed to the large volume of exports going to countries which have inconvertible currencies, and in part to the tendency of traders and others either to allow dollars to accumulate abroad or to sell them on the black market, the latter transactions enabling the new owners to purchase nonessentials or to hoard dollars. In neither case is the most effective use made of the dollars received. Europe's imports from non-European countries in 1938 were 45.5 per cent of her total imports; but in 1947 the percentage had risen to 61.4 per cent; the respective figures for exports to non-European countries were 34.9 and 42.6 per cent.[7] These suggest a greater strain on dollar resources, for imports from overseas increased much more than exports to non-European countries.

Western Europe's deficit with the Americas will depend in part upon the success with which her sales (net) to other nonparticipating countries will yield dollars with which to cover part of her deficit with the Americas. In the CEEC report, the participating countries estimated their credit balance with other nonparticipating countries over the four years at $3 billion. Although the report pointed out that should dollars be made available to the other nonparticipating countries, the deficits with the Americas

BALANCE OF PAYMENTS

would be correspondingly reduced, the CEEC in estimating its deficit with the Americas did not count on this development. In other words, the deficit that had to be covered was $22.4 billion, that with the Americas, not $22.4 billion minus $3 billion. Apparently the Harriman Committee misread the CEEC report; for that committee criticized the CEEC for its optimism in assuming that the required dollars would be made available to the other nonparticipating countries, and hence to the participating countries. In short, should the CEEC countries accumulate $3 billion of credits with the other nonparticipating countries, only a part — but one-fourth to one-half — will be convertible into dollars.[8]

A related problem is that of exports among the participating countries. It was estimated that a billion dollars of goods might fail to enter the channels of trade because, under the bilateral agreements in vogue, it would not be possible to finance trade among participating countries. Should this happen, Europe would be forced to seek goods in the Western hemisphere which might be much nearer to home and not require payments in dollars. Hence the emphasis on a system of multilateral payments which would make it possible for one country with a credit with a second country to use this to offset a debit with a third country.[9] By the end of 1947, Belgium, Luxemburg, France, Italy, and the Netherlands had approved a multilateral payments arrangement. Two types of offsets were provided: increases in balances or creation of new balances, and those involving only decreases in balances. Full membership carries the obligation to accept automatic offsets or those involving only decreases in balances under existing bilateral payments agreements. Occasional membership gives members much more discretion. Denmark, Norway, Sweden, Austria, and the United Kingdom accepted occasional membership. Since purchases among participating countries may reduce the burden on the American economy, the United States can finance this trade under the ERP legislation. Dollars made avail-

EUROPEAN RECOVERY PROGRAM

able for other purposes are reduced to the countries receiving dollars in this manner.[10]

On top of all these explanations of the adverse balance of payments, there are the immediate causes associated with the war and its aftermath, and the serious crop failures of 1947. With production much below prewar levels, the pressure was strong to sacrifice exports and stimulate imports. (In 1946–47, however, exports rose more than output. For Europe, the ratio of the exports index to the production index rose from 61 in the first quarter of 1946 to 86 in the third quarter of 1947 — at the latter time production was 99 and exports 85, where 1938 = 100.[11] See Figure 7.) Political confusion and uncertainty in Europe and Asia intensified the breakdown of trade between Western Europe on the one hand, and Eastern and Central Europe and Asia, on the other. Western Europe was thus unable to pay for its excess of imports from America with income received from exports and invisible credits from the East; and, with exports from Eastern Europe and Germany to Western Europe drastically reduced, was forced to find alternative sources of supplies.[12]

In summary, the adverse balance of payments of the sixteen participating countries is genuine. Long-run forces are germane, as is the breakdown of trade and production, the rise of import prices, losses in invisible exports, the crop failures of 1947, the segmentation of markets, a worsening in the terms of trade and, to some extent, mistaken policy.

FINANCING THE ADVERSE BALANCE, 1945–1947

United States exports attained a record level of $21 billion (annual rate) in the third quarter of 1947, and the export surplus no less than $13 billion.[13] For the year as a whole, net foreign investment averaged close to $9 billion.[14] Serious problems of financing this excess of exports plagued both foreign countries and our Government.

EUROPEAN INDUSTRIAL PRODUCTION AND EXPORTS, EXCLUDING GERMANY

By Quarters, 1946 and 1947

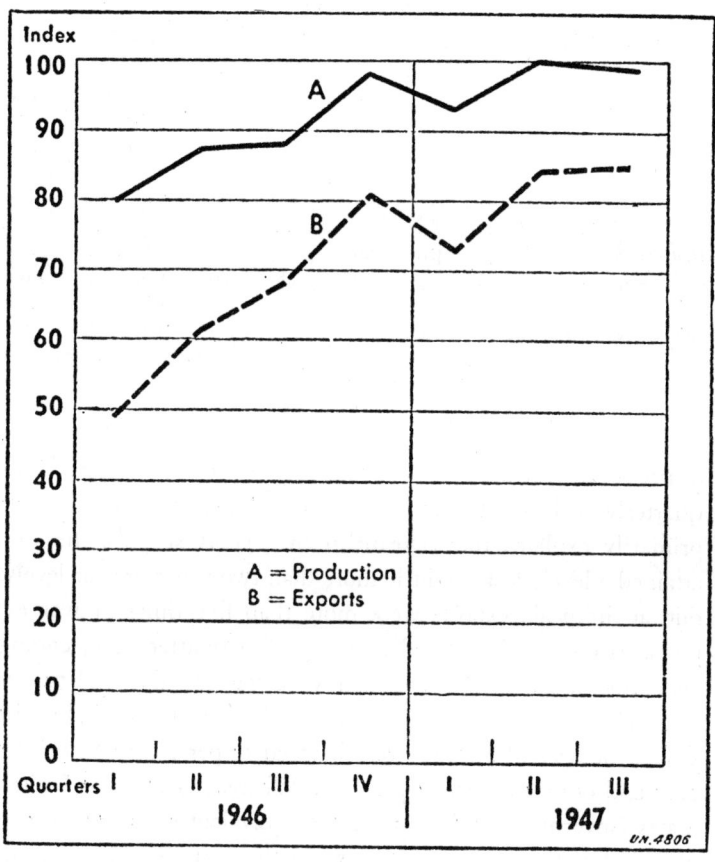

Figure 7

Note — The ratios shown are not those of the value of imports or exports to the value of production, but an expression of the relative movements of the two indexes.

[127]

EUROPEAN RECOVERY PROGRAM

A bird's-eye view of the balance of payments from June 30, 1945, to the third quarter of 1947 suggests the problems raised and the manner of solution. Table 13 and Figure 8 suggest the following

TABLE 13
United States Balance of Payments, 1945–1947 *
(*In Billions of Dollars, Annual Rate*)

	Goods and Services Exports	Imports	Export Surplus	U. S. Govt. Aid	Liquidation Short-term Capital and Gold	Private Gifts	Other Sources
1936–1938	4.1	3.6	.5	..	1.1	.2	−.8
1945 — 2nd half	13.4	7.6	5.8	5.9	−1.6	.4	1.0
1946	15.2	7.1	8.1	5.4	1.8	.6	.3
1947 — 1st 3 quarters ..	19.3	8.0	11.3	6.7	3.4	.6	.6

* Adapted from *CEA*, pp. 7, 14.

conclusions: (a) Both the export total and export surplus tended to rise: both reached a peak in the second quarter of 1947. (The quarterly peak is not shown here.) (b) An expansion of exports primarily explains the increase in the export surplus. Imports attained a level of only a little more than two times prewar levels; but, at the peak, exports were more than five times prewar exports. (c) Over the period of two and a quarter years ending September 1947, United States Government aid financed 72 per cent of the export surplus; liquidation of short-term capital in the United States and sales of gold financed 14 per cent; and private gifts and other sources, 14 per cent. Whereas in 1945 the United States Government aid financed the equivalent of the entire surplus, it financed only 60 per cent in the first three quarters of 1947. The resulting drain on liquid short-term capital and gold reserves is to be explained by the pressure put upon foreign countries by the rise in imports from this country, not matched by a corresponding increase in United States Government aid.

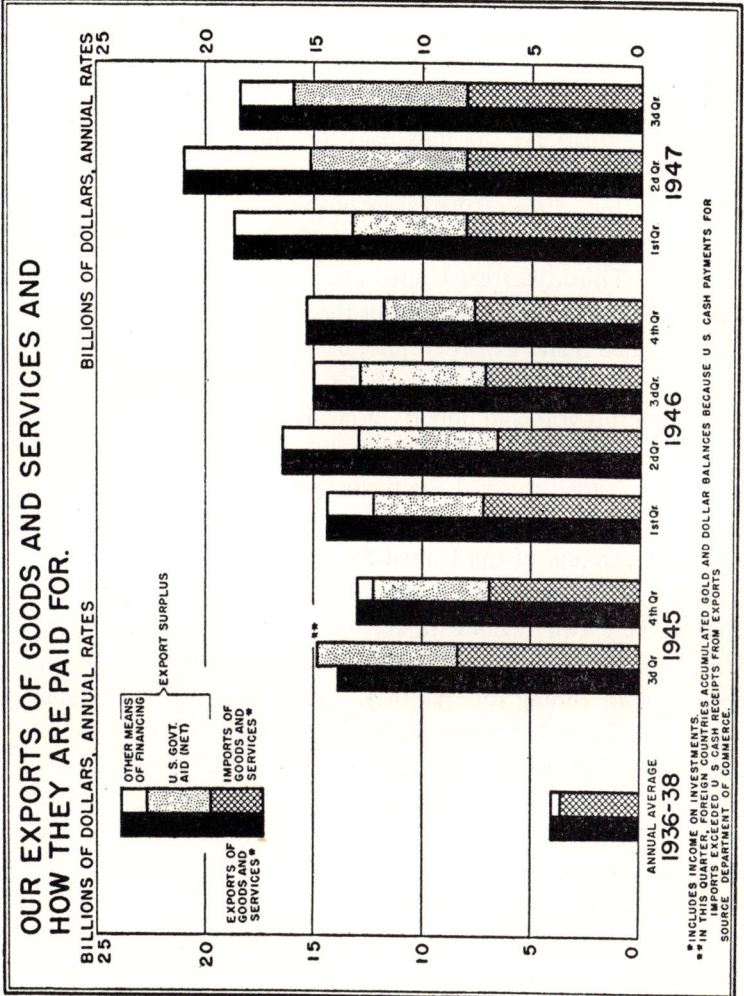

Figure 8

EUROPEAN RECOVERY PROGRAM

Since we are especially interested in Europe, her contribution to the export surplus of this country and her share of United States credits and gifts require separate consideration. First, observe that whereas in 1936–1938 Europe paid for 57 per cent of her imports from the United States by shipping goods to us, in 1947 (first three quarters) she thus paid for only about 15 per cent of her imports. Second, the financial aid to Europe accounted for more than four-fifths of the excess of purchases of Europe from this country in 1946 and for nearly all of it in the second quarter of 1947.[15] Third, whereas United States merchandise exports to Europe in 1946 were 45 per cent of the total, and Europe's share of the United States export surplus, 67 per cent, imports into the United States from Europe were but 17 per cent of United States imports in this year, and imports of goods and services and investment income, 24 per cent.[16]

Fourth, Europe received the major part of the loans and unilateral transfers made by the United States. Thus Europe obtained 72 per cent of the United States Government's unilateral transfers in 1946 and 60 per cent in the second quarter of 1947, and in these two periods 93 and 92 per cent, respectively, of United States Government long-term capital loans.[17] Fifth, in the two years ending June 30, 1947, Europe received $12.2 billion of $16.3 billion of United States Government loans, property credits, and grants. Of the total, Paris Conference countries accounted for $9.3 billion, and the Iron Curtain countries, $2.3 billion. (Many will consider the last as a rat-hole enterprise.) Of the loans and property credits, Europe received 87.4 per cent ($8 billion out of $9.1 billion) and the Paris Conference countries, 80.9 per cent, with the Paris Conference countries accounting for $7.4 billion (the United Kingdom and France alone, $6.3 billion).[18]

According to the National Advisory Council (NAC), gold, dollar balances, and foreign investments in the United States on June 30, 1947, were around $28.7 billion, of which one-half was in

BALANCE OF PAYMENTS

gold. Of this total the countries under the ERP accounted for $13.7 billion (gold, 6.6; short-term dollar assets, 2.2; long-term, 4.9). For *all* countries, *private* dollar balances at $3.2 billion as of June 30, 1947, exceeded official dollar balances at $2.2 billion.[19] These figures of the National Council do not check too well with those released by the Federal Reserve Board more recently. Gold reserves of the ERP countries were estimated at $5.7 billion at the end of 1945 and $3.75 billion at the end of 1947; foreign banking funds at $2.1 billion and $1.5 billion, respectively.[20]

It is indeed tempting to tap the gold and other United States assets held by the ERP countries at the end of 1947. Unfortunately, the assets are unevenly divided, and the *surplus* gold reserves even in the middle of 1947 were but $1.5 billion — an additional amount has since been sold. Their $3.75 billion of gold available at the end of 1947 equalled about 4 per cent of their income, whereas our $22 billion constituted about 11 per cent of our income. Furthermore, the $2 billion of short-term assets belonging to the ERP countries in 1947 were not large when compared with export trade to these countries at the annual rate of $7 billion. In 1937 all of Europe held $1.3 billion of short-term dollar assets, with exports to Europe in 1937 at about one-quarter the 1947 level; and the dollar balances privately owned are not all easily mobilized by the government. Part of the foreign assets, in fact, more than half of the long-term assets of the ERP countries in 1947, were in direct investments. These are not easily liquidated.[21]

In short, there seems to be little prospect that Europe will be able to finance herself significantly by further drains on her reserves and dollar balances and investments. This pessimism is generated by the need of minimum reserves to cover the internal circulation and temporary deficits in the balance of payments (and related to this, the increased needs with higher prices and larger trade), the uneven distribution of the assets, the conceal-

EUROPEAN RECOVERY PROGRAM

ment of a large proportion by private holders, the difficulties involved in liquidating direct investments, and the recent large losses of gold and dollar assets — at the annual rate of $4½ billion in the first three quarters of 1947.

THE PARIS PROGRAM AND SUCCESSIVE REVISIONS

According to the CEEC, the participating countries and Western Germany required $57.3 billion of imports over the years 1948–1951, the United States to provide $20.4 billion, the rest of America, $14.8 billion, and other nonparticipating countries, $22.2 billion. Whereas before the war the Americas had accounted for 45 per cent of the imports of these countries, the proportion in 1948 was to be two-thirds. The main imports from the Americas in 1948–1951 were to be the following: [22]

In Billions of Dollars

Food and fertilizer	13.7
Coal and petroleum	2.9
Iron and steel	1.3
Timber	1.0
Equipment covered by Technical Committee	3.4
Other (mainly raw materials)	12.9
	35.2
Shipping	1.7

In 1948 the deficit with the American Continent, according to the Paris Report, was to be over $8 billion. On the assumption that the International Bank would cover $918 million of the deficit there remained a total of $7.1 billion. The United Kingdom, France, and Italy accounted for two-thirds of the total.[23]

Europe's difficulties stemmed in large part from her dependence upon imports from the United States, without corresponding sales to the United States. Production and exports were indeed at

BALANCE OF PAYMENTS

an inadequate level; but on top of that, Europe's exports tended to move to markets other than the United States, with the result that the goods (net) and dollar burden rested predominantly upon the United States. The following figures (from Table 14) support this conclusion.[24] It will be noted that the deficit with the United States was to be almost three and a half times as large as the exports of the Paris Conference countries to this country; but with the rest of America the deficit was to be about three-fourths of their exports to these countries. Furthermore, as noted above, the United States was to provide about $20 billion of the imports required, the other Americas, $15 billion, and other nonparticipating countries, $22 billion. The unfortunate relation of exports and imports is evidenced by the fact that the deficit with the United States was to be four-fifths of the imports required from her; with the other Americas, two-fifths; while with other nonparticipating countries the deficit was insignificant compared to $22 billion of purchases.

For various reasons, some of which have been mentioned, the Harriman Committee scaled down the aid to be made available

TABLE 14

Deficits and Exports of Sixteen Countries and Western Germany, 1948–1951

(In Billions of Dollars)

	Deficits with	Exports to
United States	15.81	4.67
Rest of Americas	5.97	7.63
Dependencies	0.66	...
	22.44	
Financed by International Bank	3.13	...
Remains to be financed	19.31	...

Source: *CEEC*, pp. 54–56.

EUROPEAN RECOVERY PROGRAM

to the participating European countries. A statement of the assumptions made by the CEEC underlines the optimism upon which their estimates were made:

> The tentatives estimates . . . are based on a number of assumptions; these include the assumptions that their production will increase greatly, that the imports required for this will be available, that a state of full employment and full use of productive resources will be continuously maintained, that an increasing part of the needs of the participating countries and Western Germany can be obtained from Eastern Europe and from South East Asia, that the goods which the participating countries can produce for export can be sold to the American Continent and to the rest of the world, that there will be a progressive reduction in the price of imports in relation to the price of exports, and that non-participating countries will so far as necessary be able to pay for such goods in dollars.

On these assumptions, it was anticipated that an adverse balance with the American Continent of $8.0 billion in 1948 would be reduced to $3.4 billion by 1951, and the adverse balance with other nonparticipating countries of $240 million in 1948 would be converted into a credit balance of $1800 million in 1951.[25]

Emphasizing the difficulties of making precise estimates for years to come, the Harriman Committee nevertheless scaled down the deficit to be financed by the United States from $19 billion, as estimated by the CEEC, to from $12.5 to $17.2 billion. Because goods were not available in adequate amounts and because they proposed to transfer the burden in part to other countries, the Harriman Committee put exports from the United States at $2.5 to $6 billion *less*, and exports from the other Americas at $0.75 billion dollars *less* to $1.5 billion *more*, than the CEEC had estimated. The help to be given by the International Bank and the use of part of the dollar balances belonging to the ERP countries were to reduce the cost to this country. In other respects, the Paris Conference projections were held to have been overly optimistic. Prices of imports and of imports relative to exports were

BALANCE OF PAYMENTS

likely to be higher than assumed by the CEEC. (With large excesses of imports, the absolute prices of imports are much more important than relative prices of exports and imports, that is, the terms of trade.) The estimates of exports from Europe were optimistic; the assumption that the proceeds from exports by dependent countries could largely be made available in dollars was unrealistic. For these reasons, the Harriman Committee had to raise the estimates of deficits; but *on balance* the cost to the United States was scaled down.[26]

After a survey of the CEEC report and official United States reports (of the Council of Economic Advisors, of the Department of the Interior, and of Mr. Harriman's Committee) and after an exhaustive independent examination, the Executive Branch proposed an ERP to cost from $15.1 to $17.8 billion over four and a quarter years, April 1, 1948 to June 30, 1952. For the fifteen months ending June 30, 1949, the State Department's estimate was $6.8 billion, inclusive of $200 million to cover contracts for goods and equipment to be delivered after June 30, 1949. Also included in this sum were outlays for the recovery and rehabilitation of Western Germany (except for $822 million to be spent for the prevention of disease and unrest in Bizonal Germany and to be covered by the Army).[27]

The executive branch estimate for the first fifteen months, as submitted to Congress, called for an authorization of $6.8 billion. In the Foreign Assistance Act of 1948, the program was to be on an annual basis, the amounts involved being related to the fifteen months' proposals of the executive branch. On its recommendation for the fifteen-month period, the United States would not cover the major part of the deficit of $811 million of participating countries with nonparticipating countries; and loans by the International Bank, private loans, unexpended United States Government credits and assistance previously authorized, reduction of gold and dollar balances by participating countries, and

EUROPEAN RECOVERY PROGRAM

assistance from other Western Hemisphere countries should account for $1.3 billion additional. By deducting $1.3 billion and also $822 million in army appropriations for expenditure in Western Germany from the deficit of $8.5 billion for the CEEC countries and adding $200 million for covering deficits of Western Germany with nonparticipating countries and $200 million required for obligations prior to June 30, 1949, to cover contracts for shipments in subsequent periods, the executive branch arrived at an estimated cost of $6.8 billion for the first fifteen months.[28] A similar pattern is used for the four and a quarter years. Starting with a deficit for the Western Hemisphere of $19.4 to $22.1 billion and adding $0.6 billion for the Bizonal deficit with nonparticipating countries and deducting $4.1 billion for financing outside of new United States Treasury funds and $800 million for United States Army outlays in Germany, the executive branch estimated total outlays at $15.1 to $17.8 billion and requested authorizations of $17 billion.[29]

For the fifteen months ending June 30, 1949, the executive branch made the estimates found in Table 15.

For fiscal 1949 (year ending June 30, 1949), the estimates by

TABLE 15
ESTIMATED BALANCE OF PAYMENTS OF PARTICIPATING COUNTRIES AND WESTERN GERMANY, APRIL 1, 1948 TO JUNE 30, 1949 *
(*In Millions of Dollars: Surplus* [+], *Deficit* [−])

	With U. S.	With Other Americas	With Western Hemisphere	With Other Nonparticipating Countries	Total
Exports	2,255	1,758	4,013	5,516	9,520
Imports	6,989	4,824	11,813	6,633	18,446
Net adjusted balance †	−5,176	−3,351	−8,527	−811	−9,338

* *ERP State*, p. 42.
† Includes allowances for rise of prices since July 1, 1947 and net invisible items.

BALANCE OF PAYMENTS

the executive branch of the Government are to be compared with those of the CEEC and the Harriman Committee for 1948 (see Table 16).

Estimates of imports by the ERP countries from the United States ran substantially lower than those by the CEEC, and roughly at the upper limits of those by the Harriman Committee. Imports by the participating countries from the other Americas were, however, high as compared with either the CEEC or the Harriman estimates. For exports to the United States by the participating countries the estimates of the executive branch were again substantially higher, and to the other Americas roughly equal to those of the CEEC and the high Harriman estimates. It

TABLE 16

Comparison of Estimates of Balance of Payments Deficits of the Participating Countries with the Western Hemisphere for the First Year of the European Recovery Program *

(*In Millions of Dollars; July 1, 1947 Prices*)

	CEEC (1948)	Harriman Committee		Executive Branch (Fiscal 1949)
		Low Availability (1948)	High Availability (1948)	
Imports from U. S.	5926	4350	5050	5034
Imports from other Americas	3239	2960	3410	3661
Exports to U. S.	848	700	850	1063
Exports to other Americas	1311	1110	1310	1319
Unadjusted balance of payments, current account				
With U. S.	−5936	−4450	−4920	−3760
With other Americas	−2099	−1880	−2140	−2543
Total	−8035	−6330	−7060	−6303

* *ERP State*, p. 100.

EUROPEAN RECOVERY PROGRAM

is clear that the executive branch's suggested imports for the participating countries *from* the United States were lower than those of the CEEC and, from the other Americas, higher; and exports from the participating countries *to* the United States were estimated higher by the executive branch than by the CEEC and the Harriman Committee. As might be expected, the adverse balance with the United States was reduced, and that with the other Americas increased relatively, as compared with earlier estimates.[30]

Table 16 reveals that the CEEC estimates of imports from the Americas were watered down by the executive branch, in part because of the unavailability of goods from this country; and a large share of the burden in terms of goods, relative to CEEC blueprints, was transferred from the United States to the other Americas. According to the executive branch program, this country is to export less and to import more (relative to the Americas) than suggested by the CEEC. In this manner the goods cost of the program to this country is to be reduced, and dollar costs whittled down — for reasons suggested here and above. The executive branch envisages these savings despite their expectation that production goals in Europe will generally not be reached. The expected failure of Western Europe to attain its production goals will not be too serious if instead of persisting in excessive investment programs, they concentrate their reduced capital programs on projects yielding quick returns and large gains in the foreign balances, and if they divert agricultural production substantially from meat to grain.[31]

An interesting estimate was also made by the International Bank. Cutting ERP imports substantially below the CEEC estimates, the Bank also envisaged a large cut in exports by the ERP countries. The Bank reduced the CEEC estimated imports for four years by the ERP countries by $3 billion, or 5 per cent, the largest cut being accounted for by imports from the United States

[138]

BALANCE OF PAYMENTS

($2.5 billion). Imports from the other Americas corresponded to the CEEC estimate: The Bank *reduced* imports of equipment over the four years by $1.25 billion, or close to 30 per cent; of the three F's (food, fuel, and fertilizer) by $1.1 billion, or 17 per cent. As a result of the rise of prices since July 1, 1947, the decline in dollar value of imports of these reductions was cut by one-half. Although exports were reduced much more than imports, the greater significance of imports is reflected in a much larger deficit for the ERP countries than the average estimate of the Harriman Committee or that of the executive branch.[32] For fiscal 1949, the estimated deficit in billions of dollars was: Administration: 8.7; the Bank, 9.1; Harriman: Low = 7.3, High = 8.5; CEEC = 9.2.

FINAL OBSERVATIONS ON THE DEFICITS

For more than a generation, Europe has suffered from dollar shortage. In part the explanation is faulty policy making (inclusive of extravagant capital programs and unrealistic exchange rates), in part the failure of the price mechanism to work; but, in addition, structural maladjustments related to war and political disturbances and uncertainties, and the emergence of new industrial nations help explain Europe's difficulties. In the years 1946–1948, the breakdown of trade with Eastern Europe, Eastern Germany, and Asia, the crop failures, and especially higher prices for imports and losses of invisible credits were special factors intensifying the crisis.

How large the adverse balance of payments of the participating countries will be over the next four years can be estimated only subject to a large margin of error. Much will depend upon the recovery of European production, the allocation of resources between exports and domestic use, the effectiveness with which domestic resources and supplies obtained under the ERP are used, the progress made in stabilizing currencies and balancing budgets, movements in prices of exports and especially imports, the extent to which the participating countries can divert their exports to hard currency countries and stimulate imports from soft currency countries inclusive of Eastern Europe, and upon the strengthening of trade ties and currency arrangements among the participating nations, with resulting reduced demands upon the Americas. These and other factors will determine the size of the deficits.

How much of the cost will fall upon the United States economy can also be estimated only roughly. All the factors listed in the preceding paragraph are relevant. The more European imports are obtained outside the United States, and the more her exports are channeled to this country, the less the costs to the United States. By forcing foreign countries to finance a larger part of the total costs, the United States will contribute not only to reducing the cost to the American taxpayer but also to cutting our exports. For, insofar as this country finances exports to the participating countries from the other Americas, the latter obtain dollars which they use largely to buy goods from the United States. Forcing the other Americas to carry part of the financing burden will be tantamount to a reduction in the supply of dollars made available to them, and hence in the command of goods in our markets.

Another relevant issue is American commercial policy. Unless this country adopts liberal economic policies, it will not be easy for Europe, the other Americas, and other nonparticipating countries to sell the goods which will reduce the net burden. It will be recalled that this country over many years has had an excess of exports in relation to Europe and the rest of the world. At the end of 1946, the debt of the world to the United States (exclusive of World War debts) was about $21 billion. In addition, commitments still unutilized amounted to $5 billion. The annual charge by 1952, inclusive of amortization, is estimated at $1.2 to

BALANCE OF PAYMENTS

$1.4 billion; and this exclusive of new loans and commitments under the ERP.[33] Equilibrium in the balance of payments will require an excess of imports of at least $1 billion plus the amounts required to finance the ERP and other loans. The adjustment in the balance of payments required from an excess of exports of one to ten billion dollars, annually, to an excess of imports would be revolutionary, and if effected over a short time it might well be disturbing. Concerned over the disrupting effects of repayment of loans, the Council of Economic Advisors urged serious consideration of substantial assistance rather than loans under the ERP.[34]

Finally, we should underline the following conclusions to be drawn from the statistical marathon in this chapter. Western Europe's adverse balance of payments stems in small part, if at all, from a deterioration in the terms of trade; much more important is the large rise of prices of exports from this country and the Western Hemisphere generally, the conversion of a favorable invisible balance (for example, interest paid abroad) of $1.5 billion on credit account before the war to a deficit of $500 million in 1947, and the difficulties of converting currencies received for a large part of her exports into dollars. These are in addition to the general economic deterioration associated with the production crisis. It is clear, also, that European gold, dollars, and other foreign assets will not finance much of the adverse balance of Western Europe: the amounts available are not large relative to reserve requirements for currency and balance of payments purposes; and in part they cannot be mobilized. Despite the large proportion of aid made available to Europe in 1945–1947, the sixteen nations are still confronted with a very large deficit. Their exports to the United States are a small proportion of their imports from this country, both in relation to prewar imports and in relation to the imports from the other Americas. The executive branch tried to correct this situation in part by estimating

EUROPEAN RECOVERY PROGRAM

exports from Western Europe to this country from 1948 to 1952 generously and by putting a heavier burden of exporting to Western Europe upon the other Americas. In general, the executive branch was inclined to be more optimistic concerning Western Europe's capacity to export and our capacity to provide goods than was the Harriman Committee; but less optimistic on availabilities of goods in Europe or the Americas for export than the CEEC.

PART THREE
IMPACT ON THE UNITED STATES

Introduction

CONTENTS

Having dealt with the European crises, I shall now turn to the impact of the ERP upon the American economy. This introduction indicates the contents of the next four chapters. The first of these chapters (7) discusses the determinants of costs and allocations of assistance; the next (8), the financial costs, then (9), inflation and the ERP, and finally (10), shortages in relation to the ERP.

I begin this introduction with a summary of the contents of Chapters 7 and 8. The reader will find in these chapters a discussion of the financial problems raised by the ERP. Rather than summarize Chapters 9 and 10, I have dealt rather briefly in this introduction with the issues of inflation and impact of the ERP on particular markets. The reader who is not particularly interested in the inflation problem in this country, and the contributions of the ERP to inflationary pressures may prefer to read this introductory section and skip Chapter 9. He will, however, find a much more detailed and comprehensive treatment of the subject in that chapter. In this introduction, we also consider the possibility of a deficiency of demand. In particular this offers an occasion for considering a serious threat to the program: the tendency to use the ERP as a device for subsidizing exporters of products in excess supply. This introduction ends with a consideration of the effects of the ERP upon one market, that of petroleum products. (Chapter 10 deals more fully with repercussions on numerous mal-provisioned markets.) This introduction also

IMPACT ON THE UNITED STATES

indicates the effects of the ERP upon the distribution of United States exports.

Chapter 7 begins with a discussion of costs and the standards to be applied in determining the amount of aid and its distribution. Deficits in the balance of payments are an important consideration; but, as we shall see, not by any means the only important criterion. For example, the assistance given under the ERP depends also upon the relative recourse by the participating countries to purchases from the United States on the one hand, and from the other Americas on the other. One of the troublesome problems considered in this chapter is that of determining the manner of financing imports of the ERP countries. For example, how is this government to determine the choice between imports to be financed with ERP funds and those to be financed in other ways? Since ultimate costs will depend upon whether assistance is given by loans or grants, it is necessary also to consider the manner of allocating assistance between these two alternatives. Manner of financing is to depend in no small part upon the types of commodities imported; for, other things being equal, it is assumed that countries requiring food and other necessities would receive grants rather than loans. How far this formula is followed, will be made clear in later discussion.

Treatment of these problems, which requires the major part of Chapter 7, is continued in Chapter 8, where the issues are considered in a general way, such as the magnitude of the programs, the manners of providing assistance (dollars or goods?), and special problems of finance.

INFLATIONARY IMPACT

Various aspects of this problem are discussed in Chapters 9 and 10, and for this reason we may be brief. Witnesses on behalf of the executive branch and secretaries Marshall, Harriman, and Anderson, in particular, gave testimony that the inflationary

EUROPEAN RECOVERY PROGRAM

effects of the ERP would not be serious and that its introduction would not require the imposition of controls. The implication was not that controls were not necessary, for Harriman before the Senate Banking and Currency Committee had proposed allocation and other controls in crucial markets; but rather that the need for controls was associated with the general supply and demand situation, not with the ERP.[1]

The issues were well put by the House Committee on Foreign Affairs:

> These special inflationary impacts of the foreign-aid program can be mitigated or neutralized to a considerable extent by administrative programming procedures such as were developed during the war. It would be the purpose of such measures to maximize available supplies, to insure that the supplies produced were made available in fact for the most essential uses, and that other uses were deferred if acceptable substitutes were not available.[2]

In Chapter 9 we take the position that the inflationary pressures on our 1948 economy are strong; that the introduction of ERP (and, more recently, increased military expenditures) will tend to increase the dangers of substantial inflation; and that unless courageous protective measures are taken, the success of the ERP will be jeopardized, both because of the reduced value of goods made available under the program, and because of the association of inflation with the ERP and the resulting threat to the program.

The inflationary pressure is not measured merely by the ratio of ERP expenditures to total national income though this is a relevant consideration; but also by the relation of ERP outlays to such marginal items as the excess of business outlays to savings available, or the excess of government receipts over expenditures. It is well to consider, for example, the relation of the ERP to the government budget. In his budget message of January 1948, President Truman estimated the surplus for the year ending

IMPACT ON THE UNITED STATES

June 30, 1948, at $7.5 billion, and for the year ending June 30, 1949, at $4.8 billion. It now appears that in view of the large reduction of taxes voted early in 1948 and the increased demands of the military and the ERP, fiscal 1949 is likely to experience a deficit, not a surplus. (This may not appear in view of the Ponzi-like legislation, which provides the transfer of $3 billion of the 1947–48 surplus for use by the ERP.) Correct fiscal and monetary policy in the current situation would require not a reduction of taxes, but an increase. In calendar 1947, for example, a budgetary surplus of $6 billion did not preclude a 15 per cent rise of consumers' prices. Large budgetary surpluses are required to offset two inflationary factors: the excess of spendings over savings available to business and the relevant excess of exports over imports.[3] Yet at the same time that the ERP aid and increased military expenditures promise to erase the surplus, Congress voted a reduction of taxes. It is difficult to reconcile the action taken, in which the members of the House Foreign Relations Committee concurred, with the sensible views on fiscal policy urged by that committee under the expert guidance of Professor W. Y. Elliott.[4]

ANTI-INFLATIONARY POLICY

What is required in the current situation is an over-all anti-inflation program, inclusive of cautious use of monetary policy and a bold recourse to fiscal policy, by which I mean severe taxes and economy of expenditures, consistent with our broad national objectives. This is a time for debt reduction, not debt increase. The more judicious and effective these impersonal controls of our system, the less the country will have to depend upon the type of controls that are distasteful to the American people.

Allocations, inclusive of export controls, are crucial in the anti-inflationary attack. As is evident in Chapter 10, the executive branch in the evolution of the ERP, tended to avert severe pressures on scarce markets by reducing the amounts requested by the CEEC and also by diverting purchases to other countries. Yet allocations and a genuine export control system are required in order to assure Western Europe a fair share of commodities in short supply, and in order to control the use of dollars obtained in payment for offshore purchases under the ERP. Surely a genuine allocation system for steel, oil, grains, and lumber with its control of demand, would assure the most effective use of these scarce goods and preclude large inflationary pressures on these markets.

That exports, or the excess of exports, may be $1 billion less in 1948 than in 1947 does not by any means suggest that the excess of exports will not be inflationary. A large excess of exports contributes to inflation because the income earned in producing the exports is not offset by a corresponding supply of goods: the exports are not available to satisfy domestic demand. By 1947 exports were already contributing to inflation. In 1947 they were $4.3 billion, and the excess over imports, $3.2 billion above those of 1946; and the total of exports was $19.6 billion in 1947 and the excess of $11.3 billion, a record.[5] What may be accomplished by export control is suggested by the fact that in the second half of 1947, the volume of exports to Latin America was five times that of 1938, to Canada three times, and to Europe only two and one-half times.[6]

DEFICIENCY OF DEMAND AND DUMPING

One final point should be made about the inflation problem. It is generally assumed that over-all conditions over the period of the ERP will be inflationary. In the light of the institutional pressures which tend to induce inflation, and in the light of the large government commitments and the pent-up demand, this seems to be a reasonable assumption. Excessive solicitation for protecting middlemen and the encouragement of a mushrooming

IMPACT ON THE UNITED STATES

of middlemen for buying ERP goods may further strengthen the inflationary effects of the ERP.

Yet we should not rule out the possibility of deficiency of demand over the next four years. Insofar as that occurs, the mobilization of resources for the ERP may not cause inflation: goods may be produced out of factors that otherwise would have been unemployed. Moreover, it is necessary to take into account the extent to which the ERP will be provisioned out of surpluses. (We comment on this problem in Chapters 9 and 10.) Secretary Anderson frankly admitted that the ERP will be necessary to provide adequate markets for cotton, wheat, tobacco, lard, rice, fruits, and vegetables.[7] In fact, the ERP may degenerate to some extent to a program for subsidizing surplus producers.

Nowhere is the tendency to use the program as a means for subsidizing inefficiency at home and dumping more clear than in the struggle to save several hundred million dollars by transferring a limited number of ships to foreign control and foreign charters. The original executive branch proposal was gradually whittled down, first by the Senate Committee and then by the Senate; and despite the efforts of the House Committee, the Foreign Assistance Act protected the domestic industry — at least 50 per cent of the gross tonnage is to be shipped under the United States flag — and did not provide for transfers. Undoubtedly the shipping lobby must have been very effective; for the transfers and foreign chartering originally proposed were compatible with defense requirements.[8]

In the course of passage, various groups urged Congress for special favors under the ERP. One example is the producers of naval stores, who emphasized the loss of export markets and, confronted with the choice of price support or listing under the ERP, preferred the latter as a wedge to the reëstablishment of foreign markets.[9]

EUROPEAN RECOVERY PROGRAM

IMPACT ON PARTICULAR MARKETS

It is a commonplace that though the total amounts involved may not be large, the repercussions of substantial diversions under the ERP may be serious on particular markets. Chapter 10 largely deals with the problems of supply and demand in particular markets affected by the ERP. (Figure 9 may be of some interest here.) By reducing the requirements presented by the CEEC and by proposing recourse to other markets for commodities especially short in this country, the executive branch substantially reduced the anticipated inflationary effects and sacrifices associated in this country with the ERP. In grains, for example, the

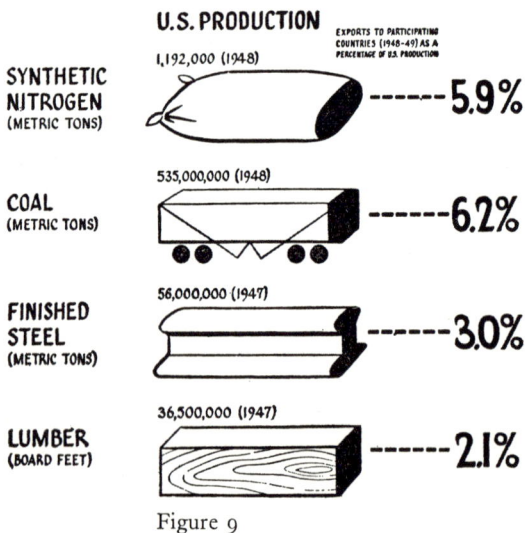

Figure 9

executive branch reduced both the total amount to be made available and the proportion to be provided by this country. Where alternative supplies were not available and serious shortages prevailed or threatened, Europe had to be satisfied with

IMPACT ON THE UNITED STATES

much less than she had asked—for example, scrap iron and machinery. In its estimates of machinery and equipment needed, the CEEC was particularly unrealistic; and the amounts to be made available were much smaller than those requested.[10] In steel, the Senate Small Business Committee complained of the excessive drains for export. The committee was concerned over exports of steel-mill products in 1947 at the rate of 7 million tons annually, or 11.1 per cent of current production.[11] The Herter Committee also pounced upon the CEEC for its large demands for steel.[12] More recently (April, 1948), the State Department further reduced allocations of iron, steel and oil.[13]

Oil was one of the biggest headaches. Only by imposing the real burden almost exclusively on the Caribbean and (especially) on the Near East, the financial costs to be borne by this country, could we satisfy a substantial part of the requirements. Senators were quick to point out that Europe was committing a serious blunder in shifting from coal to oil; and that, should trouble arise in the Middle East, the commitments under the ERP might seriously embarrass both Europe and the United States. According to Secretary Krug, even though imports into this country in 1948 would rise by 14 million barrels, exports decline by 10 million, and output expand by 95 million, the United States sources in the first year could provide only 2 to 3 per cent of the ERP requirements, and even less later; and to secure these goals some controls would be necessary.[14]

Tables 17 and 18 below summarize the main aspects of the problem. ERP countries are not to receive as much food as they would like, the exceptions being commodities likely to be in excess of supply in this country. Meat is an example of a commodity offered in substantially smaller amounts than requested—and with impending shortages in this country, Europe will have to obtain its meat under the ERP in the other Americas. Shortages here also explain the large pruning of CEEC estimates for petroleum, equipment and machinery, pig iron, scrap, and crude and

EUROPEAN RECOVERY PROGRAM

TABLE 17
COMPARISON OF SELECTED FOOD AND AGRICULTURAL IMPORT REQUIREMENTS FOR 1948–49 * AS ESTIMATED BY CEEC AND BY THE EXECUTIVE BRANCH (DEPENDENT OVERSEAS TERRITORIES ARE NOT INCLUDED)
(In Thousands of Metric Tons)

	Estimated Total Import Requirements CEEC	Executive Branch	Executive Branch Estimate as Per Cent of CEEC Estimate
Bread grains	17,988	14,270	79
Coarse grains	9,349	5,700	61
Fats and oils	2,968	2,464	83
Oilcake and meal	4,417	2,750	62
Sugar	3,053	3,056	100
Meat (including horse meat)	2,603	1,933	74
Cheese	279	249	89
Processed milk	240	346	144
Eggs	346	209	60
Dried fruits and nuts	455	493	108
Rice	352	140	40
Coffee (green)	422	435	103
Pulses	...	530	...
Fresh fruits	2,811	2,818	100
Cocoa	338	276	82
Tobacco	247	328	133
Nitrogen fertilizer	297	180	61
Agricultural machinery †	266	160	60

Source: *ERP: Sen. Rep.*, p. 23.
* CEEC estimated requirements for food and agricultural commodities were based on crop years, July 1 to June 30 of the following year. The first year of estimated requirements under the European recovery program was assumed by CEEC to relate to the crop year 1947–48. Requirements are larger in 1947–48 than in 1948–49 and following years. The CEEC assumed that full satisfaction of its 1947–48 requirements would result in much lower requirements in 1948–49 and later years. However, CEEC requirements for 1947–48 were in fact not met, and therefore the CEEC would probably want to revise its requirement estimates upward for 1948–49. In the table given above, the CEEC requirements relate to 1948–49 rather than to 1947–48. Since the 1948–49 CEEC requirements are lower than those for 1947–48, the extent to which the executive branch estimates of requirements differ from those of the CEEC is understated.
† In millions of dollars.

semi-finished steel, and will account for additional cuts later. The generous offer of finished steel relative to requests is a partial offset to the denials of non-finished products.

IMPACT ON THE UNITED STATES

TABLE 18

COMPARISON OF CERTAIN SELECTED IMPORT REQUIREMENTS FROM THE UNITED STATES FOR COMPARABLE 12-MONTH PERIODS AS ESTIMATED BY CEEC AND BY EXECUTIVE BRANCH (DEPENDENT OVERSEAS TERRITORIES NOT INCLUDED)

Commodity	Unit	CEEC, Calendar Year 1948	Executive Branch, Fiscal Year 1949	Executive Branch Estimate as Per Cent of CEEC Estimate
Petroleum (from dollar sources) *	Thousand metric tons	23,766	19,542	82
Timber	Million board feet	789	789	100
Crude and semifinished steel	Thousand metric tons	2,040	748	37
Pig iron	Thousand metric tons	182	35	19
Scrap (or pig-iron equivalent)	Thousand metric tons	1,399	††	0
Finished steel, other than sheets and tin plate	Thousand metric tons	449	1,150	256
Timber equipment †	Million dollars	10.1	9.8	97
Electrical equipment	Million dollars	150	95	63
Freight cars	Thousand units	47	20	43
Steel plant and equipment	Million dollars	100	48	48

Source: *ERP: Sen. Rep.*, p. 23.
* Total imports from dollar sources, largely outside the continental United States.
† Total timber equipment requirements in 1948, as estimated by the CEEC, were 16.4 million dollars, of which 6.3 million dollars were for dependent areas of the United Kingdom and France. In order to raise productivity in the timber-producing colonial areas, the executive branch estimated that 7.1 million dollars of timber equipment might be made available from the United States to these dependent areas in the fiscal year 1948–49.
†† Negligible.

EFFECTS OF ERP UPON DISTRIBUTION OF UNITED STATES EXPORTS
In testifying before the Senate Committee on Foreign Relations, the Department of Commerce presented an interesting table on United States exports.[15] This table throws much light on the problems under discussion. What follows is based on an analysis and rearrangement of material. (The calculations are mine.)

(1) From 1946 to the first half of 1947 (annual rates), the rise of exports to CEEC countries and others was roughly of equal proportions: 53 and 59 per cent, respectively.

(2) On the assumption that the ERP would not be approved, United States export trade in 1948 would be $9.9 billion; on the

EUROPEAN RECOVERY PROGRAM

assumption of approval, $14.2 billion. (1946 = $9.5 billion; first half of 1947, annual rate = $14.9 billion). If the ERP had not been approved, export trade in 1948 would have declined by an annual rate of $5.0 billion relative to the annual rate for the first half of 1947, and by $4.3 billion in 1948 relative to exports in 1948 with an ERP.

TABLE 19
Percentage Rise of Exports on Assumption of ERP Relative to Exports on Assumption of No ERP, 1948

	Percentage Rise Associated with ERP	Percentage of Increased Amount Resulting from ERP Going to ERP Countries
Foods	26	80
Textile fibres and manufactures	42	60
Nonmetallic minerals	77	86
Metals and manufactures	44	50
Machinery and vehicles	43	69
Chemicals and related products	80	75

Source: Based on *ERP: Sen. Hear.*, p. 297.

(3) Under the ERP, exports to ERP countries in 1948 would be $6.0 billion, whereas without the ERP the exports to these countries would be $3.2 billion, the gains associated with ERP being 87 per cent (2.8 = 87 per cent of 3.2). Although the CEEC countries in the first half of 1947 accounted for less than one-third of United States trade, in 1948 they would account for almost two-thirds of the increased exports associated with the ERP. These figures suggest both the large re-deployment of exports under the ERP and the continued high amounts for the world — in part associated with aid and in part with the validation of dollars obtained for offshore ERP purchases by the United States.

(4) Table 19 gives figures for important classes of commodities. It shows the large rise of exports in these categories and the proportion of the increase to benefit ERP countries.

7. Determinants of Costs and Allocation of Assistance

COSTS

The costs of the ERP to this country are less than the deficit estimated by the CEEC — the executive branch put the deficit in the balance of payments of CEEC countries with the Americas in the first year at $6.7 billion, as compared with the CEEC estimate of $8 billion. Executive branch estimates roughly corresponded to those based on low availabilities of the Harriman Committee.[1] In an independent survey, the International Bank put the deficit in the balance of payments at $7.6 billion, or about $1 billion in excess of the administration. And the Bank estimated ERP country exports alone at $600 million less than the Administration. Over four and a quarter years the executive branch put the deficit in the balance of payments at $19.5 to $23.0 billion, as compared with an estimate of $22.4 billion by the CEEC.[2]

Many of the details concerning the relative contributions of the United States and the other Americas will be found in Chapter 8. For example, over the life of the program, the United States is to provide about 55 per cent of the goods and 90 per cent of the funds. Insofar as the dollars put at the disposal of other countries for offshore purchases are used to buy goods in this country under the ERP, the "goods" cost will be more than 55 per cent. Total costs also depend on the price assumptions made, on the purchasing methods and similar considerations. (See Chapter 8.)

STANDARDS OF AID

Costs depend also on standards. On what criteria are we to determine how much help Europe is to obtain? Secretary Marshall's

EUROPEAN RECOVERY PROGRAM

address of June 1947 at Harvard merely suggested that "there must be some agreement among the countries of Europe as to the requirements of the situation and the part these countries will take in order to give proper effect to whatever action might be undertaken by this government." At Paris the CEEC countries estimated the goods that might be available from abroad for the participating countries and Western Germany, and from this and estimates of exports and other items in the balance of payments worked out a common balance of payments. The resulting deficits in the balance of payments checked well with computations by individual participating countries of their anticipated deficit with the Americas.[3]

It is quite clear that the ERP is not based on the theory that the poor countries should receive more aid than the wealthy ones. In the first fifteen-month program prepared by the executive branch, the United Kingdom was to receive $1760 million, or about 26 per cent of the total, and France about $1432 million, or about 21 per cent. Italy's share was to be $869 million, or about 13 per cent. The suggested distribution announced by the ECA Administrator on April 20, 1948, before the House Appropriations Committee corresponded closely to that of the executive branch, the main difference being that the former was on a twelve-month basis.[4] If the egalitarian principle were applied, Italy would have received much more help than the British; for with a population 94 per cent that of the United Kingdom, Italy in 1946 had a national income of but 30 per cent of that of the United Kingdom. That the amount of aid offered was only little more than one-half as large as that for the British is explained largely by the much smaller deficit in the balance of payments: the British deficit with the Americas was estimated at $2.16 billion for the first year, and the Italian at but $0.894 billion, and ECA obligations at $1.67 and $.901 billion respectively.[5] Apparently, the aid offered was related to the expected balance of payments.

COSTS AND ALLOCATION OF ASSISTANCE

Behind the ERP was the philosophy that each country should be helped to retrieve a standard of living which she could maintain in the post-ERP era.[6]

Had aid been given according to past efforts to adjust the balance of payments, the United Kingdom might well have fared better relative to France than she actually has under the ERP; for the reader will recall from the last chapter that the British, in their efforts to expand exports and exclude imports, advanced much more rapidly than the French. (Of course, the French may have suffered more as a result of the war.) Another consideration which may have turned the scales in favor of France is the crucial position occupied by France in the struggle against communism.

An indication of the manner of allocating ERP funds is to be had from Table 20. This table is based on income figures which

TABLE 20

ERP COUNTRIES: PERCENTAGE OF AID TO NATIONAL INCOME AND TO DEFICITS IN BALANCE OF PAYMENTS WITH THE AMERICAS

	Percentage of Aid under ERP on 15-Month Basis (April 1, 1948– June 30, 1949) to National Income (12 months)	Percentage of Aid under ERP on 15-Month Basis (April 1, 1948– June 30, 1949) to Anticipated Deficit in Balance of Payments, 1948	Percentage of 12-Month Allotment of Aid (April 1, 1948– March 31, 1949) to Anticipated Deficit in Balance of Payments, 1948
United Kingdom	5.5	67	50
France	8.0	81	64
Netherlands	16.8	112	95
Belgium	10.8	101	93
Sweden	0.7	22	19
Denmark	8.2	78	62
Norway	2.4	68	66
Italy	8.5	93	76
Western Germany	9.1	79	43
Greece	63.7	36	21

Source: National Income, *ERP: Sen. Hear.*, p. 1005; deficits in balance of payments, 1948, *CEEC*, I, 53; 15-month aid by countries, *ERP: Sen. Rep.*, p. 47; 12-month aid, *Final Report, House*, p. 90. (Calculations mine.)

are subject to a large margin of error; on anticipated deficits in the balance of payments for 1948 as presented to the CEEC by the countries involved — likely to be overestimated for obvious reasons; on the estimates of aid presented by the executive branch on a fifteen-month basis, and on the twelve-month estimates by the ECA administrator.[7] These figures are subject to periodic revision, and the results are only roughly accurate.

DETERMINANTS OF ALLOCATIONS OF FUNDS

Table 20 suggests that aid is not based primarily on need as indicated by national income or income per capita. Compare, for example, the relatively large grants to Greece and the exclusion of Portugal. (The latter is not included in the table.) Yet both countries are in the one to two hundred dollars per capita income group. Or compare the Netherlands with fifteen-month aid equal to 16.8 per cent of yearly income and Italy with but 8.5 per cent, and yet the former's per capita income in 1946 was twice that of the latter.

Obviously the deficit in the balance of payments with the Americas is decisive. The reader will observe, however, that the aid proposed varies greatly relative to the adverse balance with the Americas in 1948. In part the explanation is that the periods covered are not identical (adverse balance is for 1948, and aid for the year ending March 31, 1949); but more important is the modification of the CEEC estimates by the United States experts. It will be noted, for example, that Sweden, Greece, Western Germany, and the United Kingdom especially received much less than the CEEC estimate of adverse balances seemed to indicate they needed; and that the Netherlands and Belgium were treated particularly well (Columns 2 and 3).

The figures in Table 21 are relevant — they compare the adverse balance as suggested by the CEEC for 1948, and the estimates by the executive branch for the year ending June 30, 1949.

COSTS AND ALLOCATION OF ASSISTANCE

TABLE 21

DEFICITS IN THE BALANCE OF PAYMENTS WITH THE AMERICAS AND ECA OBLIGATIONS

(In Millions of Dollars)

	1948 — CEEC (1)	July 1, 1948 to June 30, 1949 — Executive Branch (2)	ECA Obligations (Estimates of March 1948) (3)
Countries receiving much less than indicated deficit			
Sweden	150	65	28
Greece	510	157	106
Western Germany	1270	825	549
United Kingdom	2630	1923 *	1324
Countries receiving amounts that correspond roughly to deficits			
Netherlands	630	659 †	600
Belgium	320	439 ‡	296
Others			
Italy	930	780	704
Norway	50	76	33
France	1760	1224 †	1131
Denmark	210	162	131

Source: Column 1, *CEEC*, p. 53; Column 2, from individual *ERP Country Studies*; also see *ERP: Sen. Hear.*, p. 132.
 * Dependencies — favorable balance of $260 million.
 † And dependencies.
 ‡ And Luxemburg.

In Table 21, figures in the last column (ECA obligations) are the latest revision: they include adverse balance for dependencies and relate to *ECA obligations*, that is, payments obligated for in the period, not the actual deficit in the balance of payments, nor the Treasury disbursements for the period. Obligations of funds mean the amounts made available for *contracts* to be made. Obviously, *deliveries* will not equal obligations in any one year. The State Department also published *deficits* for the fiscal year 1948–49, with the Western Hemisphere as estimated in March 1948. These figures of March 1948 diverge from those of December

EUROPEAN RECOVERY PROGRAM

1947, notable examples being: the United Kingdom, a reduction of $306 million in the deficit, or 16 per cent (the Dependencies, a reduction in the *credit* balance by $170 million, or about two-thirds); France, a reduction of $100 million in the *deficit*, or 9 per cent (the French Dependencies, a rise in the deficit of $75 million, or 56 per cent); Greece, a decline of $28 million in the deficit, or 18 per cent; Switzerland, a rise in the credit balance by $92 million, or more than five and a half times; and also a large rise for Western Germany.[8] (The comparison is not between column 2 and column 3 of Table 21, but between deficits in the balance of payments [estimated late in 1947 — column 2] and deficits estimated in March 1948.)

Obviously, there are other relevant considerations. France and Italy may receive favored treatment because they are crucial areas in the anticommunist struggle, although the correlation of aid and communist strength is not generally high; and to some extent aid is related to the kind of commodities purchased by each country.

Another related problem is the source of financing, which Table 22 clarifies. It will be noted, for example, that the United Kingdom's dollar earnings are more than half of her anticipated total imports from the Western Hemisphere, and that Swiss dollar earnings are at least equal to her imports from that area; but for Italy they are less than one-sixth and for France less than one-fifth. Sources exclusive of new United States funds and dollar earnings available to cover the dollar deficits are *relatively* large for Belgium, Denmark, France, Greece, Italy, the Netherlands, Norway, and the United Kingdom; but these sources provide nothing or relatively little for the other countries. These sources are advances from the international agencies, the Export-Import Bank, advances by other Americas, and so on.[9]

We should also consider the relative deficits of the various countries with the United States on the one hand, and with the

COSTS AND ALLOCATION OF ASSISTANCE

TABLE 22

RECAPITULATION OF TABLES SHOWING ILLUSTRATIVE COMPOSITION OF IMPORTS OF COMMODITIES AND SERVICES FROM WESTERN HEMISPHERE AND POSSIBLE SOURCES AND DISTRIBUTION OF FINANCING, APRIL 1, 1948, TO JUNE 30, 1949
(*At July 1, 1947, Prices*)

	Total Imports *	Dollar Earnings †	Possible Sources of Financing	
			Sources Other Than New United States Funds	New United States Funds ‡
	$ million	$ million	$ million	$ million
Austria	233	39	12	182
Belgium-Luxembourg	853	334	196	323
Denmark	237	45	28	164
France	1,931	369	128	1,434
Greece	262	67	9	186
Iceland	23	10	...	13
Ireland	192	40	...	152
Italy	1,160	183	108	869
Netherlands	1,136	271	160	705
Norway	253	163	56	34
Portugal	144	144	...	...
Sweden	499	423	43	33
Switzerland	535	535	...	...
Turkey	69	69	...	...
United Kingdom	4,311	2,133	418	1,760
Germany:				
Bizone	1,014	100	...	914
French zone	93	13	...	80
Saar	14	3	...	11
Total	12,959	4,941	1,158	6,860

Source: *State Department.*
* Including net dollar payments for freight and other invisibles.
† Including drawings of $72,000,000 by Portugal on its gold and foreign exchange resources.
‡ This column includes funds being requested by the Department of the Army for prevention of disease and unrest in Germany.
Cf. *State Dept. Proposed Distribution*, p. 7, for later figures. Total shipments from Western Hemisphere are now estimated at $13,565 million. The largest gains are for Belgium-Luxemburg and Western Germany; there are large reductions for Greece and Sweden. Dollar earnings are down by $473 million, the main losses being ascribed to France, the Netherlands, Norway, Sweden, Switzerland, the United Kingdom, and Western Germany. Earnings of Portugal were boosted. *It is significant that within 3 months, estimates of shipments were up by 5 per cent and dollar earnings down by almost 10 per cent.*

other Americas on the other. Countries with relatively large deficits with the latter may have to depend relatively less on United States aid; for the other Americas presumably are to advance part of the credit required to finance offshore purchases. Over

EUROPEAN RECOVERY PROGRAM

the first fifteen months, American officials estimated that about $700 million of aid would be had from the other Americas. (The International Bank was less optimistic.) Thus the United Kingdom's anticipated deficit in 1948 with the United States is $891 million and with other Western Hemisphere countries, $1032 million; in contrast, Italy's deficits are $584 million and $196 million, respectively; and France's, $903 million and $187 million, respectively.[10] On this account, it might be expected that the United States would provide larger sums of new money relative to the deficits for Italy and France and *relatively* small amounts in relation to the deficits for the United Kingdom.[11]

In summary, the allocation of funds under the ERP depends on numerous factors, the most important of which is the balance of payments with the Americas; and significant variables are the availability of dollar earnings and other sources of dollar income, and the extent to which imports come from the other Americas. Political considerations may also have influenced the allocation of ERP funds. In short, countries with large deficits with the Americas will receive dollars in large quantities under the ERP in order to finance these dollar deficits. But assistance received will be less in so far as these countries hold assets saleable for dollars, or in so far as purchases in the other Americas will be financed by interests in the other Americas.

The financial burden on the United States depends in part upon (1) the objectives of the program, (2) and, related to this, on the manner of estimating the costs involved, (3) on the extent of recourse to financing outside of the United States Treasury, (4) on the relative dependence on loans and grants. Finally, (5) a rather difficult administrative problem is raised by attempting to determine the manner of financing exports from this country. The difficulties originate in deciding on the exports to be financed under the ERP appropriations, those from foreign dollar earnings, and those from other sources of finance. Costs to the United

COSTS AND ALLOCATION OF ASSISTANCE

States taxpayer may well be influenced by allocations for purposes of financing.

In his Cambridge address, Secretary Marshall made it clear that this was to be a program of recovery as well as relief; and in his testimony before the Senate, Ambassador Douglas emphasized that in the long-run a relief program would have to be more costly than a recovery program.[12]

Estimates of costs depend in part upon assumptions concerning prices of exports and imports, availabilities of any excess of exports to non-dollar areas to cover deficits in the dollar areas, the anticipated volume of exports and imports, and the amounts to be provided by the International Bank and the other Americas. These problems are discussed to some extent in Chapter 8. It is clear that the estimates of the CEEC were optimistic on the anticipated terms of trade; and, as Dr. Richard Bissell suggests, the executive branch may have been optimistic in appraising Europe's exports and the availability of United States exports.[13]

On the basis of the balance of payments estimates, the executive branch put the deficit for the first year at $6.75 billion, the Harriman Committee at $6.88 to $7.69 billion, the International Bank at $7.6 billion, and the CEEC at $8.03 billion.[14] On February 6, 1948, the Secretary of State submitted an over-all estimate of the foreign assistance to be required for the remainder of the fiscal year and fiscal year 1949. The amounts involved were as follows:[15]

In Millions of Dollars

European Recovery Program	6800
Government and relief in occupied areas	1400
Philippine war damage, rehabilitation, etc.	133
Other foreign aid (including China)	750
Addition to President's budget of appropriations	250
	9333

EUROPEAN RECOVERY PROGRAM

In the view of the House Foreign Relations Committee, the amounts to be made available for financing the ERP countries' deficit with the Americas out of sources other than new United States Treasury funds (for example, other Americas, International Bank, and Export-Import Bank) seem conservative. The Committee points out, quite properly, that with the uncertainty of price movements and availability of crucial supplies the cost of the program even in the first year may well decline by a billion dollars below the current estimates, or rise by a billion. The International Bank, it should be noted, thinks the administration estimates for outside financing are too high.[16]

LOANS AND CAPACITY TO REPAY

Insofar as the United States Government succeeds in providing aid in the form of loans rather than grants, the burden on the taxpayer may be eased. In deciding that $1 billion of the $5.3 billion to be made available for the first year should be disbursed by the Export-Import Bank, the government put a floor under the amounts to be advanced or guaranteed; in addition, part of the remaining $4.3 billion might be advanced rather than given away. The executive branch estimated loans at 20 to 40 per cent of the total amount involved; the crucial factor in determining the form of aid was capacity to repay, and another, the nature of the imports, for example, funds for capital development should be advanced. Countries able to repay were indeed to be asked to borrow rather than to accept gifts.

That it will not be easy to apportion aid between *grants* and *loans*, because the type of commodities imported will not necessarily suggest the relative capacities to repay, is evident from the fact that the executive branch classified aid by countries on the basis of *relief* commodities and services required, and *recovery* commodities and services, the former presumably being financed by grants and the latter by loans. Yet it will be noted from the

COSTS AND ALLOCATION OF ASSISTANCE

table below, for example, that whereas recovery types of commodities account for about 30 per cent of the total, the percentages for Austria, Belgium, France, the Netherlands, and the United Kingdom are: 35, 21, 32, 56, and 15 per cent, respectively. Surely, Austria's 35 per cent, the Netherlands' 56 per cent, and the United

TABLE 23

RECAPITULATION OF ILLUSTRATIVE DISTRIBUTION BETWEEN RELIEF-TYPE AND RECOVERY-TYPE COMMODITIES AND SERVICES FINANCED WITH NEW U. S. TREASURY FUNDS AND IMPORTED BY THE PARTICIPATING COUNTRIES FROM THE WESTERN HEMISPHERE, APRIL 1, 1948, TO JUNE 30, 1949

(In Millions of Dollars, at July 1, 1947, Prices)

	Total Relief-Type Commodities and Services	Total Recovery-Type Commodities and Services	Total
Austria	118.6	63.4	182.0
Belgium-Luxemburg and dependencies	255.2	67.9	323.1
Denmark	77.8	86.3	164.1
France and dependencies	968.9	465.3	1434.2
Greece	137.3	48.6	185.9
Iceland	7.8	4.9	12.7
Ireland	102.6	49.2	151.8
Italy	719.4	149.4	868.8
Netherlands and dependencies	311.3	393.7	705.0
Norway	...	34.1	34.1
Portugal and dependencies	...	...	...
Sweden	...	32.9	32.9
Switzerland	...	...	...
United Kingdom and dependencies	1490.9	269.3	1760.2
Western Germany:			
Bizone	630.7	283.8	914.5
French zone	71.6	8.8	80.4
Saar	7.0	3.9	10.9
Total	4899.1	1961.5	6860.6

Source: *ERP: Sen. Hear.*, p. 495.

EUROPEAN RECOVERY PROGRAM

Kingdom's 15 per cent to be repaid, are not in accord with capacities to repay.[17]

Repayment was not considered merely a matter of internal capacity to finance the loan, but also a problem of transfer of local currencies into dollars. American experts were aware of the transfer problem, though nowhere was it made clear how the over-all transfer problem would be solved in dealing with individual countries, that is, the problem of converting non-dollar currencies *generally* into dollars without bringing chaos into exchange markets. Even so able a Senator as Hickenlooper could not be made to see the relevance of the transfer problem.[18]

The Senate Report summarizes the issues:

> The Committee has, however, established the criteria for determining whether assistance should be in the form of grants or loans. This determination is to depend primarily on two factors: (1) the character and purpose of the assistance [19] and (2) the capacity of the country concerned to make repayments without jeopardizing the accomplishment of the purposes of this bill. It is clear that grants should not be made to countries which have the capacity to pay cash or repay loans. It is equally clear that it would be unrealistic to require a participating country to contract dollar debts now if it does not have the capacity to pay without jeopardizing the purposes of the program. However, to the fullest extent practicable within the above tests, payment should be made on loans used in order to finance imports of capital equipment and raw materials for use in connection with capital development, and grants should be used to finance imports of supplies of food, fuel, and fertilizer and raw materials not used in capital development.[20]

IMPORT STRUCTURE AND MANNER OF FINANCING

One of the most difficult problems confronting the ECA will be that of determining the manner of financing different types of commodities. For example, in the first fifteen months, it was estimated that the ERP countries would require $12.9 billion. They would obtain the required dollars as shown in Table 24.

COSTS AND ALLOCATION OF ASSISTANCE

TABLE 24
Possible Sources of ECA Funds
(*In Billions of Dollars*)

	Original Plan *	Revised Plan †
From Dollar Earnings from Exports and Services	4.9	4.47
From Dollar Sources Other Than New United States Funds	1.2	2.14
From New United States Government Funds	6.8	6.96
	12.9	13.56

* ERP: House Rep., p. 23.
† See *State Dept. Proposed Distribution*, p. 3.

Under the Foreign Assistance Act of 1948, it is assumed that trade will be carried on largely through private enterprise.[21] Obviously, the allocation of dollar receipts will be a responsibility of each government, each importer then dealing with his government. To some extent foreign governments will purchase. *But the vital issue remains that of determining the commodities which will be paid for with ERP dollars and those to be bought with dollars obtained in other ways.* (This is not to be confused with the problem of the manner of making new dollars available — loans or grants — which was discussed above.)

The executive branch suggested the following procedure:[22]

1. Financing which might be forthcoming from sources other than new United States funds has been spread over commodities for the purchase of which it is thought most likely that loans and credits might be granted. Much is assigned to the category "Other imports," which includes heavy and specialized equipment and important industrial raw materials, and additional large sums are allocated to bread and coarse grains, fats and oils, sugar, meat, and coffee, for which other Western Hemisphere countries might extend commodity credits or make other arrangements to assist the participating countries.

EUROPEAN RECOVERY PROGRAM

2. It is assumed that new United States funds will be used, in the first instance, for selected commodities.

3. Dollar earnings of the participating countries are assigned to the remaining Western Hemisphere requirements.

In this connection it should be pointed out that the category "Other imports" is made up principally of important raw materials and manufactured goods which in almost all cases are as important to economic recovery as the selected commodities. On many of these commodities studies of requirements and availabilities are being prepared, but a miscellaneous category will always be necessary since trade between advanced industrial countries involves thousands of individual products.

The executive branch summarized the allocation of dollars as shown in Table 25.[23] From this table, it should be clear that

TABLE 25

ALLOCATION OF DOLLARS

(In Millions of Dollars)

Category	By Own $ Earnings	Sources Other Than New U. S. Funds	New U. S. Funds	Total
Food, fuel, fertilizer	755	618	4,185	5,558
Other raw materials	383	80	986	1,449
Listed capital equipment	36	53	489	578
Other imports	3,211	408	609	4,228
Other dollar payments	555 *	...	592 †	1,147
Total	4,940	1,159	6,861	12,960

Source: *ERP: House Rep.*, p. 23; cf. *State Dept. Est. Imp. etc.*, pp. 4–7 for revised estimates.
* $236 million freight and $319 million other dollar payments [*sic*].
† All freight.

countries importing food, fuel, and fertilizer in large relative amounts are to rely heavily on ERP (New United States) funds, whereas those taking "other imports" in relatively large amounts will receive relatively small aid from the ERP. In this discus-

COSTS AND ALLOCATION OF ASSISTANCE

sion, I assume that the countries involved require aid under the ERP.

On the basis of material presented by the State Department, I have checked some of the principles enunciated in Table 25 concerning the allocation of dollars. Table 26, for example, suggests the contributions of the three main sources of dollars for the most important countries. This table suggests that Sweden,

TABLE 26
Sources of Dollars, Certain ERP Countries, April 1, 1948 to June 30, 1949
(*By Percentage*)

	$ Earnings	Other Than New U. S. Funds	New U. S. Funds
Belgium	39	23	38
France	19	6	75
Greece	26	4	70
Italy	16	9	75
Netherlands	24	14	62
Sweden	84	9	7
United Kingdom	49	10	41
Western Germany Bizonia	10	..	90

Source: Calculated from materials presented by State Department in *ERP: Sen. Hear.*, pp. 119–129. Cf. *State Dept. Proposed Distribution*, p. 7 for later estimates; and pp. 159–160 of this book.

the United Kingdom, and Belgium should rely heavily on their own dollar earnings (also Switzerland and Portugal); that dollar earnings will contribute relatively little to the dollar pool of Italy, France, and Bizonal Germany; that sources other than new United States funds will provide substantial funds especially for Belgium and the Netherlands; and that recourse to dollars provided under the ERP will be especially heavy for Western Germany, France, Italy, and Greece, in that order; and *relatively* small for Sweden, Belgium, the United Kingdom (and Switzerland and Portugal).

EUROPEAN RECOVERY PROGRAM

An examination of Table 27 is of some help in explaining the sources of dollars.[24] Since the new ERP dollars are especially to finance the three F's (food, fuel, and fertilizer), it might be expected that the large differences in relative ERP help might be explained by large differences in the proportion of dollars required for the three F's. But the differences — from 41 to 49 per cent — are not wide enough to explain the large relative *grants* offered to France and Greece, as compared with those proffered the United Kingdom. Again, listed capital equipment, largely to be financed by new United States funds, does not loom large

TABLE 27
PERCENTAGE OF IMPORTS, 15 MONTHS — FRANCE, GREECE, AND THE UNITED KINGDOM

	France	Greece	United Kingdom
Food, fuel, and fertilizer	42	49	41
Listed capital equipment	6	7	2
Other imports	26	18	38
Other raw materials listed	11	4	14

Source: See Table 26 — my calculations. (All items not included.)

enough to explain substantial differences in the proportion of deficits financed by new United States funds. The large drain on dollars by the United Kingdom to finance "other imports" does help explain the relatively small contribution of ERP dollars to financing that country; for these are largely financed by "new" dollar earnings. But these imports loom smaller in the Greek budget than in the French; yet under the ERP the French receive more aid than the Greeks relative to the deficit. In view of the importance of raw materials in the total of British imports, we would also expect larger relative help to the British out of ERP funds; for raw materials are largely to be financed by ERP dollars.

This survey suggests the following conclusion: *it is not going*

COSTS AND ALLOCATION OF ASSISTANCE

to be an easy task to reconcile the broad principles of use of dollars from various sources according to the nature of imports with another principle, namely distribution of ERP dollars according to need, as revealed by alternative sources of dollars. The British, for example, will rely relatively less on ERP dollars than other countries. That they will do so, results not so much from the type of goods imported as from their large exports and other dollar earnings, and their access to credit for purchases from other American countries.

CONCLUSION

In its impact on the American economy, the ERP is bound to be of first-rate importance. It will be felt in many ways — in the provision of markets for surplus commodities, in the pressure on mal-provisioned markets, in the general inflationary effects. It is necessary to know what the program will cost; the manner of distributing aid among countries; the division between loans and grants; the allocation of exports for financing purposes among ERP dollars, earned dollars, and dollars from other sources. In making decisions, the ECA will have to know what commodities are being exported to each country, the resources available to each, the adverse balance of payments, the capacity to repay in the future. Frequently one variable (for example, capacity to pay) may suggest a loan, whereas another (for example, type of commodity) may suggest a grant. Rules of thumb will not solve the problem for the administrator. And aside from decisions concerning individual transactions or even all transactions for a single country, broad general decisions concerning the whole program will have to be made. For example, the ECA may discover a high capacity to repay for the British; and yet from the viewpoint of the over-all dollar position, repayment may be an unwise policy. In other words, the presumptive capacity of the British to repay may leave out of account the general shortage of

EUROPEAN RECOVERY PROGRAM

dollars; and pressure on them to repay would impair their capacity to meet dollar requirements of others. This follows, because with the British under pressure to find additional dollars, they will restrict access to their dollar supplies and will seek to transfer the burden to other holders of dollars.

8. The Financial Costs

INTRODUCTION

In Chapter 7 the standards of aid were considered. Relevant variables are the deficits in the balance of payments, accessibility to dollars from sources other than dollars made available under the ERP, and the sources from which the ERP countries import. Political considerations undoubtedly play a part. Yet as Mr. Henry Taylor so well showed, the deployment of ERP dollars could scarcely be justified as an attack on communism. How, Mr. Taylor asks, could the government support allotments of $5.4 billion, or 32 per cent of the total, to the United Kingdom, of $2.4 billion to Holland (with a communist vote of less than 7 per cent), of $1.4 billion to Belgium and Luxemburg, or of $150 million to Portugal if this were an anticommunist program?[1]

In the earlier discussion, we failed to comment on standards for appropriations to be made later. *Are they to be based on actual deficits in the balance of payments, or what they should have been had the country adhered to bilateral agreements and received a grade of A on effort and policies pursued?* Here is an issue of first-rate importance; and the discovery of the difference between actual deficits and "might have been" deficits will tax the ingenuity of any economist or administrator. Should actual deficits be the guide for alloting funds in the future, the ERP may become a pauperization program.

GENERAL OBSERVATIONS ON BURDEN

Having discussed the ERP from the viewpoint of Europe's recovery and the balance of payments, we now turn to an examination of the burden upon the United States. In earlier chapters the discussion touched upon relevant considerations, for example, the extent to which the burden may be transferred to the other

EUROPEAN RECOVERY PROGRAM

Americas. Our task in the next three chapters is to deal more intensively with the costs to this country. Three approaches to the problem are germane: financial costs, inflationary effects, and the drain on commodity markets and resources. Each of these problems will be the subject of a separate chapter. Obviously, the three problems are interrelated, for the financial costs and the pressure on commodity markets affect the price level; and the last, in turn, influences the financial costs.

THE MAGNITUDE OF THE PROBLEM

Earlier discussion of the balance of payments and the deficits of the participating countries suggests the amounts involved, although the estimates beyond the middle of 1949 are necessarily highly conjectural. Table 28 summarizes the amounts and the suggested financing.

TABLE 28

Proposed Financing of the Balance of Payments Deficit of the Participating Countries, April 1, 1948 to June 30, 1952 *

(In Millions of Dollars)

	April 1, 1948 to June 30, 1949	April 1, 1948, to June 30, 1952
1. Deficit (inclusive of Western Germany) at current prices	8,727	20,024–22,658
2. Deficit to be met from sources other than United States Treasury funds		
a. International Bank and other sources in U. S.†	500	2,200
b. Other Western Hemisphere countries	700	1,700
c. Participating countries on cost basis ‡	85	191–205
3. From new United States Treasury funds		
a. For procurement in the U. S.	4,627	8,545–9,979
b. For offshore procurement	2,615	6,788–8,001
4. Total new U. S. Treasury financing (inclusive of deficit of Bizonal Germany)	7,442	15,933–18,580

* *ERP State*, p. 113.
† Includes disbursements from unutilized balances of existing Export-Import Bank credits as well as new private investments and disbursements by the International Bank.
‡ Represents deficits of Portugal, Turkey, and Switzerland with Western Hemisphere countries.

THE FINANCIAL COSTS

The following conclusions can be drawn from Table 28.

(a) About one-fifth of the deficit from April 1948 to June 1952 is to be covered by sources other than *new* United States Treasury funds. But since the Treasury provided most of the resources sought from the International Bank and all those of the Export-Import Bank, the taxpayer still will meet most of the $2.2 billion under 2a in the table. Incidentally, the burden on the International Bank may be considered excessive in view of the fact that the Bank is supposed to provide funds for both reconstruction and development, and not for Western Europe alone.

(b) In all, the United States is to provide about 90 per cent of the funds under the ERP, but only about 55 per cent of the goods required (the proportion of the latter declining with time). These figures may, however, give a misleading impression, for obviously foreign countries receiving from $5.1 to $6.3 [2] billion from this country for goods to be shipped under the program will use the dollars in no small part to buy United States goods. Since this country presumably exports goods to the other Americas in payment for commodities shipped by the latter to ERP countries, it may then be asked why the goods are not offered directly by the United States to the participating countries. The answer is, first, that the goods wanted by the latter can be obtained in part only from the other Americas; second, that the other Americas may use part of the proceeds to replenish their dollar balances, and to that extent not validate dollars against goods; and, third, that export controls, in part strengthened to contend with the ERP, may be used to contain exports to the other Americas from mal-provisioned markets. In that manner, the other Americas will be forced not only to pay a small part of the finance bill, but also part of the real costs. For they will send more in goods to the participating countries than the additional amounts they will be able to obtain from this country over the next few years.[3] Finally, the other Americas (or their creditors) on the average will

EUROPEAN RECOVERY PROGRAM

probably seek goods in more ample supply than those they provide under the ERP.

In estimating the costs, the government staffs obviously had to forecast prices over the next four years. That is not an easy task, and the estimates are subject to a wide margin of error. No economist is foolish enough to assert today that export prices will not rise by 40 per cent (say) within four years or will not fall by 20 per cent. The possible or even probable range is wide indeed. Estimates for one year from now will command some respect, those for four years from now, little. The executive branch's price range for exports from the United States to the participating countries is a maximum of 107.5 (July 1, 1947 = 100) and a minimum of 85.[4] Actually prices early in 1948 had risen to about 110. A "high" assumption should surely exceed prices of early 1948. Hence on this account the estimates of probable cost limits may well be revised upwards.

A relevant consideration is the manner of purchasing. The Harriman Committee and the executive branch are clear on this point, supporting purchases through private channels. (The Foreign Assistance Act of 1948 also supports purchases from private sources.) "Private trade channels, both in the supplying and in the participating countries, should be used to the maximum extent practicable in the procurement of commodities under the European Recovery Program."[5] The amounts involved are large, for a saving of 5 to 10 per cent, or even more, which might be made as a result of central buying and purchasing in the cheapest manner, may reduce the tax bill by 1 to 2 billion dollars or more. In the war, similar issues were raised. Lend-lease and also foreign purchasing commissions to a considerable degree by-passed traders, though not so much as the official purchasing agents would have chosen. Perhaps equally important is the control of competition among foreign purchasers. Foreign countries may prefer to buy through their own agents; but unless they

THE FINANCIAL COSTS

operate through a central buying authority, the result will be chaos in mal-provisioned markets. In a more recent period competition between government and private purchasing brought about excessive rises in grain markets. A strong case could be made for monopoly buying practices, direct contacts with manufacturers, allocations between domestic and foreign buyers, and rigid control of the number of middlemen. Unless measures of this kind are taken, parasitic middlemen, their numbers increasing in response to shortages, will take command, with resulting high prices in badly provisioned markets.[6] Export merchants have no vested interest, for purchases under the ERP are largely additional to, not substitutes for, private purchases; and the middlemen serve no genuine function for the large public purchases. Without the intervention of government, the purchases would not be made. Economizers in Congress may well find a fruitful outlet for their energies here.

GOODS OR DOLLARS?

One of the perplexing issues confronting the ECA is whether the advances should be in the form of so many tons of grains, so many tons of steel and bales of cotton, or in the allocation of a blanket sum of money — a problem not easily resolved. It is easier to control the market situation if each country is offered a quota of each commodity over a given period of time. Obviously this involves allocation between domestic and foreign uses, among the various foreign countries, and even control over purchases in the United States with non-ERP funds by the participating countries, and to some extent by others. This system has its weaknesses: it involves a thoroughgoing control of distribution, for which the country is neither prepared nor enthusiastic. Emphasis on supplies rather than dollars may also be costly because less attention will be paid to prices. Finally, in many markets where quantity designations are almost devoid of meaning, the

EUROPEAN RECOVERY PROGRAM

grants will have to be made in dollars — for example, machine tools, structural steel. In fact, differences in quality and costs per unit even for the most standardized commodities (such as rice) are much greater than is generally assumed. It will, therefore, be necessary to make allocations both in quantities and dollars.[7] This is in fact achieved by appropriating money under the ERP on the basis of imports required, and controlling exports. It was proposed by both Senator R. Baldwin and Representative Herter that the orders be received on the basis of ultimate use and appropriations be based on these screened orders. It is also important that the goods arrive at their correct destinations — as they not always have in the past.[8]

SPECIAL PROBLEMS OF FINANCE

From the discussion in Chapter 7 (especially pp. 170–172) the main problems emerge; and little need be added here. First, there is the problem of how much aid is to be given to each country. Obviously, this depends on their deficits in the balance of payments and the resources other than ERP dollars to meet them. In the future, compliance with agreements with this country under the ERP may be a relevant consideration. Second, the ECA will have to allocate ERP dollars between grants and loans. Capacity to repay inclusive of the probable capacity to convert local currencies into dollars without seriously disturbing the exchange market will be a relevant consideration. Much will depend also on the type of commodities imported. It is assumed that the ECA will provide "aid" dollars to finance the three F's and "loan" dollars to finance capital equipment and raw materials to be used for capital purposes. Unfortunately, an examination of the anticipated structure of the import trade does not suggest that countries which will predominantly import the three F's under the ERP will be the ones with relatively small capacity to repay. As a matter of fact, capacity to repay over the next twenty years

THE FINANCIAL COSTS

(say) will depend on a host of factors which defy accurate forecasts: for example, the rate of recovery, the allocation of resources between consumption, investment and exports, exchange rates, the resiliency of the system of free enterprise or the effectiveness of controls under the planned economy, United States commercial policy.

To some extent, at least for the first year, the Congress guides the ECA. Of the total amount to be made available, one billion dollars is to be advanced by the Export-Import Bank. (Obviously this Bank will have to operate under special rules in administering ERP loans; for frequently the probability of repayment will not be so great as under its usual loans.)[9] In addition, provision is made for private advances guaranteed by the government and plans envisage loans by the other Americas and the International Bank. Since the major part of the assistance is to be in the form of grants, the incentive to make loans on a *commercial* basis is to that extent increased.[10]

USE OF LOCAL CURRENCIES

Interwar experience with the foreign exchanges and recent chaos in the dollar market have made it clear that Europe will not be able to repay the full costs of the ERP in dollars. But why should not the French make payments currently for grants-in-aid in francs, the British in sterling, the Dutch in guilders, and so on? This idea occurred to the CEEC, and received favorable and even enthusiastic support by the Harriman and the Herter Committees and the executive branch. To the extent that European governments should sell materials received as grants under the ERP to their nationals, the Harriman Committee recommended that the local currency should be held in trust, the equivalent gold value being guaranteed. Use of the local currencies thus earmarked should be according to agreement of the United States and the foreign government, and should include purchase of strategic raw materials for stock-piling by the United States, and encouragement of production.[11]

Use of local currencies for development purposes was a proposal of the Herter Committee. In addition to disbursing the currencies received under the ERP to cover local expenses of the United States Government, the Committee proposed that the funds

should be utilized and invested for the primary purpose of contributing to the recovery of the recipient country (under safeguards to prevent inflationary effects), to the development of any new sources of wealth therein and to the promotion of enterprises of mutual interest to the United States and the recipient country.

Out of the increased resources thus made available, the participating countries were to obtain additional exports and exchange as well as provide materials for the United States stock-piling program.[12] (This problem is discussed more fully later in this section).

In the official recommendation of the executive branch, the local currency equivalent of grants-in-aid would be deposited in a special account. On the basis of an agreement between the United States and the recipient government, these funds should be used in a manner

as will best contribute to its general program of monetary, fiscal, and other measures designed to assure a sound and stable currency and promote a maximum output of essential goods and services.

The executive branch proposed the following uses: withhold the whole or a part, assist in measures of financial reform and currency stabilization, retire national debt, cover local currency costs incident to exploration and development of additional production of materials in probable short-term supply in the United States, and meet administrative costs of the ERP program.[13] The final legislation took cognizance of these suggestions.

THE FINANCIAL COSTS

As might be inferred from the discussion in Chapter 2 (pp. 79–80), the writer does not share the enthusiasm of government agencies, the Herter Committee, or Congress for control over local currencies. They should recall that attempts by the reparations agent to sterilize, and in general control local currencies in Germany in the twenties were a constant source of irritation. They should be reminded that the amounts involved for some countries (for example, Greece) may be more than the stable value of their currency outstanding. They should be warned that control over the monetary system is one of the prerogatives of a sovereign nation, and that outside interference arouses bitter resentment. They should be instructed that there is no stopping a country facing obstinate deficits. In order to survive, governments may have to manufacture money: should the ERP tie up local currency, then European governments may manufacture so much more. The problems are much more complicated than is suggested by Ambassador Douglas when he says that governments will not be allowed to fill the void left by blocking domestic currency; for they are under obligation to balance their budgets. Communists and their sympathizers have already seized upon this provision as an infringement on sovereignty.[14] Finally, the same criticism may be directed against the proposals of the Herter Committee's financing of capital development in Europe through use of controlled local currencies as was made by the Harriman Committee and the State Department against excessive capital building as a cause of the deficit in the balance of payments of Europe. Control over local currencies might be helpful only when gentle pressure by this government is exercised upon governments welcoming outside support of stable monetary and fiscal policies.

The Foreign Assistance Act of 1948 provides for

> placing in a special account a deposit in the currency of such country, in commensurate amounts and under such terms and conditions as

may be agreed to between such country and the Government of the United States, when any commodity or service is made available through any means authorized under this title, and is furnished to the participating country on a grant basis.

The currency is to be used

for purposes of internal monetary and financial stabilization, for the stimulation of productive activity and for the exploration for *and* development of new sources of wealth, or for such other expenditures as may be consistent with the purposes of this title, including local currency administrative expenditure of the United States incident to operations under this title . . .   (S. 115, [b], [6].)

Additional difficulties may be suggested by what follows. From the discussion of the ERP in official circles, it was made clear that a primary objective of the control over domestic currency supplies would be to put pressure upon foreign governments to adopt anti-inflationary policies. Destruction of local currencies received in payment for aid under the ERP would be the most effective anti-inflationary weapon. Two issues arise. First, as Congressman Herter, Chairman of the House Subcommittee on Foreign Aid, well recognized, the policy will not be effective unless the ECA can also take over control of the monetary and fiscal policies of the countries involved.[15] This would mean such an intrusion on the sovereignty of ERP countries that they would not acquiesce, and the ECA should wisely shun it. At best, then, this deflationary attack might be used to offset other inflationary policies.

Second, it is clear that a vigorous policy imposed by the ECA for sterilizing domestic currencies might well strangle an economy. This conclusion, as shown in Table 29, is based on figures, necessarily rough, but adequate for the purpose. I limit my discussion to France, Greece, and the United Kingdom.

These figures suggest: That the annual amount of grant in local currency is roughly equal to Greece's total currency, to a

THE FINANCIAL COSTS

TABLE 29

	France ($ billion)	Greece ($ million)	United Kingdom ($ billion)
Total supply of money * (1)	3	70 }	20.8 †
(2)	8	160 }	
Rise in circulation over last year available ‡	1.7	80	.12
Estimated annual grant under ERP § ...	.9	100	.90

Source: Calculated from materials in EC Europe: Survey, p. 82; IMF, *International Financial Statistics*, February 1948; U. N., *Monthly Bulletin of Statistics*, February 1948.
 * Total supply of money is derived (1) from estimates of the ratio of stable value in 1947 to that in the prewar period by the Economic Commission for Europe applied to money value (IMF) in the prewar period (1938) adjusted to dollar value; from (2) the circulation late in 1947 converted at current exchange rates. Differences are explained in part by the fact that (1) is derived by adjustment based on movements of domestic prices, and (2) by adjustments according to exchange rates, probably overvalued.
 † Circulation end of 1947 converted at $4 = 1£.
 ‡ Gives dollar value (on basis of then dollar exchange rate) of variations in monetary supply (IMF).
 § The amount made available in first year of ERP is reduced by percentage estimated to be advanced rather than given.

substantial part of the total monetary supply of France and the United Kingdom, and exceeds the variation over the last year (for which figures are available) of the monetary supplies of two of them. Surely the ECA would not want to exercise the vast powers over the European currencies that Section 115, (b), (6) confers upon them.

It is not necessary that the local currency be destroyed. For example, it may be paid out to redeem public debt, or it may be used to expand investment activities. If it is used to redeem public debt, the process may be deflationary or even inflationary, depending upon whether the debt repaid is held by banks or the public, and the use to which the proceeds are put. In the years 1946 and 1947, the British Government obtained £1055 million from loans abroad and sales of assets to foreigners. The use to which the domestic currency obtained in exchange for assets sold or goods imported was put, in no small part determined the net effects of monetary and fiscal policy. It is quite clear, for example, that the use of domestic currency obtained through disinvestment

EUROPEAN RECOVERY PROGRAM

abroad was not used in an inflationary manner, for example, the net foreign disinvestment of £675 million in 1947 occurred in a year when the total monetary supply was roughly stable — a rise of but £30 million.[16]

In short, the program of controlling local currencies is of limited value, and is likely to prove to be a mare's-nest.[17]

CONCLUSION

Financing of the ERP raises thorny problems of all kinds. It is clear that the United States will pay most of the cash required to finance the program; but it is not equally clear that our contributions to the supplies required will be commensurate with the dollar outlay. Much will depend on the use of export controls in this country and the use made of dollars put at the disposal of other countries under the ERP. Costs in both dollars and goods will also depend on the proportion of outlays under grants and loans, and upon factors mentioned in earlier chapters — for example, the rate of recovery, American commercial policy. Unless the authorities impose a much more efficient system of purchasing than now appears likely, the costs may well be substantially larger than seems necessary: producers and especially middlemen will gain unnecessarily at the expense of the taxpayer. Estimates of probable prices under the program seem low; and to that extent the probable cost range is underestimated. Finally, the revolutionary proposal to control the use of local currencies received for exports under the ERP in order to impose correct monetary and fiscal policies and to divert commodities to the United States is likely to prove to be a boomerang. Any resulting expansion of exports will be at the expense of other exports, though possibly this may be a means of imposing a larger sacrifice upon other nonparticipating countries.

9. Inflation and the ERP

INTRODUCTION

Unless inflation, one of the most important and difficult problems of the postwar period, can be beaten, this country faces serious difficulties. Aside from the demands made on the country by the ERP, the inflationary pressures were bound to be heavy in the early years of the postwar period; but when the costs of the various foreign aid programs and rearmament are superimposed upon domestic demands, then the inflationary problem becomes acute. In the introduction to Part III we briefly dealt with the major issues. Here our task is to elaborate.

The outcome of the ERP depends in no small part upon the successful attack on inflation. Should inflationary forces cumulate, the monetary costs of the program would rise, the pressure to renege on European aid would gain strength, and the ERP would be in jeopardy. A further rise of prices at the rate of the increase in 1947 over 1946 would increase the cost of the program from $20 billion (say) to at least $30 billion. This estimate is based on the unlikely assumption that an annual rise in prices of 15 per cent would not accelerate to a higher rate, and also that the increase in the consumers' price index measures that in prices of goods purchased under the ERP. Actually, the pertinent rise for commodities purchased under the ERP is much larger than that given by the consumers' price index.

OVER-ALL FACTORS: INCOME AND THE COST OF THE ERP

In relation to net national income of $203 billion and gross national product of $232 billion in 1947, or in relation to the *rise* of net national income of $161 billion since 1932, the four to six billion dollars that may be required annually under the ERP is

EUROPEAN RECOVERY PROGRAM

not a large amount, as it is less than 3 per cent of this country's annual flow of goods and services. Surely, we can afford this sacrifice. The cost may be even less insofar as the resulting excess of exports should come from unemployed resources. In general, of course, the prospects are that the goods will be delivered in the midst of a full or over-employed economy. But even under present economic conditions, some part comes from surpluses; and if there were no ERP, the drastic decline in exports would result in unemployment or reduced output, insofar as resources in export industries are not easily or quickly transferred to active industries. These offsets, to be sure, probably are not very large. Should a depression develop in this country in the next few years, however, then the exports may to a substantial extent come from resources that otherwise would remain unemployed. In the absence of alternative measures to stimulate the economy, the net effect of the additional exports under the Marshall Plan might then be an expansion of output in excess of the amounts required under the plan. When unemployment is substantial, the problem is not one of reducing demand but rather of increasing it; and at such times, the argument *for* the ERP may be its contribution to sustaining demand just as at present one strike against it is that it contributes to excessive demand.

Clearly the inflationary effects, when viewed in the relation of the cost of the ERP to the output of the economy, do not seem to be large, a conclusion which is reinforced when comparison is made of the export surplus in 1947 and the cost of European aid in 1946 and 1947 with the anticipated export surpluses in 1948 and later years. In 1947, for example, the cost of the annual rate of withdrawal of British loans, other European aid, and the cost of German occupation was more than $5 billion: in 1946, the total of United States Government aid was $5.4 billion; in the first three quarters of 1947 (annual rate), $6.7 billion; and in the latter period, exports had reached $19.3 billion (annual rate) and export

[186]

INFLATION AND THE ERP

surplus, $11.3 billion. These figures should be compared with estimates by the executive branch for the fiscal year 1949 of total exports at under $18 billion, an export surplus of less than $10 billion, and about $5.5 billion required of the United States Treasury under the ERP.[1] These figures may explain the official attitude that the ERP will not greatly strengthen inflationary pressures nor be the decisive factor accounting for increased controls.[2]

Over-all figures are, of course, to be used with caution. It is necessary to consider not only the impact on particular markets (as we shall do in the next chapter), but also some additional aspects of the over-all figures. When compared with $230 billion of gross national product, the inflationary effects of expenditures of four to six billion dollars yearly may not seem serious; but when comparison is made with the marginal factors which determine whether an economy is inflationary or not, the amounts are more important. The significant issue is the relation of receipts to expenditures in each important segment of the economy. Excesses of receipts tend to bring inflation, and deficiencies, deflation.

In the second half of 1947, for example, the following occurred (annual rate): (1) consumers saved $11.8 billion out of their income; (2) business spent $13.9 billion on private domestic investment in excess of the amounts available out of undistributed profits and additions to reserves; (3) net foreign investment was $8.2 billion (this corresponds to an excess of expenditures over receipts); and government receipts were $6.0 billion in excess of expenditures. It is readily seen that against the excess of receipts of $18 billion of government and consumers, an excess of exports or of net foreign investment of eight to ten billion dollars is a significant item.

In discussing the relation of the costs of the ERP to national income, we should not leave out of account the effects of the plan upon foreign economic and political conditions. Should it succeed in contributing towards the rebuilding of Europe's economy, then the resulting rise of income would help sustain American exports and enable Europe ultimately to pay her way in a world of high incomes and trade. The political aspects are even more important. World War II cost this country $350 billion. Another war would cost considerably more: not only because the war would not be paid for out of additional output as World War II was largely in this country, but also because future warfare will be much more devastating. We can be certain that in the event of World War III, we shall not raise our income from $70 billion (as in 1939) to $160 billion (at the peak of World War II), and $203 billion in 1947. Even in stable prices, our income is up around 75 per cent since 1939. We shall not then pay substantially out of unemployed resources as we did in the last war. Another war should cost us at least twice as much as the last war, say, $150 billion a year over five years; or if it is a knockout war, an optimistic guess would be the loss of half to three-quarters of our income over a period of at least ten years or, say, $1500 billion. It is well to ask whether we should take the prudent risk of spending $25 billion over ten years (assuming that aid will taper off for five years after 1952) in order to save $1500 billion (say); on the assumption that the stabilization of a democratic Europe will contribute substantially to saving us from a war.[3]

In summary, the cost of the ERP is likely to be small in relation to our income in prosperity; and should be offset by favorable effects of the resulting spending upon our economy in depression. This cost is not additional to expenditures in 1946–47, but rather is a program to continue payments by government into the next four years. Against the economic gains of a prosperous world and against the vast costs of a third world war, the amounts involved are a prudent investment for a prosperous and peaceful world. But we should not leave out of account the significance of the export surplus in contributing towards an over-all excess of receipts over expenditures.

INFLATION AND THE ERP

INFLATIONARY EFFECTS OF THE ERP

Undoubtedly one of the most serious aspects of the plan is its contribution to inflation. By fall 1948, the cost of living was more than 70 per cent above the 1939 level, and 30 per cent above that of June 1946. Even an annual withdrawal of but four to six billion dollars of goods under the ERP may contribute significantly towards inflation; and especially since much of the demand is concentrated in areas where serious shortages already exist and where demand is intense. Here again, however, we emphasize the fact that the drains are not significantly in excess of those for 1946 and 1947 and that they may well be less. The excess of exports is likely to decline though the proportion of the excess financed by government aid may well rise.

How much the ERP will contribute to inflation depends upon the corrective measures taken to deal with this problem. The main contribution to inflation comes from *excessive* expenditures on consumption (*total* was $174 billion annual rate in the first half of 1948), on gross private domestic investment (total was $37.2 billion), and not primarily from net foreign investment ($7.9 billion), and certainly not from the $5 billion to be anticipated as the annual costs of the ERP. Against $210 billion of consumption and investment demand, the $5 billion required annually under the ERP is a relatively unimportant item.

The way to deal with the inflationary problem is not to deny aid under the ERP, but rather to treat the over-all supply and demand conditions. With total demand deposits adjusted and currency outstanding up by more than two times since 1939, many are reconciled to a corresponding rise in prices. Actually, history does not confirm this close relationship of money and prices. Over the 140 years of our history preceding World War II, the supply of money rose by 1750 times, income by only 110 times, and prices actually fell by 25 per cent. Even granting that the

EUROPEAN RECOVERY PROGRAM

measurement of long-run price changes is subject to serious errors, American history clearly does not suggest the inevitability of inflation with expanding supplies of money; the increases are absorbed in rising output and in a propensity to hold cash at an increasing rate in relation to income.

TIME FOR ACTION [4]

Inflation is the most pressing economic problem confronting the country. That conclusion would hold even if prices rose no further in 1949 and 1950; for large adjustments are required to correct distortions already induced by inflation. Prices for consumers in the middle months of 1948 were 70 per cent above the 1939 level, and food prices were more than 110 per cent above the 1939 level. Since the end of price control in the middle of 1946, consumers' prices had risen by 30 per cent, and food prices by substantially more.

It is time to make a concerted attack upon this social disease, using all weapons that are available in the anti-inflationary arsenal. In 1948 it is necessary to assure the average American that his dollars are not going to be frittered away in rising prices; for whispering campaigns of impending shortages, of continued rises in prices are beginning to gain momentum. Only ignorance of what goes on, or inertia on the part of those who know the advantages of buying today rather than tomorrow, saves the country from a calamitous rise in prices, from a galloping inflation. The country cannot count on such good luck much longer.

THREE ALTERNATIVE APPROACHES

First, do nothing and allow the forces of inflation free play until the collapse comes. Were this course followed the highest bidders would obtain available supplies of goods; and the failure to act would result in large doses of inflation, even on current standards, and ultimately a collapse and radical correctives. Greece is

INFLATION AND THE ERP

a case in point. By 1946, the prices of eleven domestic commodities in Greece had risen by 110 times over prewar prices, of eleven industrial products by over 309 times. But little was done to correct this situation.

Second, it is possible to invoke drastic remedies. The example of the capital levy on money recently carried out in the USSR immediately comes to mind. Stalin was aware of the large excesses of money relative to goods at controlled prices. He solved the problem by reducing the supply of outstanding money, exchanging new money for old (with some exceptions), at the ratio of 1 new for 3 *or* for 10 old rubles. Here was a bold step heartily supported by the conservative London *Economist.**

A third solution is the effective use of all available weapons in order to exclude drastic measures later — and that applies to the substantial inflation in this country. Our inflation is serious, but can be contained. My inclination is to depend on monetary and fiscal policy as much as possible; for the more effective the task done through these attacks, which require the least interference in the daily life of the citizen, the less the task required of controls. Of this we may be sure. Failure to use monetary and fiscal weapons effectively will result either in a rising tempo of inflation, and the drastic remedies already used in Russia, Greece, Hungary, Belgium, and Czechoslovakia, and being considered in France and Great Britain, or in a vast extension of controls. Use of fiscal and monetary instruments may be compared to area or saturation bombing; for their use will reduce the total supply of money and spending, with the result that the areas of infection will be greatly reduced. The need for attacks on particular mar-

---

* An even more drastic remedy is called for when the supply of money reaches fantastic heights. From the end of 1939 to June 30, 1946, Hungarian circulation in pengos had risen 6,277,271,176,000,000,000,000 times (6.2 × 10^{21}), and the official exchange value of the dollar from 5.7 in December, 1939 to 2.97 × 10^{22} in June, 1946. The only outcome is (and was) a virtual demonetization of all outstanding supplies.

kets (comparable to strategic bombing) will be reduced *pari passu* with the general attacks. *I urge, therefore, the strongest possible use of fiscal and monetary policy to enable the government to limit the use of distasteful controls.*

REDUCE DEMAND NOW

Reduce demand now when demand is excessive, and encourage demand later (that is, shift it in time) when demand will be deficient — that is the essence of the problem. In *pure economics*, it is a simple problem. It does not follow just because the country has three times as much money or liquid assets as in 1939, that prices have to rise by 200 per cent. Against the rise of money, we can put an increase of 75 per cent in output. But even more important, as noted above, with a rising standard of living the public tends to hold an increasing part of its income in cash — that is, unless the management of the economy impairs its faith in the future of the dollar.

RESULTING INJUSTICES

Inflation is unwelcome because it brings injustices and distortions, and with these, political struggles and distress. One can well imagine what a ⅔ rise in prices, and a rise of more than 100 per cent in the price of food means to three million veterans and their families living on pensions, to two million beneficiaries of federal old age insurance, to four million receiving public assistance, to 12.9 per cent of the nation's families with incomes of less than $1000 per year and the 28.2 per cent with incomes of less than $2000 per year.

The damage done depends upon how the inflation affects different groups. Although family incomes are up about 75 per cent over 1935-36, the gains are very uneven. Millions obtained no rise (for example, pensioners), and millions, much smaller increases since the war than the rise in the cost of living, although per

INFLATION AND THE ERP

capita *real* gross income and per capita disposable net personal real income on the average by 1947 had risen by about 50 per cent. Those dependent upon government, for example, clerks, teachers; upon institutions, such as professors, laboratory workers; and the white collar worker generally — all of these receive a reduced value in goods though total output per capita is up by about 50 per cent.

We now turn to causes and cures in some detail.

THE EXPANSION OF MONEY AND CREDIT

Since the supply of money and deposits, largely as a result of the war, has increased by about two times, an obvious way out is a reduction in the supply of money, or more broadly a vigorous credit policy. Few are disposed to go so far as to recommend a *reduction* of the total supply of deposits and money; and few would not like to stop the expansion of money. In the three and a half years ending June 30, 1948, loans of American insured commercial banks rose from $21.3 to $39.7 billion.[5] In these three and a half years, the rise of loans exceeded in absolute and relative amounts the expansion in the highly inflationary period, 1922 to 1929. Clearly the rise, coming when deposits and liquid assets of business and consumers were at record levels, was disconcerting and should have been checked. This was, moreover, not the only form of credit which had expanded. In the years 1946 and 1947, mortgage credit on housing had increased by more than $9 billion, and the rate of current mortgage lending had risen from about $550 million to about $1 billion per month. Consumer credit was up from an average of $6.6 billion in 1945 to $14 billion in summer, 1948. Mortgage loans and consumer credit loans are not primarily made by commercial banks, and, therefore, their control requires not merely control of the total supply of money, but also control of the use to which money may be put. A strong case can be made for scrutiny of loans on housing and for consumers

EUROPEAN RECOVERY PROGRAM

generally. Here, of course, policy makers run up against a conflict of major objectives: should they discourage the provision of housing for veterans, or yield on the inflationary front? Actually, a judicious control policy might have yielded veterans adequate housing at the expense of nonessential construction and would have been consistent with adequate inflation control.

ORTHODOX MONETARY CONTROL AND THE GOVERNMENT BOND MARKET

The more general and important issue is, should the orthodox control of money supply be exercised at this time? Should the Federal Reserve banks, for example, sell government securities to offset the consequences of the continued inflow of gold, and *in addition* sell government securities with a view to reducing reserves of member banks, thus forcing the banks to reduce their loans and raise the rate of interest? As part of this policy, the reserve banks might discourage the sales of government securities from banks to reserve banks. Bankers, on the whole, do not seem to favor such strong measures. In fact, forgetful of earlier inflationary episodes, they seem to be content with mild persuasion to discourage speculative loans. Eight professors of the University of Chicago, in a letter to the *New York Times* of January 11, 1948, urged upon the reserve banks the use of these orthodox weapons, apparently irrespective of what happens to the government bond market.

Governor Eccles of the Federal Reserve Board, however, was concerned over the adverse effects of these policies upon the government bond market. He was also dubious that a rise in the rate of interest, in the present circumstances, would seriously reduce the amount of spending by business. I am inclined to agree with Eccles. The government has a commitment to protect the bond market, not only to the current holders of bonds, but also to the taxpayers. That, as the Chicago professors contend, the banks

INFLATION AND THE ERP

would gain from a fall in the price of securities, does not in my opinion strengthen the case for a free bond market. A chaotic bond market which would seriously interfere with the refunding program in the years to come, and in this kind of a warlike world, would be a most unfortunate development. It would be much better to resort to unorthodox measures, which include immobilizing part of the reserves of banks and also part of the government short-term securities, both as additional reserves against deposits. In this manner, the authorities might achieve the minimum required control of monetary supplies, with adequate protection of the bond market.[6]

FISCAL POLICY

Monetary policy is a tool of limited possibilities. One of the main advances of economics in the last generation has been to show the limits of monetary policy. *First, it is not nearly so precise a tool as fiscal policy.* An analyst can make reasonable estimates of the effects on spending and on the economy of a cut in income tax by $2 billion or 10 per cent; but his estimates of the repercussions of a reduction in the supply of money by 10 per cent would be subject to a much larger margin of error.

Second, the relation of money and prices is not so simple as our distinguished colleagues of the University of Chicago seem to think. Our interwar experience taught us nothing if it did not teach us that changes in the supplies of money may be nullified by opposite variations in velocity. For that reason, it is necessary to supplement monetary policy by direct attacks on demand.

Hence the importance of fiscal policy. *Correct fiscal policy in the present situation calls for maintenance of present tax rates, or preferably, if this were politically palatable, a rise in rates.* Prudent fiscal policy also calls for economies in public spending. In periods when demand is excessive, the government can make a substantial contribution by taking in more than it pays out, an objective achieved by imposing heavy taxes and keeping expenditures down. This should be the primary objective of fiscal policy, though necessary functions (for example, adequate military expenditures) should be carried on. Respectable fiscal policy then would contribute towards a substantial reduction of the national debt. It does not become the past opponents of deficit financing and a rising public debt to stump now for policies which tend to keep the debt at a higher level than is necessary.

A continued high level of taxation would be all the more welcome if Congress were prepared to delegate to the Executive the right to alter tax rates (income and payroll) and to adjust certain categories of expenditures, both within prescribed limits, on the basis of indexes of economic well-being. Should that power be delegated under adequate safeguards, then fiscal policy might be used with maximum effectiveness — a sudden economic storm heralding a decline might *quickly* be treated by a reduction in taxes and a rise in expenditures.

Finally, many confuse the long-run objectives of sound tax policy with the immediate requirements. It may well be that taxes on risk-taking are now too high to yield an adequate volume of investment in the long run. But in the current situation, taxes are surely not too high. How can they be when, for example, corporate profits after taxes had risen from $4 billion in 1935–1939 to $17 billion in 1947; and when private investments for two years had been running at the record level of $30 billion per year? High levels of investment are one of the most inflationary factors in the situation, for they provide, not the goods currently needed, but goods in the distant future. It would be a serious mistake to cut taxes in order to encourage investment in 1948 or 1949.[7]

The meager anti-inflationary legislation of the special session of Congress in the summer of 1948 reflected an unwillingness to come to grips with the problem. Control of consumer credit and a small rise of reserve requirement could not possibly stem the

INFLATION AND THE ERP

tide. Congress had already made a serious error in reducing taxes. In contrast, the Federal Reserve had disposed of at least $3 billion of assets to offset the inflationary effects of large inflows of gold.

OTHER CORRECTIVES

Given an effective monetary and fiscal policy, I repeat, the need for controls will be reduced. I am not, however, optimistic that the appropriate monetary and fiscal policies will be forthcoming; and, therefore, I fear either that controls on a more ambitious scale than here proposed will be necessary, or that the inflation bacillus will be allowed freedom to spread.

In some markets, I see no substitute for direct controls. It would be very helpful to allocate essential and scarce commodities, for example, steel, oil, grains, and lumber.[8] As part of the allocation program, the government should continue export control, thus assuring adequate diversions to export markets and the most effective use of the exports. In export markets, allocations should be implemented by direct government purchases for the ERP program. In view of the demand to be made by the ERP, it is especially important to exclude nonessential purchases from mal-provisioned markets. Indeed, the ERP requires only 2 to 3 per cent of the nation's output and is not likely to increase the foreign drain over the 1947 level; but in particular markets (such as machinery, iron and steel, grains and foods generally, fertilizers) the demands may be serious. It would be well, for example, to favor Europe against other markets. (In 1936–1938, Europe received 42 per cent of United States exports; in the first three quarters of 1947, only 36 to 37 per cent. South America's share rose from 9 to 16½ per cent.) Scarce commodities should be distributed according to essentiality: grain for feed, not alcohol; wood for veterans' homes, not for luxurious summer hotels; oil for heat at the expense of excessive pleasure driving. Allocations reflect shortages and secure economies: by excluding nonessential

EUROPEAN RECOVERY PROGRAM

demands they keep prices down. In some instances, however, the pressure of demand will continue so strong that it may be necessary to introduce rationing and price control. I hope this will be the exception rather than the rule.

CONTROLS FURTHER DISCUSSED

Surfeited with controls, the American public through their representatives in Congress demobilized them with excessive speed in the years 1945-46. In no small part, the rise in prices since 1945 is to be associated with the mistaken control policies in the early postwar period. So great was the repugnance to controls that the government in 1947 did not use its allocation powers to strengthen its export controls. In the latter part of 1947, Congress began to retrace its steps; and with inflationary pressures increasing and the growing awareness of the need of integrating export and political policies, the importance of reinstituting controls became evident. In the discussion of the ERP, the Council of Economic Advisers, the Harriman Committee, and the Select Committee on Foreign Aid (Herter Committee) all acknowledged the need of extending controls though there was little sentiment for the comprehensive wartime controls. Early in 1948 the Senate Banking and Currency Committee held hearings on five bills which would reimpose controls, including a bill introduced by Senator Taylor for a general price freeze and administration bills for limited price and other controls.[9]

Above all, it was held necessary to extend and strengthen controls in order to weaken the inflationary forces, and also to obtain equitable distribution of scarce supplies. Other important objectives were conservation of scarce resources, controlled distribution to achieve political objectives, and fair access to scarce supplies among business units.

Undoubtedly the major problem of control in relation to the ERP will be export control, and its supplementation by allocation

INFLATION AND THE ERP

control. Most scarce commodities are now under export control; but the administration requires strengthening, new power, and, in general, improvement. Congressional failure to appropriate adequate sums caused much of the difficulty. Figure 10 gives some indication of the relation of output and capacity in industries, where the main reliance will have to be in economy of use.

One of the most serious problems confronting the Office of International Trade of the Department of Commerce is the problem of integrating export with price policies. Obviously, with supplies allocated to export markets but a small percentage of requirements, and with demand for these commodities highly inelastic, prices of exports tend to rise far above domestic levels. Trafficking in export licenses becomes a profitable business. Temptation to buy licenses becomes almost irresistible when, for example, applications for reinforcing bars in the second quarter of 1947 were 100 times the export quota. In chemicals, export prices rose several times above domestic prices. Again, a world struggle develops for our small contribution to rice moving in international markets when world demand is twice world supply; and intense demand raises skyward world prices of our small exports of nitrogen.[10]

Export price control is not the answer; for without domestic price control, it is not workable, and would certainly be sabotaged. But even as part of a general control system, both of prices and supply and demand, export price control is extremely difficult to administer. As one who was in charge of export price control in the war, I can vouch for the difficulties.[11] It is particularly annoying to American sellers, forced to keep margins down, who find middlemen abroad making the gains denied them. Unless domestic price control is introduced here and prices controlled all along the line abroad, export price control is out of the question. It remains to be seen whether the Department of Commerce's new policy of taking price charged into account, in giving

CAPACITY AND PRODUCTION
Many industries are operating at close to practical capacity.

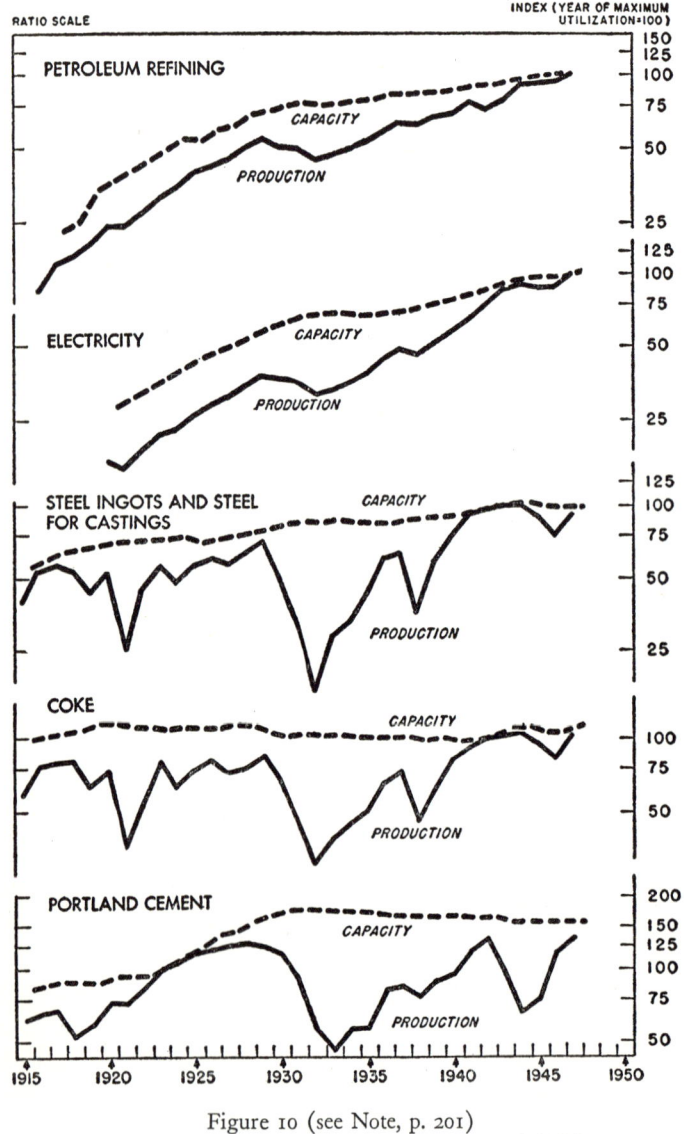

Figure 10 (see Note, p. 201)

INFLATION AND THE ERP

export licenses, will be administratively workable; and, if it is, whether it is fair, unless resale prices are controlled abroad. *My suggestion is concentration of purchases by government agencies of all supplies required under the ERP, and free pricing generally for other purchases.*

An effective system of export commodity controls will be a *sine qua non* for the most equitable and effective distribution of scarce supplies under the ERP; and, if implemented by other allocation controls, will reduce the pressure on export markets. What is especially required is a diversion of exports to Europe at the expense of other areas. It will be recalled that Europe's share of United States exports declined in 1946-47 relative to the prewar period. (Cf. Figure 11.) The relation of control and Europe's participation in United States exports is evidenced by her taking 70 per cent of our exports under control and only 27 per cent of uncontrolled exports (in the third quarter of 1947, the respective percentages were 61 and 32 per cent). Even if one admits that the figures are subject to some reservations and that allocations contributed to the results attained, they are nevertheless significant.[12] A Department of Commerce estimate of November 1947 yields some interesting results: For commodities that were exported to all countries at an annual rate of $14.9 billion in the first half of 1947, the estimate is that $14.2 billion would be exported in 1948. Exports to the ERP countries would rise from 4.9 to 6.0 billion dollars, and to other countries decline from 10 to 8.2 billion dollars, or a rise percentagewise for the former would be from 33 per cent to 42 per cent. For food, the exports to ERP countries would rise from $1.2 to $1.4 billion, and to others, decline from $1.3 to $1.0 billion.[13]

Note — Capacity and production for each industry have been plotted so as to touch at the year when the ratio of production to capacity reached its maximum. Such points correspond approximately to operations at the limit of practical capacity, though rated or theoretical capacity would in most cases be higher. All 1947 figures are estimates based on incomplete data.

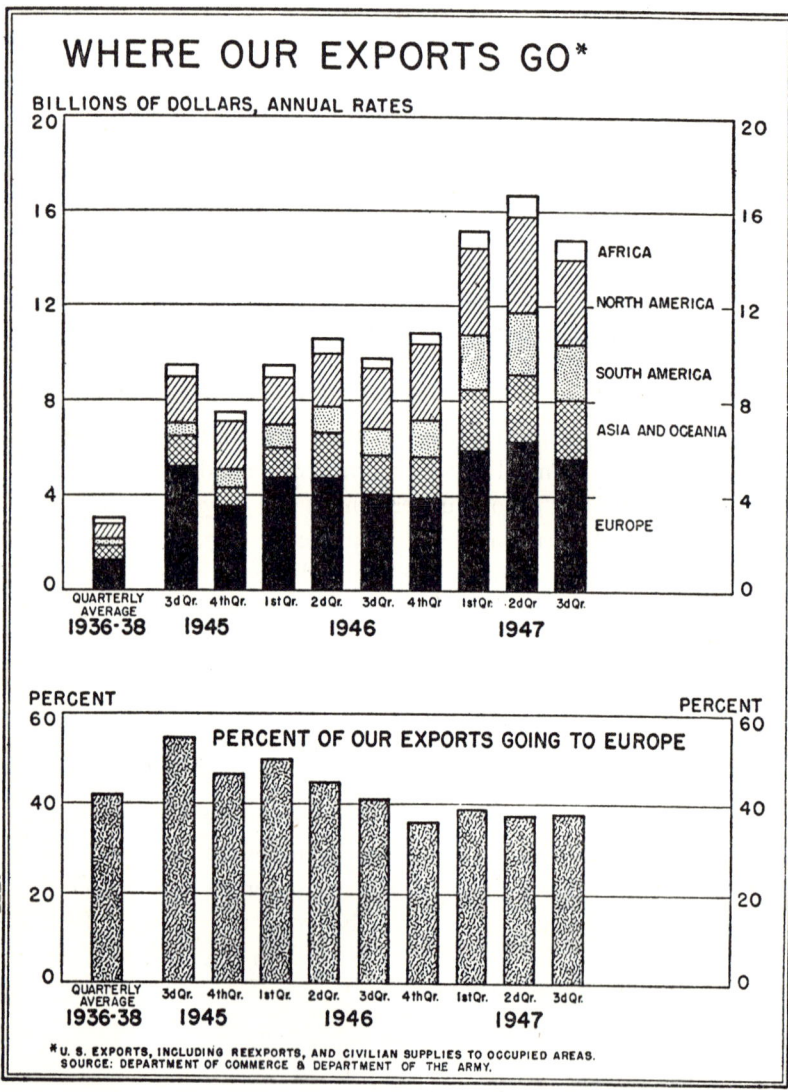

Figure 11

INFLATION AND THE ERP

It is clear that under the ERP, export controls will be strengthened; and they will have to be integrated with the ERP. In the last few years, it has largely been a problem of determining the amounts of scarce items that can be spared for export. Now it will be increasingly imperative to assure that what goes out does the most good in terms of the objectives of the ERP. Even before the ERP the Department of Commerce strengthened its export controls, for instance, requiring validated rather than consolidated or blanketed licenses as in the past.[14]

In a statement before the Senate Banking and Currency Committee, which had three bills stipulating a freeze under consideration, I advised against a price freeze at this time. Even the price freeze of 1942 had been no great success. In 1948 the conditions were even less propitious. I mention only three factors: the absence of war conditions and resulting moral pressures, the vast accumulation of excess purchasing power in 1948 as compared with 1942, and, finally, the unavailability of the related controls without which price control is likely to be ineffective.[15]

THE BUDGETARY PROBLEM AND THE ERP

In January 1948 the President estimated budgetary receipts for fiscal year 1948 at $45.2 billion and expenditures at $37.7 billion, surplus at $7.5 billion. For fiscal year 1949, the budgetary surplus was put at $4.8 billion. International affairs and finance would cost $5.5 billion in fiscal 1948 and $7.0 billion in fiscal 1949.[16]

Because of these anticipated budgetary surpluses, it might have been possible to retire substantial amounts of public debt in the calendar years 1948 and 1949. However, a substantial program of tax reduction and an expansion of military outlays spoil the chance of a large reduction of debt. This is unfortunate because under inflationary conditions, large budgetary surpluses might still not prevent inflation. In the inflationary milieu of 1946–47,

EUROPEAN RECOVERY PROGRAM

for example, the country experienced large budgetary surpluses and substantial rises in prices; for prices depend on *total* demand, not on the relation of government receipts and expenditures.

Correct fiscal policy would surely demand that, despite the heavy requirements of ERP, substantial amounts of debt be retired, or, at the very least, that 1947 tax rates should be maintained. Then it *might* be possible to combine a balanced budget, the financing of the ERP, and increased military expenditures; but ideal policy would go much further than that. *The ERP should be financed out of additional taxes;* for unless it is, the effects budgetwise would be inflationary: the budgetary surplus would be reduced and hence the contribution of government excess of receipts to staving off inflation and paying off debt would be less. Even should the ERP be financed out of additional taxes of $5 billion yearly, the program, in its *over-all* effects, would still be inflationary; for private expenditures would not fall by $5 billion, but by substantially less. Hence total expenditures would rise. Actually the tax cut of 1948 plus the rise in the military budget are likely to convert a surplus in fiscal 1948 into a deficit in fiscal 1949.

For later years, the issues are not quite so clear. Much depends on the success with which inflation is treated, and therefore on the continuance of favorable economic conditions. Should a collapse follow a rise of prices after (say) 1948–1950, then the government would probably incur large deficits once more; then the ERP may well contribute to a growth of public debt, rather than obstruct a decline in the debt. Even this is not clear, however. If we fail to substitute domestic stimulative measures of equal effectiveness, the excess of exports induced by the ERP would raise incomes and, therefore, tax capacity. In a period of substantial deficiency of demand, national income should then rise by much more than the outlay under the ERP,[17] and even *additional* Treasury income may exceed the outlays under the ERP.

INFLATION AND THE ERP

Purists in fiscal policy should be consistent. Thus critics of the ERP on the grounds of adverse effects upon the budgetary situation might well support a policy of high taxes and large debt reduction in the current inflationary situation. Any increase of debt in the ensuing period of deflation would to that extent be more palatable.

CONCLUSION

This country's economic future depends in no small part on how we deal with the serious inflationary problem which confronts us. The outcome will depend primarily upon the courage and wisdom shown by the government, and secondarily on the restraints exercised by capital, labor, and the farmers. With or without an ERP, we must cope with the inflationary problem. There is no substitute for high production and control of demand. The fifteen to twenty billion dollars required under the ERP over the next four years, or the twenty-five to thirty billion dollars that may be required to solve the dollar problem once and for all in the next ten years may well be the straw, or better, straws, that break the camel's back; but the main burden on the camel is of domestic origin. It is well to recall that of a gross national product of $210 billion in 1944, domestic civilian use accounted for but 59 per cent; but of a gross national product of $231 billion in 1947, the proportion taken by domestic civilian use had risen to around 90 per cent. In highlighting the inflation, the budget, and the conservation of resources, the ERP may well mobilize the anti-inflationary forces of the country and contribute towards solving the inflation problem.

The essence of the problem is control of demand, which is high because of vast accumulations of purchasing power, because of a backlog of demand, and a level of demand originating in current income far from matched by a corresponding flow of consumers' goods. Many hold the thesis, and erroneously, that high levels of

EUROPEAN RECOVERY PROGRAM

output are the way out. Far from it. Compare 1932 and 1947, the latter year with its output three times that of 1932, and consider price movements in these two years. Businessmen who predicted in 1945 that lifting controls and raising output would stop inflation have proved to be even more wrong than the officials who forecast in 1945 a serious depression in 1946 and 1947.

Cautious control of supplies of money and credit; qualitative restrictions on the use of credit; high taxes and economies in public expenditures; control of the use of scarce resources, with particular emphasis on discouraging excessive investment and nonessential use generally; a resulting stability of prices, with pressure upon labor and farmers to desist from inflationary policies — these are the roads to price stability and economic and political stability. (It will be noted that I do not have much confidence in moral suasion on businessmen to reduce prices.) If these policies are used effectively, price and rationing controls need not be very extensive. As a private citizen and as an economist speaking for the public welfare, I urge Congress especially to reverse the politically attractive policy of tax reduction.

10. Shortages in Relation to the ERP

INTRODUCTION [1]

The subject matter of the last chapter was related to general supply and demand conditions: we proposed treatment of excess demand, with a view to keeping prices from rising further, the government to use every weapon available, inclusive of monetary and fiscal policies and controls. The more effective the monetary and fiscal measures directed to removing excess purchasing power, the less recourse will have to be had to controls. Yet to some extent it will be necessary to rely on controls. No general measures, short of a reduction of purchasing power which would paralyze the economy, could possibly remove inflationary pressure in a market for a necessity of life, with supplies 20 per cent (say) short of demand at current prices. Recent studies in the elasticity of demand for farm products, for example, suggest that a decline of 25 per cent in output would ordinarily raise prices by 100 per cent. Hence the need for allocations and possibly other controls in particular markets. Allocations are effective because they exclude nonessential demand; but unless they are effectively administered or (and) supplemented by price controls, black and grey markets emerge. Excluded purchasers bid for supplies until a point is reached where legitimate recipients of supplies under allocations are tempted to divert supplies to nonessential users: for example, this becomes evident in a trafficking of licenses.

This chapter is concerned primarily with shortages in particular markets associated with the ERP.[2] That the ERP countries were denied part of the supplies asked, and that to a substantial degree the United States will satisfy Europe's requirements under the ERP through offshore purchases, will contribute towards easing

EUROPEAN RECOVERY PROGRAM

of the pressure on many markets in this country. But in the absence of a serious economic collapse, shortages, which may be aggravated by bad weather or interruptions of production, will continue to prevail in many markets.

EXPORT DRAINS

Obviously if exports are a fairly large part of total production of commodities in short supply, the ERP should contribute substantially to inflationary pressures. In order to give the reader a proper perspective, I reproduce two tables (30 and 31) from a document submitted by the executive branch.[3]

Table 30 shows that for 1948–49, foods and tobacco exported from the United States to the participating countries would account for close to 40 per cent of the imports from this country. For the entire period of four and a quarter years, these commodities are scheduled to require more than $5 billion, or close to 40 per cent of the total goods to be shipped *from the United States*. Other items of large significance are cotton ($1957 million), or about 15 per cent, and petroleum, largely from sources other than the United States ($2305 million), about 18 per cent.

The expert will note at once that shipments from the United States are to be determined in no small part by the availabilities in this country. For example, exports of dairy products ($533 million) are related to seasonal excesses, those of tobacco ($911 million) and dried fruits ($96 million) to our surplus supplies. Rather large exports of agricultural machinery ($545 million) are explained by their anticipated contributions to the rise of output in Europe and, therefore, to reduced demands for food from this country. Coal is a rather large item ($599 million), and particularly in 1948–49 ($297 million), but the amount involved is not large in relation to this country's output. Exports of iron and steel were to be $921 million, the major part, finished steel, $720 million. Embarrassed by shortages in scrap, this country refused to

SHORTAGES AND THE ERP

export scrap in significant quantities and instead offered the CEEC countries more finished steel than they had requested.

When serious shortages prevail here and supplies might be found elsewhere, the United States Government would lean heavily on the other Americas. (See Table 31.) In grains, shipments by the other Americas account for $5.4 billion in comparison with $2.6 from the United States. In fats and oils (and oilcake and meal), the former contribute more than three times as much as the United States. According to the recommendations of the executive branch, the other Americas were to contribute $1353 million of meat in comparison with but $61 million from the United States. In agricultural commodities, the other Americas were to provide about $11.4 billion, whereas the United States was to provide $7.2 billion; but in coal, timber, iron and steel, trucks, machinery, and equipment, the respective exports were to be $913 million and $3.5 billion. (These figures relate to *exports* from the United States and other Americas to the ERP countries — a total much larger than aid to be given under the ERP.)

It is clear then that exports from the United States under the ERP are to be less damaging, in part because the CEEC demands are not to be fully met, because the contributions of this country are related to supply conditions, and where supplies are deficient here and are available in adequate amounts in the other Americas, the burden of shipping goods is shifted to the latter. Furthermore, the ERP countries are to receive an increased proportion of United States exports.

I submit Table 32, a comparison (for the anticipated life of the ERP) of the import programs of the CEEC and the recommendations by the United States executive departments. Again, this table suggests the manner in which the original CEEC requirements were adapted to the needs of the American economy. With food and fertilizer scarce, the executive agencies proposed to cut American exports below the amounts requested and to raise the

TABLE 30

VALUE OF SELECTED IMPORTS OF THE PARTICIPATING COUNTRIES (INCLUDING DEPENDENT AREAS) FROM THE UNITED STATES, JULY 1, 1947, PRICES

(In Millions of Dollars)

Commodity	April-June 1948	1948–49	1949–50	1950–51	1951–52	Total
Bread grains	218.3	535.5	509.7	411.6	411.6	2,086.7
Coarse grains	5.8	82.9	120.0	133.0	133.0	474.7
Fats and oils	20.0	80.4	88.0	97.4	97.4	383.2
Oilcake and meal	4.4	17.7	22.6	22.6	27.1	94.4
Sugar	6.5	21.4	17.3	10.5	11.0	66.7
Meat	1.7	6.0	12.1	17.9	23.8	61.5
Dairy products	75.2	160.0	105.7	101.5	90.3	532.7
Eggs	12.0	24.0	12.0	12.0	12.0	72.0
Dried fruits	6.9	26.6	25.2	17.6	20.0	96.3
Rice	1.1	6.1	6.1	6.1	11.9	31.3
Coffee	…	…	…	…	…	…
Other foods	9.2	64.6	61.2	80.4	80.4	295.8
Tobacco	52.5	210.0	217.4	215.6	215.6	911.1
Cotton	142.5	438.3	437.6	458.7	480.5	1,957.6
Nitrogen	2.4	14.0	7.8	…	…	24.2
Phosphates	.6	2.5	2.5	2.5	2.5	10.6
Potash	…	…	…	…	…	…
Agricultural machinery	…	136.3	161.5	131.8	115.5	545.1

Table 30 continued next page

Coal	92.3	297.0	135.1	49.6	24.9	598.9
Coal-mining machinery	...	81.9	52.7	37.6	34.5	206.7
Petroleum*	121.3	530.6	546.2	570.5	537.0	2,305.6
Timber	24.0	96.3	93.1	88.0	76.4	377.8
Iron and steel:						
Finished steel	44.6	182.1	186.9	179.3	126.6	719.5
Crude and semifinished	11.9	47.2	47.2	47.2	43.5	197.0
Pig iron	.3	1.3	1.3	...	...	2.9
Scrap	.4	1.6	...	...	...	2.0
Rich iron ore	...	...	...	...	...	...
Trucks	19.7	80.9	40.1	33.9	33.6	208.2
Freight cars	...	60.0	18.0	...	...	78.0
Steel equipment	...	48.1	48.2	48.2	48.2	192.7
Timber equipment	...	16.9	22.2	11.7	11.7	62.5
Electrical equipment	...	95.0	100.7	85.0	65.0	345.7
Total	873.6	3,365.2	3,098.4	2,870.2	2,734.0	12,941.3
Assuming high prices	939.1	3,617.6	3,330.8	3,085.5	2,939.0	13,912.0
Assuming low prices	939.1	3,617.6	3,098.4	2,654.9	2,323.9	12,633.9

Source: ERP; Sen. Hear., p. 115; also see *State Dept. Est. Imp., etc.*, especially pp. 6–7 and 7.43 and 7.44.
* Total imports from dollar sources, largely outside the continental United States.

TABLE 31

VALUE OF SELECTED IMPORTS OF THE PARTICIPATING COUNTRIES (INCLUDING DEPENDENT AREAS) FROM THE OTHER WESTERN HEMISPHERE COUNTRIES, JULY 1, 1947, PRICES

(In Millions of Dollars)

Commodity	April-June 1948	1948-49	1949-50	1950-51	1951-52	Total
Bread grains	177.5	669.0	712.3	777.4	777.4	3,113.6
Coarse grains	52.6	411.0	562.1	626.7	626.7	2,279.1
Fats and oils	55.8	222.2	217.1	237.2	237.2	969.5
Oilcake and meal	33.5	135.1	147.5	163.8	158.0	637.9
Sugar	67.2	200.7	175.7	178.2	178.7	800.5
Meat	77.3	308.1	322.3	322.7	322.9	1,353.3
Dairy products	11.3	28.7	25.2	25.2	20.8	111.2
Eggs	16.1	33.2	9.0	17.3	20.1	95.7
Dried fruits	.3	.5	.8	.7	1.7	4.0
Rice	7.9	32.7	32.7	32.7	35.7	141.7
Coffee	22.7	133.9	155.6	134.4	155.1	601.7
Other foods	16.8	77.4	78.5	84.6	84.6	341.9
Tobacco	6.3	24.6	21.9	20.7	20.7	94.2
Cotton	41.9	167.3	195.3	203.7	210.0	818.2
Nitrogen	4.4	22.0	17.8	8.0	8.0	60.2
Phosphates	...	...	...	...	...	...
Potash	...	...	...	...	...	...
Agricultural machinery	...	22.4	26.5	23.2	18.7	90.8

Table 31 continued next page

Coal	...	...	...	...	...	...
Coal-mining machinery	...	...	...	...	...	...
Petroleum*	...	...	...	...	...	...
Timber	42.5	170.6	172.2	145.0	132.0	662.3
Iron and steel:						
Finished steel	...	...	...	...	...	...
Crude and semi-finished	5.4	21.7	21.7	21.7	21.7	92.2
Pig iron	...	...	...	...	...	...
Scrap	1.7	7.1	7.1	12.0	12.6	40.5
Rich iron ore	3.2	13.0	4.0	3.4	3.2	26.8
Trucks	...	...	...	...	...	...
Freight cars	...	...	...	...	...	...
Steel equipment	...	.1	.1	...	...	.2
Timber equipment	...	...	...	...	...	...
Electrical equipment	...	...	...	...	...	...
Total	644.4	2,701.3	2,905.4	3,038.6	3,045.8	12,335.5
Assuming high prices	676.6	2,836.4	3,050.7	3,190.5	3,198.1	12,952.3
Assuming low prices	676.6	2,836.4	2,832.8	2,734.7	2,512.8	11,593.3

Source: ERP: *Sen. Hear.*, p. 117. For individual countries (quantities and values) see: State Department, ERP: *Confidential Supplement to Commodity Reports*, Vols. A–E (1948), which gives imports from the United States, other Americas, and other countries, and also exports from ERP.
* Included under imports from United States.

EUROPEAN RECOVERY PROGRAM

TABLE 32

IMPORT PROGRAM OF PARTICIPATING COUNTRIES (AND WESTERN GERMANY) FROM THE AMERICAN CONTINENT, 1948–1951

(*In Billions of Dollars, July 1, 1947 Prices*)

	From U.S.A. CEEC	From U.S.A. Exec. Dept.	From Other Countries CEEC	From Other Countries Exec. Dept.
Food, fertilizer	5.4	5.1	8.3	10.6
Coal	0.7	0.6	...	...
Petroleum products	2.2	2.3	...	...
Iron and steel	1.2	0.9	0.1	0.2
Timber	0.4	0.4	0.6	0.7
Equipment	3.3 *	1.6 ‡	0.1 *	0.1
Other	7.2	2.0	5.7	0.8
Total	20.4 †	12.9	14.8	12.4

Sources: Adapted from *CEEC*, pp. 44 and 55; and *ERP State*, pp. 115, 117.
* Total equipment given for *all* Americas.
† This total includes only $3.3 billion for equipment covered in technical committee. The total equipment is $4.5 billion; the difference may be covered in other imports.
‡ Includes machinery, trucks, etc.

amounts from the other Americas by about 25 per cent above CEEC estimates. The CEEC countries were to obtain the petroleum requested from the United States; but from sources primarily outside of the continental United States. Europe's requests for equipment especially were scaled down, the large reduction being explained in part by the scarcity of these items in this country, and the fear that ambitious capital development programs in Europe might generate serious inflationary effects. The CEEC countries were not to obtain the iron and steel sought, and particularly were to be denied scrap. (For the entire period, the executive branch offered 6.4 million metric tons of finished steel against 2.3 millions asked, but much less than one-half as much crude and semifinished iron and steel, and virtually none of the scrap asked.) [4]

EXPORTS AND PRICES

In his testimony before the Senate Foreign Relations Committee, Secretary of Agriculture Anderson tried to show that the large exports under the ERP would not seriously influence prices.[5] "As

SHORTAGES AND THE ERP

far as wheat is concerned, I think it is safe to say that the wheat price ought not to be influenced by the Marshall Plan." [6]

Secretary Anderson did not seem very convincing on this issue, and although most of the senators commended him for his convincing statement, Senator Hickenlooper probed for the correct answer.[7]

[Senator Hickenlooper] Now I am concerned about the impact of taking this tremendous amount of wheat for a specific purpose and not necessary in the ordinary economic channels of international trade. We are pointing this entire tremendous 23 percent of the American wheat production exported abroad for a specialized purpose which is bound to go into a specialized economy, and not in the normal channels of trade, and I think that is a thing we will have to think about; it is bound to affect our agricultural economy, I think.

Now I would like to ask you just another question or two about the pressures that not only these grains but some of the other foodstuffs would bring. It has seemed apparent to me in the past that it was the evident shortage of corn that contributed very seriously to the rise in the price of wheat, and the anticipated shortage for our full domestic needs here of both corn and wheat, and that they, in turn, have a direct effect upon the price of meat in this country, and a direct effect upon the marketing light of both cattle and hogs . . .

But I have been very much convinced that it was the definite shortage, over-all shortage of grains in this country that has been the direct cause, that is one of the direct contributing causes, of this inflationary spiral in foodstuffs.

[Secretary Anderson] I simply say that I think the supply of wheat in this country was sufficient so that it need not have had violent fluctuations and rises. When we know that there is remaining in this country 950,000,000 to 1,000,000,000 bushels of wheat, we know that that is a lot of wheat. And even if the export program ran 450,000,000 or 500,000,000 bushels, there would still remain more wheat than we normally use, more wheat than we normally grow, a terrific amount of wheat.

[Senator Hickenlooper] But it would indicate to me that there must be some anticipated substitute use for wheat in this country or it could not possibly, with a surplus, support these very high prices. I do not know that I can put my finger on it, but there is some reason other than just speculative activity or something of that kind that is sustaining this tremendous price of wheat, and it must be a shortage situation; otherwise it could not be sustained this long, in my judgment.

Tables 33 and 34, submitted by Secretary Anderson, do not support his position, the first suggesting that the exports were to absorb a very large part of the difference between total available supply and domestic disappearance (including carry-over). The ERP program was, in general, to account for more than one-half of the exports. It is absurd to contend when, of a total available supply of 34.3 million metric tons of bread grains, domestic use accounts for 25.9 million, 8.4 million tons are available for export, 8.1 million tons are to be exported and the ERP is to absorb 5.5 million tons, that the ERP does not make a significant contribution to higher prices. A similar conclusion relates to other commodities: for example, even the 5 per cent of supplies of fats and oils for export, three-fifths of which was to be exported to ERP countries. Speculation contributes to higher prices, as Anderson contends; but the speculators bid up prices on the basis of anticipated supply and demand conditions; and if they are too exuberant, their fingers are likely to be burned.

Table 34, which compares agricultural exports to ERP countries over the years as a percentage of production, also supports the general contention that these exports contribute significantly to inflation. For bread grains, the exports to ERP countries were 7.7 per cent in 1934–1938, 34.3 per cent in 1946–47, and anticipated at 32.4 per cent in 1947–48, and 27.4 per cent in 1948–49. In fats and oils and cheese, also, the proportion of exports tends to rise. But we shall export much less meat.

Secretary Anderson's testimony, correctly interpreted, and the accompanying statistical tables underline the point that drains under the ERP will seriously affect prices on many markets.

TABLE 33

ESTIMATED UNITED STATES SUPPLY AND UTILIZATION OF SPECIAL COMMODITIES, 1948-49 FISCAL YEAR

Commodity	Unit	Total Available Supply	Domestic* Disappearance (Including Carryout)	Quantity Available for Export	Estimated exports	
					Total	To ERP Countries
Bread grains	{1,000 metric tons	34,232	25,875	8,357	8,070	5,470
	{Million bushels	1,280	968	312	300	205
Coarse grains	{1,000 metric tons	118,354	115,878	2,476	2,200	1,100
	{Million bushels	5,406	5,296	110	100	45
Total grains	{1,000 metric tons	152,586	141,753	10,833	10,270	6,570
	{Million bushels	6,686	6,264	422	400	250
Rice	1,000 100-pound bags	23,000	11,650	7,850 †	7,850 †	400
Fats and oils (including butter).	Million pounds	12,485	11,760	645 ‡	645 ‡	322
Oilcake and meal	1,000 metric tons	6,015	5,830	185	185	150 §
Meat ‖	Million pounds	23,200	23,125	75	75	0
Horsemeat	Million pounds	100	50	50	50	50
Eggs (shell equivalent)	1,000 metric tons	3,474	3,404	70	70	40
Cheese	Million pounds	1,370	1,160	210	210	200
Processed milk	Million pounds	4,940	3,840	1,100	1,100	625
Fresh fruit	1,000 short tons	18,000	17,300	700	700	366
Dried fruit	1,000 short tons	600	422	178	140	121
Pulses	1,000 short tons	1,045	795	250	250	150
Sugar	1,000 short tons	10,000 ¶	9,800	200	200	152
Tobacco	Million pounds	5,350	4,675	675	595 **	503 ††
Cotton	1,000 bales	14,800	11,300	3,500	3,500	2,400

Source: *ERP. Sen. Hear.*, p. 350.

* Based on estimated available supplies. With the exception of meat and eggs, will permit per capita food consumption equal to or greater than 1947 for applicable commodities.
† Does not include 3,500,000 bags estimated shipments to United States territories.
‡ Does not include 80,000,000 pounds shipments to United States territories.
§ Does not include production from oilseeds imported into ERP countries.
‖ Dressed weight plus offal.
¶ Includes Puerto Rico and Hawaii.
** Export weight equivalent of 520,000,000 pounds.
†† Export weight equivalent of 439,000,000 pounds.

TABLE 34

Estimated Food and Agriculture Exports from United States under European Recovery Program

Commodity	Unit	1934-38 [1] Amount	1934-38 Percent of production	1934-38 Exports to ERP Countries[2] Amount	1946-47 [1] Amount	1946-47 Percent of production	1946-47 Exports to ERP Countries[2] Amount	1947-48 [1] Amount	1947-48 Percent of production	1947-48 Exports to ERP Countries[2] Amount	1948-49 [1] Amount	1948-49 Percent of production	1948-49 Exports to ERP Countries[2] Amount	1949-50 [1] Amount	1949-50 Percent of production	1949-50 Exports to ERP Countries[2] Amount	1950-51 [1] Amount	1950-51 Percent of production	1950-51 Exports to ERP Countries[2] Amount	1951-52 [1] Amount	1951-52 Percent of production	1951-52 Exports to ERP Countries[2] Amount
Bread grains	1,000 metric tons	1,583	7.7	860	10,940	34.3	6,443	12,054	32.4	8,250	8,070	27.4	5,470	8,000	27.1	5,190	6,700	23.5	4,175	6,700	23.5	4,175
	Million bushels	58	...	32	402	...	237	[3] 450	...	[3] 305	300	...	205	300	...	195	250	...	155	250	...	155
Coarse grains	1,000 metric tons	979	1.3	654	4,202	3.7	2,426	1,600	1.9	825	2,200	2.1	1,100	2,200	2.1	1,600	2,200	2.1	1,775	2,200	2.1	1,775
	Million bushels	44	...	29	189	...	109	[3] 70	...	[3] 35	100	...	45	100	...	70	100	...	80	100	...	80
Total grains	1,000 metric tons	2,562	2.7	1,514	15,142	10.5	8,869	13,654	11.1	9,075	10,270	7.7	6,570	10,200	7.6	6,790	8,900	6.7	5,950	8,900	6.7	5,950
	Million bushels	102	[4] 5.4	61	591	7.5	346	[3] 520	9.1	[3] 340	400	6.6	250	400	7.3	265	350	7.9	235	350	7.2	235
Fats and oils	Million pounds	4,440	[4] 5.4	[4] 219	708	7.5	284	900	9.1	450	645	6.6	322	711	7.3	353	773	7.9	390	705	7.2	390
Meat[5]	Million pounds	6,216	61.2	[4] 787	499	2.0	235	150	0.6	(8)	75	9 0.3	0	100	9 0.5	50	150	9 0.7	100	200	0.9	100
Horse meat[10]	Million pounds	2	20.0	2	89	46.0	34	150	67.0	100	50	50.0	50	100	50.0	50	50	50.0	50	50	50.0	50
Eggs (shell equivalent)	1,000 metric tons	[11] 1	[11] 1	(8)	227	7.4	160	210	6.8	180	70	2.4	40	50	1.7	20	50	1.8	20	50	1.8	20
Cheese[12]	Million pounds	1.3	2.0	...	152	12.6	142	210	17.5	200	210	17.5	200	140	11.7	130	135	11.2	125	130	10.9	120
Processed milk[12,13]	Million pounds	38.0	1.4	1.5	970	23.1	570	1,100	25.8	625	1,100	25.8	625	910	21.3	410	800	20.9	300	830	19.4	330
Fresh fruit	1,000 short tons	590.6	4.6	342.0	655.0	3.9	[14] 210.0	460.0	2.8	90.0	700.0	4.2	366.0	750.0	4.5	403.0	925.0	5.3	570.0	925.0	5.4	579.0
Dried fruit	1,000 short tons	191.6	36.0	142.0	130.3	28.0	87.8	[15] 220.0	33.3	[15] 180.0	140.0	28.0	121.0	120.0	24.0	114.0	150.0	19.0	80.0	100.0	19.0	91.0
Pulses	1,000 long tons	6.4	1.0	...	189.0	20.0	90.0	214.0	19.0	145.0	250.0	25.0	150.0	175.0	19.0	105.0	150.0	17.0	105.0	125.0	15.0	105.0
Tobacco[16]	Million pounds	[17] 420	[17] 32.8	[17] 293	[18] 663	[18] 32.6	[18] 520	475	25.0	401	520	33.7	439	540	32.8	454	535	31.7	445	535	31.7	448
Cotton	1,000 bales	5,296	35.1	3,273	3,640	42.1	1,898	2,500	21.4	1,150	3,500	29.9	2,400	3,500	29.2	2,396	3,750	31.2	2,514	3,750	31.2	2,633
Timber[19]	Billion board feet	[20] 1.72	[20] 3.0	[20] .54	[18] .69	[18] 1.0	[18] .27	[21] 1.50	[21] 2.0	[21] .72	1.30	2.0	.78	1.20	2.0	.73	1.10	2.0	.66	1.00	2.0	.51
Nitrogen[22]	1,000 metric tons	(23)	(23)	(23)	61.0	10.1	26.3	55.6	8.8	23.2	(23)	(23)	23.0	[15] 55.6	[15] 8.8	23.0	(24)	(24)	(24)	(24)	(24)	(24)

NOTES TO TABLE 34

Source: *ERP Sen. Hear.*, pp. 310–311.
[1] Fiscal year basis.
[2] Exports to European recovery program countries exclude dependent overseas territories.
[3] Based on current estimates of total export availability from United States of 520,000,000 bushels of grain.
[4] 1937–41 average.
[5] Dressed carcass weight plus edible offal.
[6] Total exports; 1935–39 average.
[7] Product weight, 1938 only.
[8] Negligible.
[9] Computed on basis of meat production, including edible offal, in neighborhood of 22,000,000,000 pounds per year.
[10] Production will depend on quantity of horse meat required for export.
[11] 1934–38 are calendar years.
[12] Estimated maximum availability of supplies for export, 1947–48 and 1951–52.
[13] Includes canned milk and dried milk.
[14] Preliminary.
[15] Estimated.
[16] Percent of production converted from farm sales weight to export weight equivalent.
[17] Average 1935–39.
[18] Calendar year 1946.
[19] All timber products (except fuel wood) converted into board feet equivalents of actual wood volume.
[20] Calendar year 1937.
[21] Estimated calendar year 1947.
[22] Includes only commercial production. Army production at ordnance plants in 1947–48 is estimated at 230,000 tons of which 47,000 is scheduled for Western Germany. Balance to other occupied areas.
[23] Not available.
[24] No exports of commercial nitrogen after 1948–49 to European recovery program countries planned.

EUROPEAN RECOVERY PROGRAM

Pressures under the ERP are significant enough to justify strong measures in particular markets — for example, allocations as a minimum, and, in exceptional cases, price control and rationing as a maximum.

One should not conclude from the discussion thus far that the major factor in the rise of prices has been exports on the anticipation of the ERP. Far from it. With relatively few exceptions, exports remain a small part of our total output. Against total exports of goods and services of $18 billion and an export surplus of $10 billion for fiscal year 1949, the country may expect a gross national product of $240 billion.[8] Hence the net "loss" of goods and services is but 4 per cent of the gross national product, and the exports financed under the ERP and shipped from the United States less than 2 per cent. (The relevant variable in comparing trade and income is the excess of exports, for imports reduce inflationary forces.) The Council of Economic Advisers has argued with force that domestic demand is the most important factor, and has shown that price movements in the last year or two have not correlated closely with variations in exports.[9] Nevertheless, the diversion to foreign markets may be a serious matter. If this country is short 10 per cent of requirements of nitrogen, then a foreign demand of close to 10 per cent of production may well contribute towards a rise in prices of several times the foreign demand. In recent periods, exports of bituminous coal accounted for 7.7 per cent of this country's production; electrical machinery, 6.8 per cent; freight cars, 19.5 per cent; rolled steel products, 9 per cent.[10] In these markets foreign drains are a substantial factor.

In short, the export demand or the drains under the ERP are far from being the most important single factor in bringing about inflationary conditions; but when superimposed upon demands already in excess of supply at current prices, and particularly in markets where demand is insistent, export demand will seriously affect prices — unless corrective measures are taken.

SHORTAGES AND THE ERP

AGRICULTURAL MARKETS [11]

So far we have concentrated on general price problems raised by large exports under the ERP, though in doing so, we necessarily had to comment to some extent on the effects in individual markets. It is time to give more attention to parts of the program, not in order to burden the reader with much detail but rather to indicate some general principles. The major demands of the CEEC countries are for agricultural commodities, the executive branch estimating the value of agricultural supplies (inclusive of machinery) to be provided by the United States over the four and a quarter years at about $7½ billion, an amount equivalent to about 40 per cent of the total estimated costs of the program to the United States.[12] We, therefore, start with a discussion of agricultural markets.

Europe's agricultural shortages are the result of mal-use of soil in the war, of the absence of incentives to move supplies to the cities (industrial products are either unavailable, or to be had at excessive prices), of the breakdown of trade with Eastern Europe and Asia, of the unavailability of foreign exchange, and, finally, of the drought in Europe and the poor corn crop in the United States in 1947.

Obviously, a many-sided attack is required to deal with the problem of agricultural deficiencies. Three facts will highlight the shortages confronting the sixteen CEEC nations. First, deficit areas will require six to seven million tons of cereals this year in excess of last year merely in order to attain consumption levels of 1946–47. Second, whereas in the years 1935–1939 the Far East exported four to five million tons of foodstuffs annually, in 1947 their required imports (net) are estimated at six and a half millions.[13] Third, even in the current consumption year, the caloric intake in the participating countries will be but 2500 per day, about 85 per cent of prewar consumption, with urban communi-

EUROPEAN RECOVERY PROGRAM

ties averaging but 2300 calories. This compares with a daily intake of 3450 calories in the United States.[14]

Both the Harriman Committee and the executive branch were critical of the agricultural program offered by the CEEC, a criticism stemming in large part from the serious effects which the fulfillment of the program might have upon the American economy. They would have Western Europe expand its cereal program at the expense of livestock output; for the latter costs more in resources. They would also drastically cut the proposed imports of agricultural machinery over the four and a quarter years from about $1.2 billion to about $600 million. The CEEC had asked for imports of agricultural machinery equivalent to four times the entire current export of the United States; and besides, Europe could not absorb machinery at that rate. Even with contributions of machinery and fertilizers below the amounts asked, American experts held that the ERP countries had underestimated their favorable effects on the output of cereals. It was nevertheless clear to the executive branch that the agricultural objectives of the ERP countries would not be achieved even though cereal output in the sixteen countries should exceed the CEEC estimates.

Table 35 summarizes the differences between European and American experts concerning what would be available. Europe will have to be content with substantially smaller imports of grains and meat, and with drastic reductions in fats and oils; but she may have about as much sugar as she requests; and even more milk, dried fruits, and tobacco.

Figures in Table 35 are subject to periodic revisions with the changing situation. In fact, important revisions became available in April 1948. In the latest materials presented, not only did the State Department revise estimates of availabilities but included estimates for numerous important commodities previously not separately itemized, especially various nonferrous metals (exports

TABLE 35

ESTIMATED IMPORTS OF SELECTED AGRICULTURAL COMMODITIES *

(In millions of metric tons)

	Apr. 1–June 30, 1948 United States	1948–49		1949–50		1950–51		1951–52	
		CEEC	United States	CEEC	United States	CEEC	United States	CEEC †	United States
Bread grains ‡	5.2	19.6	16.0	18.7	16.7	17.9	15.9	…	15.9
Coarse grains ‡	.8	9.9	6.0	11.1	8.0	11.7	8.8	…	8.8
Fats and oils	.2	1.9	1.1	2.2	.9	2.3	1.1	…	1.1
Meat	.4	2.3	1.8	2.4	1.8	2.5	1.8	…	1.9
Sugar	.7	2.2	2.3	2.3	2.1	2.3	2.0	…	2.1
Canned and dried milk	.15	.21	.32	.21	.21	.21	.17	…	.14
Dried fruit	.05	.23	.22	.21	.21	.14	.24	…	.21
Tobacco	.07	.17	.27	.17	.28	.17	.28	…	.28
Cotton	.3	…	1.1	…	1.2	…	1.3	…	1.3
Nitrogen	.03	.23	.18	.08	.12	§	.04	…	.04

Source: *ERP State*, p. 85.
* Imports from nonparticipating countries only, except where otherwise specified.
† Not available. Crop years covered by the CEEC ran from 1947–48 to 1950–51 (4 years) and did not include 1951–52.
‡ Total imports from all sources including participating countries.
§ CEEC estimated a net export surplus for participating countries.

[223]

EUROPEAN RECOVERY PROGRAM

from the Americas in 1948–49 = $319 million), wool ($77 million), cotton cloth ($85 million), hides, skins, and leather ($132 million), chemicals ($242 million), machinery ($469 million), vehicles ($208 million), petroleum equipment ($127 million), ocean freight ($1100 million). Miscellaneous commodities now only equalled 13 per cent of the imports (inclusive of the invisible debits) for the fiscal year 1948–49.

Important changes reflect especially the improved grain situation (though coarse grains do not seem to be on the revised program for 1948–49), and the shortages in several areas. For the United States, the amount of bread grains to be made available jumps from $535 to $722 million; but the decline in coal is from 297 to 271; for petroleum products, from 531 to 479; for finished steel, from 182 to 123; and for trucks, 81 to 58. For the other Americas the rise for bread grains is from $669 to $1126 million; for fats and oils from 222 to 257; but meat is down from 308 to 273, and coffee from 134 to 97.[15]

That it is important for Europe to concentrate more output on cereals, is evident from Table 36 presented by the Cabinet Committee on World Food Supplies. It will be noted that of estimated export availabilities, 1947–48, wheat flour accounts for 72 per cent of the calories but only 49 per cent of the dollar cost. Meat, poultry products, and fish, however, provide but 1.5 per cent of the calories and cost 15 per cent of the money outlay. The average cost per 100,000 calories is 14 times as much for meat, fish, and poultry as for wheat flour.

In order to understand the recommendations of the executive branch concerning American contributions to the ERP, it is necessary to consider American farm policy. Although the Malthusian specter raises its head occasionally, the dominant note still seems to be fear of excesses. Continued gains in technology and the emergence of substantial amounts of nonagricultural unemployment will once more, in the views of most farm econo-

SHORTAGES AND THE ERP

mists, bring surpluses and produce market collapses. Present shortages in grains are so serious that this philosophy does not carry its usual influence. In 1946–47, there were 6984 million bushels of grains available in this country; but for 1947–48, the

TABLE 36
Estimated Export Availabilities, 1947–48

	Trillions of Calories	Percent of Total	Probable Cost	Percent of Total	Average Cost Per 100,000 Calories
			Million dollars		*Dollars*
Wheat, flour	32.9	71.9	1066.0	49.0	3.24
Coarse grains	4.6	10.1	146.1	6.7	3.15
Rice	1.3	2.8	85.8	3.9	6.77
Beans and peas	.7	1.5	32.2	1.5	4.81
Edible fats, oils, and peanuts	3.0	6.6	153.9	7.1	5.06
Dairy products	1.7	3.7	253.5	11.7	14.81
Dried fruits	.6	1.3	46.3	2.1	8.15
Citrus juices	.1	.2	18.5	.8	24.74
Vegetables (including potatoes)	.2	.4	46.3	2.1	22.54
Meat and poultry products and fish	.7	1.5	328.0	15.1	46.02
Total	45.8	100.0	2176.6	100.0	4.75 *

Source: *ERP, Sen. Doc.*, p. 130.
* Weighted average.

estimates were but 6231 million bushels. Hence the United States could spare but 470 million bushels (12 million tons) for export for 1947–48, or about 2 million tons less than in 1946–47.[16] (Again, we should note the upward revision of estimates of grain available for export from this country and the other Americas.) Moreover, reëxamining the CEEC estimates of grain deficits, the United States officials reduced the CEEC deficits from 11.1 to 6.9 million tons of grain in 1947–48, and from 4.6 to 0.8 million tons in 1950–51.[17]

EUROPEAN RECOVERY PROGRAM

Fear of surpluses in many markets colors the United States recommendations for exports from this country under the ERP. There is indeed a danger that the government will use the ERP as a means of disposing of agricultural surpluses abroad. It should be said parenthetically that if the alternative is restricted output, then the ERP, as a source of demand, might keep output up. The taxpayer would then absorb the costs of "conservation" and "restriction" payments to the farmers under farm policies not supplemented by the ERP, and would pay the farmers for ERP supplies under a farm program implemented by the ERP program. Insofar as the ERP accounts for increased production of farm products, it does not contribute to reduced supplies and higher prices for this country.

An examination of the official documents, *Commodity Report, ERP*, reveals the interrelation of farm policies and the ERP. In fats and oils, the United States is not prepared to offer much help. Europe is dependent upon foreign countries for one-half of its supplies; but in 1947 oil supplies entering international trade were but 3.2 million tons as compared with almost 6 millions before the war. Though Europe was consuming from 70 to 90 per cent of the prewar oil supply in the more favored countries and less than 60 per cent in others, and though prices were from three to seven times greater than before the war, the European countries were forced to accept much less than they required. The United States offers 3 per cent of its oil supplies to the ERP countries.[18] Demand is too high in this country to countenance large diversions. Again, as in grains, the primary consideration is shortages, not excesses.

Sugar is another matter. Attempts to expand output in Europe are not received with approval by American analysts who anticipate a world surplus of one million tons in 1947–48, and increased surpluses later. Contending that some of the European countries should not increase their output of sugar at the expense of pro-

SHORTAGES AND THE ERP

ducing alternative products which may be grown with greater effectiveness, the American Government questions the wisdom of European sugar policy. In the role of "arbiter" between the large exporting areas and the deficit areas of Europe, the United States assumes a role which does not well become her.[19]

Europe is not to receive much help from this country in replenishing its meat supplies, although in 1947 she was producing but one-half of prewar output, and was dependent on imports even before the war. Import requirements rose from 2.2 million tons in 1934–1938 to 2.4 in 1947–48, and are anticipated at almost 3 million tons in 1950–51. The United Kingdom accounts for 75.85 per cent of the import requirements of the participating countries and 25 per cent of the rise from 1947–48 to 1950–51. Germany's rise of requirements is three times as great as Britain's: from 12,600 tons in 1947–48 to 488,000 tons in 1950–51. That the British contracted for most of the available supplies for years to come, and at favorable prices, and that the British consumption is 100 pounds per capita while other participating countries on a meat importing basis consumed but from 25 to 70 pounds per capita, raise interesting problems. Should the ERP, for example, support the relatively high meat consumption in the United Kingdom? Whatever the merits of this controversy, the point to be made here is that, although in 1947 meat production in the United States was 23 billion pounds and consumption 157 pounds per capita (as compared with 133 pounds in 1939), nevertheless we are prepared to export to ERP countries only $6 million worth of meat in 1948–49 and $60 million in the four and a quarter years. (in 1943 our total exports were more than 2 billion pounds.[20]) While there was adequate demand at home and prices were highly inflationary, this country was not enthusiastic about diverting supplies to Europe — and particularly if the commodity was not an absolute necessity.

This country is prepared to provide the requested supplies of

EUROPEAN RECOVERY PROGRAM

fresh and dried fruits as well as dairy products and tobacco. In fact there is an indication of a willingness to offer more than is asked. An official document concerning tobacco frankly states: "The program from the standpoint of the United States is of vital importance in order that customary outlets may be maintained." The authors of the CEEC report are reprimanded for their unrealistically *low* estimates of German requirements, and the proposed increase in tobacco output for Italy, Greece, and Turkey is ridiculed: these countries are reminded that American tobacco is increasingly popular.[21]

Interests of our farmers are clearly reflected in the cotton program. Europe is to obtain what she requires. In fact it is made clear that after several years of reductions in carry-overs, supply and demand are now roughly in balance, and without the ERP, it is feared that large surpluses will once more reappear. This country, therefore, will provide about 39 per cent of the imports of ERP countries. Though the carry-over in 1946 was but 40 per cent of that before the war and prices three to four times as high, the official position is that American contributions may still have to be revised upwards.[22]

ENERGY SOURCES

Outlays for energy sources are to be large under the ERP, the total imports of coal, petroleum, and equipment, and for products required for hydroelectrical development from the United States accounting for about three and one half billion dollars, or about one-third to one-fourth of the total given for selected commodities. American policy seems to be to provide the participating countries with the coal requested as well as the major part of the equipment for energy production, but to deny them a large part of the petroleum requested. Fearful of the effects of large drains of petroleum products upon the American economy, the United States authorities urged a large cutback from the demand for

SHORTAGES AND THE ERP

petroleum products (a further cut was proposed in March, 1948), greater reliance on coal, and shifting of demand for petroleum from the Western Hemisphere to the Middle East. The participating countries were denied petroleum with an energy equivalent of 155 million tons of coal. Yet, according to the executive branch of the United States Government, the European program to raise coal output from 440 million to 585 million tons in the years 1947 to 1951 admittedly will be reached only under optimum conditions. For the United Kingdom, the projected rise is from 199 million tons in 1947 to 249 million tons in 1951, or 25 per cent in volume, and 20 per cent per man-shift. In order to make sufficient energy available, the United States is prepared to provide 6 per cent of its coal output in the current year; and to *make available* $850 to $905 million of petroleum equipment as compared with a *need* estimated at $588 million by the CEEC and of $1.5 billion by the United States executive branch.[23] (The latter's estimate is high, because the CEEC left out of account the equipment required by United States companies operating in the ERP countries.)

In presenting their analysis of the petroleum situation, United States officials underline the small drains on the American economy to be countenanced by the United States Government. In fact, the United States is well on its way to becoming a major oil importing nation. This country will be the largest importer of petroleum products in the world by 1951, accounting for as large imports as the three largest European importing countries combined, and for an amount equal to about 60 per cent of the imports of all participating countries and their dependent overseas territories. According to the executive branch, United States exports of petroleum products in 1951 will account for 4 per cent of the imports of the participating countries, as compared with 30 per cent in 1938, 26 per cent in 1946, and 11 per cent in 1948. In absolute amounts, United States exports to these countries will decline from the 1938 amount of 77 million barrels and the 1946 level of 59 million barrels to 35 million barrels in 1948 and 15 million barrels in 1951. Participating countries will meet their requirements for petroleum from *dollar* sources primarily out of imports from American companies *operating abroad. It is abundantly clear from this statistical summary that the American Government will not accede to any drains of petroleum products from this country which would significantly affect our supply and demand and price situation.* Yet in 1951–52, oil requirements of the participating countries should be less than one-fifth of those of the United States.[24]

CEEC figures and American revisions are as follows:[25]
Petroleum consumption, 4¼ years recovery period
CEEC estimate   = 300 million tons
U. S. revision   = 227 million tons

This reduction should be considered in the light of average energy consumption *per capita* (hard coal equivalent) of 2.52 tons (oil = 0.29) for the participating countries and 8.09 tons (oil = 3.10) for the United States. Our per capita consumption of all energy supplies is more than three times that of the ERP countries; that of oil, 11 times. Under the assumed conditions, the supply of petroleum available for United States use will rise from 224 million tons (hard coal equivalent) in 1938 to 454 million tons in 1951; and for the participating countries from 50 to 82 million tons. The increase for the United States would be about 100 per cent; for the participating countries, more than 60 per cent. In view of the present and impending shortages, the American Government in fact advises Europe to slow down conversion from coal to oil.[26]

It is part of American policy to put a larger part of the burden of supplying oil upon other parts of the world; and the ERP fits into the country's oil strategy. With proven reserves of 2920 mil-

SHORTAGES AND THE ERP

lion tons, this country produced 253 million tons in 1946 and an estimated 255 million tons in 1951, or about 8 per cent of proven reserves in 1946, and probably less in 1951. The Middle East, however, with proven reserves of 3600 million metric tons produced but 44 millions, or 1.2 per cent of proven reserves in 1947, and an estimated 85 million tons, or about 2.4 per cent, in 1951.[27]

Concern over the large drains on American reserves explains in part the diversion of shipments under the ERP from the Western to the Eastern Hemisphere. While in 1946 the Western Hemisphere supplied 77 per cent of Europe's petroleum imports and the Middle East 23 per cent, it is estimated that by 1951 the latter will provide over 80 per cent of Europe's needs and the Western Hemisphere, less than 20 per cent. Hence the reduced contributions of the United States under the ERP, which were noted earlier.[28] As mentioned above, exports to these countries will decline from 77 million barrels in 1938 to 35 million barrels in 1948, and to 15 million barrels in 1951. The last is but 0.8 per cent of the United States production as compared with 6.4 per cent in 1938.[29]

American oil policy is well tethered to the ERP. We urge Europe to moderate her demands for oil; we suggest that she rely more heavily on other sources of energy and also on other areas. In the modern world, access to oil is a must for both military and industrial purposes. Our American civilization is now built around oil. In 1946, the United States accounted for about two-thirds of world use of petroleum products, and her rise of demand from 1938 to 1947 was two and a half times the consumption of all participating countries in 1947; and by 1951, United States consumption should be double that of 1938.[30] In view of our large demands, the question may be raised whether or not we have been generous enough in dealing with European requirements. Willingness on our part to introduce temporary

[231]

EUROPEAN RECOVERY PROGRAM

controls in order to reduce wasteful consumption of oil products might not only make larger supplies available to Europe, but might also increase the life of our reserves, and help keep inflationary pressures down. Indeed, part of the purchasing power not used on tight markets (such as oil) will be shunted to other markets, though, it is assumed, to less crowded markets.

IRON AND STEEL

Iron and steel are the last items to receive special consideration here. Agricultural products and machinery (about $7.5 billion), energy, inclusive of equipment (about $3 billion), and iron and steel (in excess of $1 billion) account for about $11½ billion of supplies to be provided under the ERP from the United States over the four and a quarter years to be covered. This amount compares with the "selected" commodities of $13 billion studied by the executive branch and the $15.1 to $17.8 billion appropriations required by the Executive. This survey, then, covers the most important items, both in amounts and in the difficulty of the problems raised.

Iron and steel are crucial materials in the modern economy: and they are of particular importance under the ERP because of their intimate relation to the ambitious investment programs of the CEEC countries, and because of the serious shortages prevailing in the United States. The American officials were critical of the CEEC estimates for many reasons: the production program could not be realized; the equipment requested could not be spared in this country and besides, once the volume of iron and steel imports was reduced, it would not be possible to use the amount of equipment asked; and the United States could spare no scrap, and very little semi-finished iron and steel. In part to compensate for the denials, the United States was prepared to provide more finished iron and steel than was requested. Since finished products are more expensive than the raw materials, this

SHORTAGES AND THE ERP

might be considered as an attempt to protect the American iron and steel industry at the expense of the taxpayer.

An examination of Table 37 and Figure 12 shows the large differences between CEEC and United States estimates of steel output, differences that tend to become smaller in the later years.

TABLE 37

FINISHED STEEL OUTPUT

(*In millions of metric tons*)

	CEEC Program *		United States Estimates	
	Participating Countries excluding Western Germany	Participating Countries	Participating Countries, excluding Western Germany	Participating Countries
1938	18.4	34.1	18.4	34.1
1947	21.0	23.7	21.0	23.7
1948–49	29.6	34.0	24.0	28.6
1949–50	30.6	36.9	27.0	33.7
1950–51	32.6	40.4	29.2	37.6
1951–52	34.2	43.9	30.9	40.6

Source: *ERP* State, p. 81.
* CEEC estimates are given for calendar years.

Against the CEEC estimate of a rise of iron and steel output for CEEC countries of 40 per cent in 1948 over 1947, the United States estimates the increase at only 20 per cent. By reducing the amounts to be consumed and exported by the ERP countries, the executive branch fits the supplies made available to demand. They note, however, that serious problems are raised by the resulting failure of these countries to reëstablish their substantial export position in iron and steel. Basic industries, it is held, will require only 40 to 50 per cent of anticipated steel consumption, and, therefore, the enforced economies need not be serious if proper allocation is made.[31]

A scrutiny of the iron and steel program is especially germane for an understanding of the capital expansion program. The total cost of expansion and modernization programs in iron and

EUROPEAN RECOVERY PROGRAM

steel for the participating countries is estimated at $2.2 billion, about 40 per cent of which represents iron and steel production equipment. The United States is asked to provide $400 million of equipment. Although the Harriman Committee urged strong efforts to meet these demands for equipment, the executive branch proposed to satisfy only about one-half.[32]

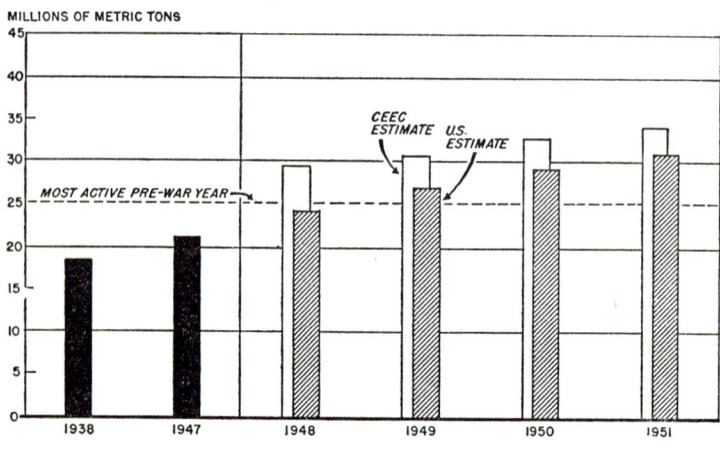

Figure 12

Shortages in the United States were decisive in the formulation of American policy. With steel ingot production in 1947 at the record peacetime level of 84 million tons (but 7 million short of capacity), the country was still suffering from serious shortages: the output of automobiles with capacity of 6 million was at the rate of 4 million; the oil and gas industry was facing a serious shortage of pipe; and steel prices were at high levels, with black and gray markets growing. Sheets, strip, tinplate, pipe, and tubes appeared to be the tightest items. Shortage of scrap, the most

SHORTAGES AND THE ERP

serious bottleneck, explains the far below capacity production of ingots. Scrap at forty dollars a ton had reached an all-time high. These facts explain the recommendations that virtually no scrap be made available, that about 40 per cent of the requested crude and semi-finished scrap be provided, and that exports of finished products exceed the amounts asked for (see Table 38). The decline in *dollar* value for all iron and steel products, relative to CEEC proposals, was from about 1165 to 830 millions or less than 30 per cent.[33] In March 1948, as noted above, the State Department reduced allocations of finished steel output further from $182 to $123 million.

CONCLUSION

It is clear that the recommendations concerning the supplies to be made available, inclusive of the distribution among commodities and among supplying countries, were determined largely by the requirements of the American economy. Where the burden could not easily be shifted to the other Americas, the only alternative was to whittle down the amounts asked. Where there were shortages, actual or impending, the disposition was to deny the CEEC countries a substantial proportion of supplies requested. Examples are iron and steel and grains. Where, on the other hand, there were more likely to be excesses in the American economy, the Executive proposed to provide all (and frequently) more than was asked. Examples are tobacco, cotton, and dried fruits. Europe then would become a sink for American excesses, the taxpayer paying the bill. American policy is to keep down the demand for scarce items, and, notably, for grains, meat, petroleum, machinery, and iron and steel. In agricultural commodities, it is possible to shift a large part of the burden to other commodities and hence the denials to Europe are substantial but not decisive. Europe will have to do with much less petroleum than was required, despite significant shifts to other areas. Alternative

TABLE 38

ESTIMATED IMPORTS OF STEEL AND OTHER INDUSTRIAL ITEMS *

Item	Unit	Apr. 1 to June 30, 1948, United States	1948–49 CEEC	1948–49 United States	1949–50 CEEC	1949–50 United States	1950–51 CEEC	1950–51 United States	1951–52 CEEC	1951–52 United States
Finished steel	Thousand metric tons	451	1,272	1,802	534	1,769	300	1,630	250	1,152
Crude and semi-finished †	Thousand metric tons	316	2,863	1,266	2,921	1,266	3,105	1,266	3,013	1,208
Scrap iron and steel ‡	Thousand metric tons	36	1,514	146	1,878	125	2,206	115	2,346	115
Steel-making equipment §	Million dollars		100	48	100	48	100	48	100	48
Timber *	Million dollars	130	520	521	580	581	625	627	665	665
Freight cars §	Thousand units		47	20	42	6	14	...	...	...

Source: *ERP State*, p. 89.
* Imports from nonparticipating countries, except where otherwise indicated. CEEC data are for calendar years 1948–51.
† CEEC data adjusted to ingot equivalents for purposes of comparability.
‡ These estimates do not include any scrap-iron and steel imports from the United States.
§ Imports from the United States.

SHORTAGES AND THE ERP

sources of iron and steel are not available; and, therefore, reductions below requested amounts are equivalent to reductions in total amounts available. In general, this conclusion stands out: the sacrifices imposed on the United States in terms of goods should not be serious; and had this country been willing to introduce moderate measures of conservation and allocation, greater amounts might have been made available for Europe. The result would have been a more rapid recovery for Europe and a more rapid improvement of her balance of payments.

PART FOUR

ECONOMIC RECOVERY

Introduction

In the opening chapter (Highlights) and in chapters 1, 3, and 6, various aspects of the European crisis were discussed, and particularly in the opening chapter and Chapter 1 the likelihood of an adequate recovery within the next four years was considered. The next chapter deals in greater detail with the European recovery in the years 1945–1947, with the retardation of the advance in 1947, and especially with the barriers to further recovery. It is necessary to consider the goals set up by the participating countries and their likelihood of reaching them; and the probability of solving the inflation, output, and balance-of-payments problems. This chapter contains an over-all analysis of the relevant problems as well as a detailed discussion of the five most important countries, accounting for about three quarters of the income of the ERP countries. Largely factual, this chapter is not required reading. The impatient reader may prefer to omit parts of it, and particularly the latter parts, other than the conclusion.

11. Economic Recovery?

INTRODUCTION

In their Paris meeting during the summer of 1947, the sixteen participating countries announced ambitious goals for the next four years.[1] Among their objectives were a strong production effort, "the creation and maintenance of internal financial stability as an essential condition for securing the full use of Europe's productive and financial resources," the development of economic cooperation between the participating countries, and a solution of the problem of the participating countries' deficit with the Americas.[2] That the targets cannot be attained with ease, is evident from the comparison of the objectives for the years 1947–1951 with the attainments of the United States economy from 1940 to 1944: for coal, the European rise was to be 33 per cent, for the United States the gain had been 34 per cent; the respective figures for steel were 60 and 31 per cent; for electric power output, 39 and 61 per cent.[3] The European experts were silent on a vital aspect: the large amount of unemployment in the United States in 1940, which made possible spectacular gains in the following four years.

In order to achieve the goals set, it would be necessary to make the fullest possible utilization of economic factors, and in particular to reduce wastages due to unemployment or production below full capacity, and to stimulate transfers of unemployed workers to countries short of manpower. Financial and monetary reform was to be an adjunct to the production policies, for with purchasing power much in excess of goods available at current prices, the incentive to work a full day was lacking. Why earn more money when it is not possible to spend it on desired goods, or else to purchase only at exorbitant prices on black markets? A rise in the level of employment, induced in part by increasing the numbers at work and the hours per worker, would have to be supplemented by gains in productivity, in turn associated with full (not over-full) production, with modernization of plant, with expansion of capital facilities, with priority in the use of scarce resources according to the requirements of the programs, and in particular with a redistribution of the factors in favor of the more productive and more essential industries. Relaxation of trade barriers and improved manner of liquidating balances across natural frontiers would also contribute towards higher man-hour output. In short, what was required was more workers, longer hours, and a rise of output per man-hour. Without these, the goals would not be reached.

A rise in output would not suffice to solve the problems of the sixteen countries, for the crisis was one of output *and* balance of payments. In order to solve the latter problem, it is necessary not only to produce more, but also to sell more abroad or (and) buy less from abroad. That the Paris Conference was interested in solving the balance of payments problems was evident in the reduction of the projected deficit of the sixteen countries and Western Germany with the American Continent from $8.04 billion in 1948 to $3.40 billion in 1951; and in a rise of exports to the United States from $850 million in 1948 to $1480 million in 1951, and to the rest of the American Continent from $1310 to $2460 million, or a total rise in excess of 80 per cent.[4]

AN APPRAISAL OF CEEC OBJECTIVES [5]

As the executive branch noted, the aid under the ERP would not amount to more than 3 to 5 per cent of the income of the participating countries and about one third of their total imports, with two-thirds of these imports being paid for out of their own

ECONOMIC RECOVERY?

resources. The big question mark was the anticipated rise of output, which had to be a multiple of the aid made available.

According to the executive branch,

> the production goals set forth in the CEEC report appear, on analysis, to be reasonable and attainable although it is probable that the participating countries will be unable to achieve certain specific goals within the span of the four and a quarter year recovery period.[6]

In foods, particularly in meats, fats and oils, and sugar, goals would not be reached. Anticipated indexes for 1950–51 (1934–1938 = 100) were: meats CEEC — 88, United States estimate — 80; fats and oils, 98 and 91, respectively, raw sugar, 114 and 108. By pruning the livestock program and by taking other appropriate measures to raise output of cereals, the participating nations might produce 105 of bread grains by 1950–51 in place of the 101 estimated by the CEEC (prewar index = 100).[7] Executive branch estimates of energy consumption for the years 1950–1952 were below those of the CEEC, the former estimate being especially low for the output of hydroelectric power — 181 was the United States estimate for 1951, whereas the CEEC projection was 190 (1938 = 100); for petroleum, the respective figures for 1951–1952 were 174 and 207 (1938 = 100). The explanation of the pessimism of the United States authorities is the unavailability of capital required to provide the additional capacity in power and petroleum. In finished steel, also, the United States estimated indexes (1938 = 100) were substantially below the CEEC projection: the former range from 7 to 16 per cent less per year over the years 1948–49 to 1951–52. Because of the shortage of coke and the unavailability of scrap, which is not to be shipped as requested under the CEEC program, the goals in steel also would not be reached. In the crucial commodity, coal, the targets were more than 30 per cent above 1947 output. The executive branch warned that they would not be reached unless conditions were very favorable.[8]

EUROPEAN RECOVERY PROGRAM

Failure to reach goals in industries which touch the economy at almost every point may indeed be serious. In iron and steel, power and coal, the achievements may well fall below goals by 10 per cent, the deficiency generally being equivalent to about one-third of the total rise in nonagricultural output anticipated over the four years. In turn, the deficit in industrial output would affect agricultural output adversely.

Perhaps even more important are the effects upon exports, which would suffer disproportionately from the retardation in the rate of advance of industrial output. With exports in 1947 about 10 per cent of the income of the countries involved, a deficit even of 10 per cent in national output might well reduce exports by 50 per cent — on the assumption that half of the decline would be reflected in a reduction of exports. A rough estimate suggests a national income of $75 billion for the participating countries in 1947–48, and $100 billion projected for 1951–52. (Estimates of income in 1947 run as high as $100 billion.) Exports in 1947–48 may well be $7 billion, or 10 per cent of income in 1947–48, and $11½ billion, or 11–12 per cent in 1951–52. Should output fail to attain the anticipated level by 10 per cent, then exports in 1951–52 might well decline to 6 to 7 per cent of incomes.[9] Export targets were ambitious even on the assumption that the anticipated rise in output would be achieved. Let us consider the export program.

Exports to the American Continent and to others were estimated by the CEEC, in billions of dollars, as follows (*CEEC*, pp. 51, 56):

	U. S. A.	Rest of American Continent	Other
1948	0.85	1.31	4.30
1951	1.48	2.46	....

A rise of about 75 per cent of exports to the United States, and close to 90 per cent to the other Americas, is ambitious indeed.

ECONOMIC RECOVERY?

Even under these favorable assumptions, the deficit of the participating countries with the American Continent would be reduced only from $8.04 billion in 1948 to $3.4 billion in 1951. Against the deficit of $3.4 billion remaining in 1951, the participating countries anticipated a favorable balance on current account of $2.8 billion with *other* nonparticipating countries.[10]

These figures should be compared with those of the executive branch (at current prices). They put the balance with the American Continent at $8.5 billion in 1948–49 (compare with the $8.04 billion for 1948 estimated by the CEEC) and at $3.4 to $4.4 billion in 1950–51 and $2.4 to $3.6 billion in 1951–52.[11] These estimates are not greatly divergent from those of the Paris Conference. In the study of exports and other items in the balance of payments, however, the American experts disagreed with their European colleagues. First, as has been noted, the Paris Conference was overly optimistic concerning changes in the terms of trade. Price history since July 1947 confirms the suggestion of over-optimism; and the enlarged military program of the United States in 1948, together with the effects of the aid programs, surely postpone the anticipated decline of overseas prices which was to contribute so much to improved terms of trade for Europe. Second, the Harriman Committee suggested that the estimates of the Paris Conference on exports to the Western Hemisphere should be cut by one-sixth.[12] But the executive branch did not support this revision. Third, and perhaps more important, the executive branch was much more optimistic concerning exports of ERP countries than the CEEC, the Harriman Committee, and the International Bank. In the latest revision of figures, for example, the State Department estimated exports and receipts on invisible account of participating countries in relation to the Western Hemisphere at $4995 million — $2820 million vis-à-vis the United States and $2175 million vis-à-vis other Western

EUROPEAN RECOVERY PROGRAM

Hemisphere countries. These figures, which relate to fiscal year 1948–49 and include $1840 million for invisible items, should be compared with exports of only $1.16 billion to the Americas in 1948 and $2.83 billion in 1949, according to the CEEC estimate. Exports to the United States were to be about $1.6 billion in 1948–49 according to the State Department, and only about $1 billion according to the CEEC. In addition, other earnings of ERP countries vis-à vis the United States were to be more than $1.2 billion.[13]

It will not be easy for the participating countries to provide the exports required under the program. It was estimated by the executive branch that in view of the unfavorable terms of trade, the losses of foreign investments and earnings on shipping and other services, these countries will have to export 30 per cent more in order to obtain imports approximately as large in physical terms as in 1938.[14]

Consumption, government expenditures, investment, and exports account for annual output. Let us consider consumption first. In the opinion of the American analysts, the projected standard of living assumed under the ERP was not too high, although the executive branch concluded that the rise could not be so rapid as had been hoped. Even by 1951, Europeans would not live as well as in 1938. It was generally understood that pressure to reduce the standard of living further would have unfortunate effects upon the production effort. Second, there was little disposition to urge economy in government inclusive of military outlays. In appraising the programs for investments, the American experts were critical. They were fearful of the inflationary effects of diverting large resources into investment; for this would increase the excess of disposable income over the flow of consumers' goods. Nor were they prepared to deprive America of capital goods in short supply here, which would have been required to meet the CEEC requests. Programs to devote 17 per cent or even

ECONOMIC RECOVERY?

more to investment seemed excessive for countries in a rather impoverished state; and particularly since inflation was one of the most serious problems. That the capital had to be provided to a considerable degree out of United States resources, did not strengthen the United States support for European investment programs. The upshot was recommendations to the sixteen nations to moderate their capital program, to concentrate it more on the vital industries (for example, coal and agriculture), and to rely more on repairing available plants and equipment rather than on modernization and replacement.[15]

ACCOMPLISHMENTS

In the discussion that follows, I shall concentrate on five countries, namely, the United Kingdom, France, Italy, Bizonal Germany, and the Netherlands; since these five countries account for most of the deficit in the balance of payments, for four-fifths of the income of all ERP countries, and an equal proportion of the assistance required, there will be no great loss in concentrating on them.

Income. In 1939 the five countries accounted for about four-fifths of the income of the sixteen nations inclusive of Western Germany. In 1946, the proportion was probably closer to three-quarters, the relative reduction being explained primarily by the large losses suffered by Western Germany and Italy and the substantial reduction of income in France.[16] Obviously, the figures are very rough.

Deficits in the Balance of Payments. According to the CEEC, these five countries would account for $7.22 billion of the deficit with the American Continent out of $8.46 billion for the ten most important countries to receive aid under the ERP. (The relatively unimportant countries omitted were Austria, Iceland, Ireland, Luxemburg, Portugal, and Turkey.) In fact, the deficit with the American Continent for 1948 for all countries under

EUROPEAN RECOVERY PROGRAM

the program, when adjusted for unavailability of supplies and the deficits of dependencies, was estimated roughly at $8 billion.[17]

Executive branch estimates of the deficit of the five major and all ERP countries are shown in Table 39.

TABLE 39

DEFICIT OF ERP COUNTRIES ON CURRENT ACCOUNT WITH WESTERN HEMISPHERE, 1948–49 (15 MONTHS ENDING JUNE 30, 1949) AND 1948–52
(*In Millions of Dollars*)

	1948–49	1948–52
Five major countries inclusive of Bizonal Germany	6,596	17,504
Dependencies of five countries	+96*	+970*
Percentage of total — five countries	82	84
Percentage of total — five countries and dependencies	81	79

Source: Based on materials, *ERP: House Hear.*, Vol. 1, p. 206.
* Credits.

OVER-ALL TRENDS

Before turning to a study of the five crucial countries, I shall briefly discuss recent trends for all ERP countries. In 1946 real national income was substantially below prewar income: in Austria, about 50 per cent of that before the war; in Greece and Italy, about 60 per cent; France and Netherlands, between 80–90 per cent; the Scandinavian countries and Switzerland, at or above prewar income. With a high proportion of resources going to government and capital, the amounts available for consumption were smaller than indicated by income figures.[18]

In many countries, even late in 1947, industrial output was below prewar output, though large gains had been made in 1946; and in the first half of 1947, the monthly rise for five ERP countries for which figures were available was 1.9 per cent. A deterioration was reflected in a monthly decline of 1.7 per cent for these five countries in the third quarter of 1947. For six of the ERP

ECONOMIC RECOVERY?

countries, the rise was resumed in the last months of 1947.[19] Average output in 1947 was higher than in 1946.

Production in many industries was spotty, even in those countries where industrial output in 1947 was above or close to prewar output. For example, in Norway the industrial index in the spring of 1947 was 115 (prewar years = 100). The index for steel and metal working had risen to 167; but for woodpulp and paper,

TABLE 40
INDUSTRIAL OUTPUT, 1945–1947
($1937 = 100$)

	4th Quarter 1945	4th Quarter 1946	3rd Quarter 1947	Last month available, 1947
Austria	...	...	40–50 (1st Qu.)	...
Belgium	50	81	82	...
Denmark	81	104	103	120*
France	67 (1st Qu. 1946)	90	89	97†
Germany — U. S. Zone	20 (1st Qu. 1946)	45	50	49*
British Zone	28 (1st Qu. 1946)	33	37	40†
Greece	39	71	68	...
Ireland	96	112	109 (2nd Qu.)	...
Italy	28 (1st Qu. 1946)	54	72	...
Netherlands	57	89	91	102*
Norway	81	110	106	115*
Sweden	104	108	108	108†
United Kingdom	..	100	100–120 (2nd Qu.)	

Sources: U. N. *Economic Report, 1945–47*, pp. 131–32; U. N., *Monthly Bulletin of Statistics*, February 1948, pp. 24–27.
 * December.
 † November.

the index had fallen to 75, for ore and metal production to 72, for canning to 55. Progress was uneven in every country. In the generating of electricity, output everywhere, with a few minor exceptions, was substantially above that before the war; but whereas electric generating capacity had risen 7.5 to 8 per cent per annum in the years 1925–1938, the expansion since had been but 5 per cent per annum, a rise much below what was required.

Bottlenecks were an important cause of the unsatisfactory level of output. Steel production for thirteen countries (inclusive of four non-ERP countries) was but 55 per cent of 1937 output in 1946 and 63 per cent in 1947, while planned expansion would have brought the output up to 114 per cent of 1937 output, and 127 per cent by 1951. But we now know that this expansion will not take place.[20] Shortages in steel are bound to affect many industries.

A decline in agricultural output also had unfortunate effects; for without adequate supplies of food and raw materials, output was bound to suffer. In 1945, the crops were disastrously low. The Economic Commission for Europe estimated agricultural output at 63 and 75 per cent of prewar volume in 1945–1946 and 1946–47 respectively.[21] In 1945–46, bread and coarse grain output of Europe as a whole was but 60 per cent of prewar output; and in 1946–47, output of grains and potatoes had risen to 74 to 77 per cent of prewar output. For 1946–47, the decline in output of all grains relative to prewar volume was 30 per cent or more for eleven of the seventeen countries listed. Belgium's output was but 51 per cent of prewar output; France's, 59 per cent; the Netherlands' and Norway's, 80; Sweden's 63; Greece's, 66; Italy's, 68; and Germany's, 64. The United Kingdom and Switzerland, however, raised their output to 156 and 141 per cent of that before the war.[22] For all countries participating in the Paris conference, production of fats and oils in 1945–46 was only two-thirds of prewar production; and the proportion of meat production was similar. Output of milk declined by 27 per cent; butter by 30 per

ECONOMIC RECOVERY?

cent; of other milk products, 52 per cent; and of eggs, 37 per cent.[23] Then came the disastrous crops of 1947. In Europe, exclusive of the USSR, the production of wheat fell from 42.3 million tons (1934–1938 average) and 32.9 million tons in 1946 to 25.8 million tons in 1947. Production of rye was about 60 per cent of prewar volume and of potatoes, about 75 per cent.[24] Especially large losses were suffered in Western Europe.

Consumption levels were far below prewar levels, and particularly in fats and oils, meats, and sugar. In Western Europe calorie intake was maintained by relying increasingly on grains and by mixing in more coarse grains. In eastern and southern Europe the reduction of calories was more serious. The CEEC estimate of consumption for countries participating in the ERP is shown in Table 41.

TABLE 41
Consumption by ERP Countries
(*Kilograms Per Capita*)

	Prewar	1946–47	1947–48
Bread grains	192	158	159
Fats and oils	24.1	13.3	17
Meat	42.9	27.7	30
Potatoes	236	190	228

Source: *CEEC*, p. 77.

With reduced supplies and large amounts of liquid assets — the result of government deficits — there was a strong pressure on prices.[25] Several countries, for example, the Scandinavian countries, and the United Kingdom, succeeded well in keeping the cost of living from rising even as much as 100 per cent above prewar levels. The achievement was remarkable in Norway in particular, for the supply of money was ten times greater than before the war. In Belgium, Czechoslovakia, and the Netherlands the rise in wholesale prices by 1947 had reached from

EUROPEAN RECOVERY PROGRAM

250 to 300 per cent of prewar prices. The cost of living in Poland had risen by 150 times in mid-1947. Several countries resorted to monetary purges: In Greece, one old drachma was exchanged for 50,000 million new drachmas; in Yugoslavia, 250 million new dinars were exchanged for 6,000 million old notes; in Czechoslovakia, exchange was limited to 500 new crowns to each person, with remaining balances frozen; and in Hungary, drastic measures were taken to stabilize prices through a reduction in monetary supplies. By July 1946, the volume of circulation had reached 6.2×10^{21}. France and Italy, with prices up to about ten and sixty times the prewar level, continued to encounter difficulties in 1947. In Germany the use of money as a medium of exchange had virtually ceased before the monetary purge of the summer of 1948.

The advance of monetary inflation in 1947 was not serious as a rule. Of the ERP countries, France, Italy, and Greece alone showed rises in circulation that might be considered large relative to the economic movements of the period. The rise of circulation in the Netherlands, Switzerland, and Sweden was small, and for Norway appropriate; and several showed a net decline over the year. Similar generalizations apply to price movements. Italy, France, and Greece were the danger spots; for other ERP countries, there were small rises or even declines. (In Ireland the cost of living rose about 10 per cent.) [26]

One of the disturbing factors in the situation was the failure of wages to respond to the increase in the cost of living, a loss softened by rationing and recouped in part by cost-of-living subsidies.[27]

INDIVIDUAL COUNTRIES: THE UNITED KINGDOM [28]

The United Kingdom is the most important country of those participating in the Paris Conference: its anticipated trade deficit with the Americas for 1948 is 30 per cent of the total for the sixteen countries and Western Germany; and its income is about

ECONOMIC RECOVERY?

one-third of the total. Hence British prospects and fulfillment of goals under the ERP will be of prime importance.

National income is the most important single index of economic well being. In 1938, British national income (or net national expenditures) was £4,671 million; in 1946, £7,974 million, a rise of more than 70 per cent. A more recent survey puts national income at £8,200 million in 1946, £8,600 million in 1947, and (estimated) £9,000 million in 1948.[29] Output even in 1946 *seemed* to be above the 1938 level, for income rose more than prices. According to one estimate, income was 15 per cent above prewar levels. In a controlled world a comparison of income and price movements may be misleading, however.[30] As of early 1948 the United States Government estimated that an expansion of production of 25 per cent above current levels would be required to achieve the expansion of exports necessary to pay for imports even at a standard of living somewhat lower than in wartime.[31]

Unfortunately for Britain, over-all income figures are not an adequate guide to the British economic situation. The distribution of the income is also a matter of importance. A rise of income not accompanied by gains in consumption may have adverse effects on output. It is clear that consumption accounts for a declining part of the national income.

These figures (Table 42) suggest that consumption expenditures are relatively much less important than they had been; and capital expenditures substantially more important. (It will be noted, however, that in the light of the large amounts of disinvestment in the six years 1940–1945, investments in 1946 and 1947 were modest.)[32] It is also clear that without large contributions from the sale of foreign assets and foreign loans, the amounts available for investment and consumption would have been substantially lower. In 1947, the net foreign disinvestment was equal to 50 to 60 per cent of the total investment.

Consumption expenditures, corrected for price changes, sug-

[253]

gest that consumption is roughly at prewar levels. Over-all figures, however, conceal the change in distribution among groups and the enforced modification of the goods consumed. The public is not pleased with the substitution of additional entertainment

TABLE 42

Use of British National Income — Percentage

	1938	1947 Provisional	1948 Estimated
Current expenditures			
Personal consumption	78	70	69
Government current expenditures	16	24	22
Additions to assets			
Net capital formation at home	7	14	12
Less external disinvestment ..	−1	−8	−3
National Income	100	100	100

Source: *Economic Survey for 1948*, p. 46.

and liquor for clothing, food, and housing denied them. Nor do the relatively well-to-do feel compensated for the losses they suffered by the gains of others. From 1938 to 1946, lower income groups increased their private income after payments of direct tax by 95 per cent; but middle and upper income groups by only 31 per cent — the former is given by wages, pay of armed forces, and social security benefits and other transfer payments; and the latter by salaries, rents, interest, profits, and professional earnings.[33] But even the low-income groups are not pleased with the results, though in the United Kingdom, weekly wage rates at the end of 1947 were 70 per cent above the 1939 level, while the cost of living had risen by but 33 per cent.[34] Wages were high on an absolute scale, and also high relative to prices; but increased taxes and the unavailability of goods reduced consumption to about the prewar level. Large reductions for 1947 and 1948 in per capita consumption were evident in all important foods but

ECONOMIC RECOVERY?

grains and potatoes; and the declines in meat, eggs, oils and fats, sugar, vegetables, and fruits were substantial.[35] In summary, the relatively small proportion of current output available for consumption, and particularly the serious shortages in vital commodities, point to a deterioration in living standards, and a weakening of incentives.

Before we turn to the problem of the British economy in relation to the ERP, two other aspects of the current situation require consideration. First, there is the problem of suppressed inflation. At the end of 1947, total purchasing power had risen by 150 per cent over the prewar level, wholesale prices by 100 per cent, weekly wage rates by 70 per cent, and the cost of living by 33 per cent. The government had succeeded in keeping prices down by increasing taxes, stimulating savings, and by controlling prices, rationing, allocating, and relying on consumer subsidies. Continuance of heavy taxation which promises a large budgetary surplus in 1948 should reduce the pressures; but inflation continues to threaten the economy. Much will depend upon the use to which the government puts the local currencies received for supplies imported under the ERP. Should this money be used to reduce floating debt held by the Bank of England and joint stock banks, the anti-inflationary effects would be large; but if it is used to purchase government securities in the hands of the public or (worse) for ordinary expenses, then the effects would be inflationary. (In the years 1946 and 1947, the government had received *net* $3000 million in local currency for goods received under foreign aid.) [36]

Another factor of importance is the reduced contribution expected from abroad, that is, from foreign loans or sales of assets abroad. Whereas £380 million and £675 million were available in 1946 and 1947, respectively, the estimated amount for 1948 is only £250 million. The receipt of goods from abroad which do not have to be paid for currently and are not offset by corresponding earnings at home has an anti-inflationary effect; and especially if a substantial part of the local currency received for these goods is not put back into circulation. A reduction in net imports is an inflationary factor as is the large volume of investment; for the diversion of resources to investment results in a rise of income relative to the supply of consumption goods made available. The rise of investment is large despite the announced reduction for 1948. Total capital formation is estimated at £1350 million in 1946, £1900 million in 1947, and £1800 million in 1948, domestic sources providing £970, £1225, and £1550 million respectively. These investments may well exceed savings and therefore be inflationary, although as against an excess of spending over saving of £410 and £30 million in 1946 and 1947, public authorities plan to contribute an excess of savings (excess of receipts) of £275 million in 1948. That part of the investment used to replenish badly depleted inventories will help reduce the inflationary pressures in the next few years. From the end of 1942 to the end of 1946, the number of weeks' stock at current consumption rate had fallen from 5.7 to 2.9 weeks for coal, from 24 to 10 weeks for soft wood, from 16 to 12 weeks for hard wood, from 8.9 to 4.4 weeks for steel.[37]

It is scarcely necessary to comment on the vital problem of the balance of payments, a variable related to output, consumption standards, allocation of resources to investment, inflation, and finally to the attainment of export targets. Export targets for the *end* of 1948 (volume) are 154 of 1938 volume; the actual amount in 1947, 108; and the anticipated amount for 1948, 130. Another important target is a rise of exports to the Western Hemisphere to 114 (1938 = 100 and 1947 = 91). It is also proposed to save hard currencies by reducing the volume of imports from the Western Hemisphere from 44 per cent in 1947, to 34 per cent (annual rate) in the first half of 1948. The current adverse balance, it is hoped, will be reduced from an estimated £675 million

ECONOMIC RECOVERY?

in 1947 to £136 million in the first half of 1948; the net reduction in reserves from £226 million in 1946 and £963 million in 1947, to £222 million (forecast) for the first half of 1948. In considering these estimates, the reader should recall that the planned deficit on current account for 1947 was £350 million and the actual deficit, £675 million.[38]

British targets as presented to the CEEC are given in the table below. In general, the government proposed large increases in output although grains were an important exception. The executive branch was not equally optimistic, substantially reducing the British estimates for iron and steel, livestock and dairy products, farm machinery, and other items. In part, the difficulty will be unavailability of imports; and in part, mal-use of resources — for example, excessive expansion of livestock products at the expense of grains. The executive branch discussed the CEEC estimates, not the Cripps program of the autumn of 1947 which assumed no ERP aid, would drastically reduce imports and resort to bilateralism, and still would show a dollar deficit of one billion dollars in 1948. But anticipated rises submitted in the official *Economic Survey for 1948* checked well with those submitted to the CEEC six months earlier. In 1948, output of coal was to rise by 8 per cent, steel by 10 per cent, cotton yarn by 22 per cent, worsted yarn by 23 per cent, bread grains (acreage) by 18 per cent. The planned increase in exports of textiles from the second half of 1947 to the end of 1948 was to be 74 per cent for cotton yarns and manufactures, 97 per cent for woolen and worsted yarns and manufactures, and 45 to 68 per cent for other classes of textiles.[39]

From all of this, it is not easy to conclude that the British will achieve the objectives set. They will not only have to increase output, a goal related to the success of heroic man-power measures, and to rising productivity in turn related to availability of capital and continued monetary stability; but they will also have

TABLE 43

PRODUCTION ESTIMATES FOR SELECTED KEY COMMODITIES
AS SUBMITTED BY THE UNITED KINGDOM TO CEEC

	Unit	1938	1946	1947	1948	1949	1950	1951
Industrial Commodities								
Coal	1,000,000 metric tons	231	193	199	214	227	239	249
Locomotives	units	478	725	657	870	1100	1150	1200
Trucks	1,000 units	70	136	124	142	155	155	155
Freight cars	1,000 units	n.a.	28	38	59	76	76	76
Iron and steel								
Finished	1,000,000 metric tons	8.2	9.6	9.6	12.0	12.1	12.3	12.4
Crude and semifinished	1,000,000 metric tons	10.6	12.9	12.7	14.0	14.2	14.5	15.0
Pig iron	1,000,000 metric tons	6.8	7.8	7.9	8.6	9.1	9.3	9.9
Scrap	1,000,000 metric tons	6.0	7.9	7.1	6.9	7.1	7.3	7.5
Iron ore	1,000,000 metric tons	12.0	12.4	10.7	12.6	13.2	13.3	13.9
Tractors*	1,000 units	15	33	60	125	226	260	275
Other agric. machinery*	1,000 metric tons	30	115	150	200	300	340	375
Agricultural Commodities*								
Bread grains	1,000 tons	1751	2271	2038	1882	2025	1832	1918
Coarse grains	1,000 tons	2886	5817	5299	5344	5267	4962	4753
Fats and oils	1,000 tons	200	101	117	150	166	171	172
Oilcake	1,000 tons	0	2	0	43	72	72	72
Meat	1,000 tons	1411	973	944	933	1034	1121	1188
Eggs	1,000 tons	257	166	171	194	230	283	376
Nitrogen	1,000 tons	137	251	240	246	252	252	252
Phosphates	1,000 tons	150	319	311	336	361	365	370

Source: ERP: *Country Studies: The United Kingdom*, p. 40.   n.a. = not available.
* First column figures are 1934–38 averages. For the following years the figures are for consumption years, which correspond to United States fiscal years.

ECONOMIC RECOVERY?

to find markets for a vast increase of export goods. It is only necessary to compare the declines (Table 43) or small rises in 1947 over 1946 for coal, locomotives, trucks, iron and steel, and tractors with the large rises expected in 1948 to suggest the need of caution. The target for all exports for 1947 was 140 (1938 = 100), the actual level, 108; it is now proposed to raise the volume to 136 in the second half of 1948, and 130 for the year. High levels of production, moderate investment programs, restricted consumption, low costs, and a large expansion of export markets will all be required if goals are to be reached.[40]

FRANCE

In the size of its deficit and the amount of aid required, France is the second most important country participating in the ERP. According to the United States experts, Metropolitan and Overseas France and the Saar face a deficit on current account of $1233 million in 1948–49 with the Americas, and $368 million additional with other nonparticipating countries; and for the period April 1, 1948, to June 30, 1952, of $3389 million, and $1303 million, respectively.[41] From the political angle, France may well be the most important single country; for here the struggle between communist and noncommunist forces is at its height, and the outcome is likely to be decisive.

After years of deprivations and economic rape by the Germans, France made a remarkable recovery from 1944 to 1947. Industrial production had risen from 20 (1938 = 100) in the third quarter of 1944 to 90 by the end of 1946; and a global index yielded a rise from 41 to 90. The industrial index for 1947 averaged 96; and by 1946, the gross national product had rebounded to within 12 per cent of the 1938 level. In that year the output of equipment exceeded the 1938 level; but unfortunately that of food was at but 73 per cent of that level, of clothing, textiles, and leather 78 per cent, and other durable goods 75 per cent. In the middle of 1947, output of several crucial items was still below prewar standards: coal, 88; iron, 95; leather and hides, 76; paper and cardboard, 84. Handicapped by low labor productivity which, in mid 1947, was only 80–85 per cent of that before the war, by war damage and removals estimated by the French at $21 billion (1938 prices), and by food budgets of but 75 per cent of the prewar amount, the French performed remarkably well in this period.[42]

Recovery of production alone is not enough. Inadequate supplies are available for consumption, with unfortunate effects on output and the political situation; excessive allocations are made for investment — excessive not in terms of needs but in terms of availability, while the amounts diverted to export are insufficient. A combination of reduced output and less than optimum distribution of resources had serious repercussions: the disproportionate resources used for investment tended to strengthen the inflationary forces, as did the over-all shortages and bottlenecks; the inadequate level of exports aggravated the balance of payments problem, to which inflation had greatly contributed.

Perhaps inflation is the core of the French problem; for it reflects the output crisis, the mal-allocation of economic resources, and the problem of the balance of payments; and in turn contributes to these malaises. Inflation is revealed in a rise of food prices in November 1947 by fifteen times over those of 1937; and in an increase in the general wholesale price index by eleven times.

Distortions resulted from the inflationary process. Thus in 1946, *real* wage rates were 40 per cent below prewar rates though real output had dropped by but 10 per cent.[43] These figures reflect the large claims on the economy of investment and government; and also shortages of consumer goods and failure of wages to respond to rising prices. Of course, the result was a

ECONOMIC RECOVERY?

breakdown of workers' morale, loss of incentives to work, and reduced output.

Inflation also had unfortunate effects upon the balance of payments. From 1938 to 1947, prices, for example, had risen six times as much as in the United States; and with the January 1948 devaluation, the price of the dollar in francs had also risen by about six times — from about three cents in 1938 to less than half a cent in early 1948. Actually the revision of the value of the franc has been tardy; and world prices of French products still seem to be high, a reflection of the inadequacy of French index numbers or (and) a deterioration of her international position. A combination of an overvalued currency, inadequacy of resources for export markets (in part associated with intense consumption and investment demands at home), loss of European markets, depletion of capital assets abroad and losses of invisible earnings, unavailability of supplies from normal sources — all of these contribute to France's unfortunate international economic position and particularly to her rapid depletion of reserves. According to the International Monetary Fund, the volume of French exports in 1946 was but 43 per cent of the 1938 volume, while imports were 112 per cent of the 1938 amount. In 1947 (first 10 months), however, exports were over 80 per cent of 1938 volume, and imports, about 120 per cent.[44]

Inflation is caused in part by the large demands made upon the economy by the Treasury; and inflation, in turn, contributes to these demands. In the early liberation period, the amount of purchasing power relative to output and the flow of goods at controlled prices was excessive. But as the United Nations has shown, the removal and weak administration of controls and the rise of output tended by 1946 to reëstablish an equilibrium between money and prices: the excess of money was now absorbed by a large rise in prices and output.

Yet the inflation threat continues. Investments tend to exceed savings. Large government deficits (negative savings), savings by consumers, and the resources made available by net imports (equivalent to savings) — these, the total of savings, are not equal to the investments required in the French economy. It is estimated that savings requirements in proportion to consumption were 33 per cent in 1946 as compared with 23 per cent in 1938. Yet savings were smaller. This large increase of savings required is explained in part by the rise in dissavings of government (excess of expenditures over receipts) and the additional investments required relative to 1938; and the proportion would have been 8 per cent additional, had it not been for the large net imports.[45]

With prices continuing to skyrocket in 1947 (the rise in wholesale prices was about 30 per cent from December 1946 to December 1947), it is not surprising that the French Government took drastic measures to revolutionize its tax system and moderate its investment program. With rates of income taxes that compare favorably with the United States, French direct taxes yield only 3 per cent of income, whereas the percentages are 10 and 20 per cent in the United States and the United Kingdom. Despite the large rise of prices, the French Government also prepared through its "Guillotine Committee" to cut public expenditures by 10 per cent. They also are prepared to restrict credit, control its use, and continue allocations. Investment is to be confined to the proceeds of internal loans and the franc proceeds of foreign assistance. These are the attacks upon an inflationary gap estimated at $1.6 billion for the first half of 1948 alone.[46]

In the next few years, the French will have to expand their output greatly, improve consumption standards, stop the inflation and expand exports substantially relative to imports. Unless they achieve these interrelated goals, they will fail to make an adequate contribution to the ERP. They will also have to join European programs of economic cooperation: for example, customs union, common investment projects.

ECONOMIC RECOVERY?

In assessing French programs as presented to the CEEC, the United States experts were much less optimistic than the French. Domestic output is the vital matter; for aid under the ERP will not exceed 5 per cent of France's gross product. Against the recommendations of the French experts, the United States proposed a rise, not a fall, in production of bread grains: by 1946 output of rye and wheat had fallen to three-quarters of prewar output. Recovery depends upon adequate output of grains. Experience has also proved that the recovery of industrial production would not equal that proposed under the Marshall Plan. According to that plan, industrial output by 1950 was to reach 160 per cent of 1938. American technicians estimated the potential output at 110 by the end of 1948, and 140 by 1952. Even these levels can be attained only by a substantial rise of labor supply, a work week 15 per cent longer than before the war, a rise of productivity of 5 per cent per year until prewar productivity is attained. (By mid-1947, man-hour output was 80 to 85 per cent of prewar output.) In the revised plan, investment will be much less than the 20 per cent of current national income contemplated by the French Government. Attainment of coal targets depends on the retention of one-third more man-power than before the war, and a rise of productivity by 25 per cent. An estimate of 10.4 million metric tons of crude and semifinished steel in 1948 is far above actual accomplishments in 1947 of but 5.8 million tons. Output in 1948–49 may reach 7.3 million tons, far below that anticipated in 1947. And yet exports will have to rise from $500 million in 1948–49 to $1 billion in 1952. France will have to continue to shift exports from textiles to products of heavy industries, the latter greatly in demand in an impoverished world; and shift exports to hard currency countries and obtain imports more largely from Europe. Recovery will depend upon a willingness to forego consumer durable goods at home, a reduction in costs in part associated with ERP, and continued prosperity abroad.[47]

EUROPEAN RECOVERY PROGRAM

ITALY [48]

Italy, like France, faces a serious communist threat; and like France, she has a large deficit in her balance of payments. For 1948–49 her adverse balance on current account with the Americas is estimated at $780 million dollars and from April 1, 1948, to June 30, 1952, at $2913 million. In the last year, however, a credit balance of $227 million with other nonparticipating countries equals 40 per cent of the anticipated adverse balance of $562 million with the Americas. Should it be possible to convert these credit balances into dollars, the adverse balance would be manageable by 1952.[49]

In many other respects, Italy's situation is similar to that of France. Inflation is the core of the problem. Budgetary deficits are even more serious than in France. In 1946–47, the estimated deficit of the government had risen to 610 billion lire, as compared with those of 300 and 397 billion lire in the two preceding years. Government expenditures in 1946 were 32 per cent of the national income; but government revenue, only 9.7 per cent.[50] In 1946 and 1947, with controls largely abandoned or functioning imperfectly, Italy attempted to contend with inflation: tax measures, restriction of credit inclusive of compulsory purchase of securities by banks and compulsory transfers of deposits, restriction of government outlays to receipts from non-inflationary sources of financing — these were to be the gateways to stability. In fact, after prices had risen to sixty-five times those of the prewar period, doubling in the year ending September 1947, the Einaudi anti-inflation program brought about a phenomenal drop of 20 per cent late in 1947, or from sixty-five to about fifty-two times the prewar level. Tax receipts in fiscal 1948 are to provide 18 per cent of national income, whereas the yield was but 11 and 13 per cent in 1945 and 1946.[51]

In some respects, the Italian problems are peculiar. First, there

ECONOMIC RECOVERY?

is serious unemployment which is associated with the release of millions previously in the service of the Fascist State, the army and war industries, with the shortage of plant and materials, with the large rise of population, and with the absence of outlets for the excess. Second, the recovery was much slower than in France. In 1946, national product was but 68 per cent of that in 1938; agricultural product but 80 per cent of the prewar product; industrial product but 45 per cent of that before the war. (There was further improvement in 1947.) Third, the loss of European markets was perhaps more costly to Italy than to most other countries. Whereas Italy had obtained 62 per cent of her imports from Europe in 1938, she received but 20 per cent from this source in 1946. Germany and Southeastern Europe, which had purchased about 30 to 40 per cent of Italy's exports before the war, were virtually lost as customers. On the other hand, the United States, which in 1938 had provided 12 per cent of Italy's imports and purchased about 8 per cent of her exports, supplied 60 per cent of her imports in 1946 and was a market for 18 per cent of Italy's exports.[52]

Italian recovery depends largely upon an expansion of output, an improved distribution of consumption goods, in part to be achieved by controls, limitation of investment to the savings available, and balancing of the government's budget. Should these goals be reached, then the help under the ERP might well be effective. That Italy's program is an ambitious one is confirmed by proposals to raise exports from $700 million in 1947 to $1.9 billion in 1951–52; output of bread grains in 1951–52 by 40 per cent over 1947–48; and agricultural output generally by more than 25 per cent; fertilizers by a few hundred per cent above the output of 1938 and 1946; cotton textiles by 51 per cent, woolen textiles by 41 per cent, and artificial fiber textiles by 33 per cent above prewar production; fuel and power by 100 per cent more than before the war; finished steel output, 87 per cent above 1938.

EUROPEAN RECOVERY PROGRAM

These are ambitious goals even allowing for substantial though hesitant gains in 1946; and the United States technicians express doubts concerning the possibility of fulfilling the plans in many sectors of the economy.[53]

BIZONAL GERMANY

Bizonal Germany is the subject matter of this part of the chapter. The French Zone is less important and its recovery has been somewhat slower than that of Bizonal Germany; and the Saar is rapidly being integrated into the French economy. Since the Russian Zone is not to profit directly from the ERP, there is no need to consider it. An examination of prewar industrial exports will give some indication of the relative importance of the areas:[54]

Million Reichsmarks

United States and United Kingdom	2676
France	376
USSR	1038
Berlin	313
Saar	77
Area East of Oder-Neisse (Polish)	193
Total	4673

The importance of Bizonal Germany and the difficulties encountered there are suggested by the following facts. The CEEC had estimated its deficit in the balance of payments for 1948 at $1.5 billion ($1.15 billion with the Americas). United States experts were less pessimistic: they put the adverse balance of payments at $1017 million for the year 1948–49, and $3580 million for the period April 1, 1948, to June 30, 1952. They estimated that at first, imports of machinery and equipment would rise spectacularly, later, materials to be processed, and finally food. Even at the end of the period, however, the per capita food con-

ECONOMIC RECOVERY?

sumption would be 25 per cent less in quantity than before the war. That the United States experts programmed a rise of exports from $169 million in 1948–49 to $778 million in 1951–52, underlines the difficulties confronting Bizonal Germany. (This rise to almost five times the 1948–49 level compares with an expansion to seven times estimated by the CEEC: from $275 million in 1947 to $1.8 billion in 1951–52.)[55]

Bizonal Germany's problems are not unlike those of many other European countries. She also is hampered by a disorganized currency system, by the breakdown of European trade, by inadequate production and consumption. Incentives are lacking; and because of Germany's central position in Europe her impoverishment seriously affects the rest of Europe.

That Germany is not a free agent, that she is subject to drains on reparations account, that she has been dismembered, that the pressure of population on resources has greatly increased, that no strong German government exists, that morale is at a record low — all of these intensify her difficulties. Fear of Germany's rearmament contributed to the plans for de-industrialization which now are generally recognized as unworkable. In successive moves, the United States and the United Kingdom retreated from their original pastoralization program for Germany; until now the relatively high Level-of-Industry goal of August 1947 may be considered a target for Bizonal Germany to shoot at but not one likely to be reached for many years. Under the earlier Level-of-Industry Plan, Bizonal steel production was to be limited to 4.7 million ingot tons; under the August 1947 plan, to 10.7 million tons; production in the peak prewar year was 17.8 million, and in 1946, 2.7 million tons.[56]

In no area are the goals more ambitious and the hopes more likely to be disappointed, than in Western Germany. First, the monetary system is in a state of collapse. The mark retains high value for rationed commodities; but for unrationed commodities

EUROPEAN RECOVERY PROGRAM

it is almost valueless. Germans barter even in relations among business firms: producers exchange their products for raw materials and for consumer goods for workers. Second, recovery in production was disappointing even on postwar European standards. In November 1947 industrial production was but 44 per cent of prewar production. The low output of coal is especially harmful. Third, food rations are altogether too low to maintain the population in health and to obtain maximum production. Indigenous production provided but 1000 calories daily for controlled distribution in 1947; food imports in the fiscal year ending June 30, 1947, yielded another 670 calories, and unrationed black-market foods, 300 calories more. Reduced food consumption greatly affects efficiency and accounts for absenteeism. Fourth, the absence of adequate administrative machinery tends to keep production down. No strong government other than the military exists in Germany. The military government, hampered by directives to save dollars, is responsible for some mal-use of Germany's limited resources. Fifth, Bizonal Germany's trade is unbalanced even on present standards. Her volume of coal exports is but one-third of prewar volume and that of other exports but 5 per cent. In the first nine months of 1947, Bizonal imports were $500 million, and exports $136 million. Sixth, Germany still has an excess of plant and equipment relative to materials and man power available. That is to say, Germany cannot make the most effective use of the capital resources available largely because of the difficulty of obtaining required supplies of raw materials and food.[57] (This paragraph was written just before the drastic monetary reform of the summer of 1948.)

Yet the United States experts seemed fairly optimistic. They improved on the CEEC program which estimated a rise of grain output of about 30 per cent from 1948–49 to 1951–52. They were however, less sanguine than the CEEC on the import program. The CEEC program for coal plans a rise of output from 149

ECONOMIC RECOVERY?

million tons in 1948–49 to 193 million tons in 1951–52; the United States experts estimated the rise from 156 to 198 million tons. Even in steel output, the United States experts were optimistic: they raised the CEEC estimates by 12, 12, and 13 per cent in successive years. The experts anticipated a reactivation of the economy in industrial output: production was to rise to 60 per cent of the 1936 level in 1948–49 and 100 per cent by 1951–52. It was proposed to increase output of machinery by 120 per cent, steel goods by 200 per cent, textiles by 150 per cent, and chemicals by 67 per cent in the four years ending 1952–53. The CEEC also stressed the need for financial reform, not only to provide incentives for dishoarding goods, but also to make it profitable to export goods. At present, incentive to sell on domestic markets is greater than that to sell abroad.[58] Perhaps the monetary reform of the summer of 1948 will help.

THE NETHERLANDS

Having discussed four large areas in some detail, we may treat the Netherlands briefly. Her adverse balance on current account for 1948–49 is estimated at $765 million ($659 million with the Americas) and for April 1, 1948, to June 30, 1952, at $2775 million ($2513 million with the Americas). Production is still far below prewar levels; and the Dutch situation is aggravated by large military expenditures abroad, by the loss of shipping, and by the failure to obtain the support from the Netherlands East Indies, Germany, and the United Kingdom to which her economy is geared. For example, exports from the Netherlands East Indies in the past helped pay for the substantial excess of imports to the Netherlands. Now these exports have largely disappeared. The Netherlands has an ambitious program to raise output in the next few years. For example, they propose to raise the output of finished steel to two and a half to three times that of 1938. Their consumption in 1947 was but three-quarters of prewar consump-

EUROPEAN RECOVERY PROGRAM

tion; and yet through a subsidy program and price, wage, and distribution controls, the inflation problem seemed well under control.[59]

CONCLUSION

In general, the estimates of the CEEC were too optimistic, both in their output and export goals. In the light of the advances in 1947, it seems improbable that an over-all gain of 30 per cent in output will be achieved. Failure to reach the output targets will result in an even greater than proportionate deficiency in exports. We need not repeat here the mistakes made by the CEEC. We should add, however, that whereas they had put the rise of exports to the United States over the four years of the ERP at 74 per cent, for the other Americas at 88 per cent, the United States experts estimated the rise of exports to this country at about 50 per cent from 1948–49 to 1951–52, and for the other Americas at close to 85 per cent.[60] In view of the enthusiastic development programs and the relatively small rise of real incomes in Latin America, the projected expansion of exports to the other Americas seems unrealistic. Besides, the Paris experts were too optimistic concerning the convertibility of Latin-American currencies.

In the five countries accounting for the major part of the deficit and of aid to be given under the ERP, the prospects are not so bright as the CEEC suggested. In all of them, the rise in projected output seems large compared to attainments over the last year. Export goals are ambitious even on the assumption of favorable world economic conditions and the successful resistance to protectionist movements; for over a period of a few years, these countries propose to raise their exports from one-third to six times.

Inflation is a real or a serious threat in each of these countries. In the United Kingdom and the Netherlands, the skillful use of controls has damped the inflationary pressures, whereas in Italy

ECONOMIC RECOVERY?

and France a combination of large budgetary deficits, serious shortages, and unrealistic investment programs, without the support of effective control systems, account for a rise of prices of dangerous proportions. The United Kingdom seems to have inflation under control; but it will face a serious test in the next year or two when the net import surplus will be reduced greatly and, therefore, investment will have to be offset *pari passu* by a rise of savings or a reduction of consumption expenditures. In France, moderation of the investment program, tax reform and a rise of consumption goods may weaken the inflationary forces. In Germany, nothing short of generous subsidies by this country and a complete overhauling of the monetary system will reëstablish a normal functioning monetary system. It remains to be seen how many of these countries will stop the advance of inflation short of complete collapse. Investment exceeds savings everywhere; and yet consumption is at levels which do not allow further reduction without serious political consequences.

Concluding Remarks

Since this books starts with a chapter giving the highlights and there are numerous summaries in the volume, a lengthy conclusion is not necessary. Here, however, are several points that cannot be emphasized too strongly:

1. Political and military developments are likely to be decisive. Sabotage of the ERP by the USSR and her communist sympathizers is a genuine threat; and communist attitudes and policies relative to the ERP may well determine the extent to which the program will have to be supplemented by military aid.

2. With favorable political conditions, there is every reason for expecting the ERP countries to resume their expansion of output. Western Europe may well achieve a rise of 25 per cent in national income in the next four years, following one of similar proportions in 1945–47. Much will depend, however, upon monetary and fiscal developments. Since June 1947 the countries confronted with serious inflationary dangers, have made progress. But the drastic remedies required have not generally been forthcoming; and until further economic recovery is made and governments strengthened, the vulnerable economies are likely to continue to rely on half-hearted measures. Yet a frontal attack on inflation is a *sine qua non* for substantial and speedy recovery.

3. The big question mark is the state of the balance of payments of the participating countries. Even with recovery and substantial gains of income by 1952, there will probably still remain a large deficit of Western Europe with the United States. American authorities are inclined to exaggerate the gains to be had from a devaluation of European currencies and they underestimate the difficulty of attaining equilibrium once more for an

CONCLUDING REMARKS

area which less than ten years ago was paying for one-third of its imports with dollars, largely no longer available. Even should Western Europe improve its balance of payments by $5 billion annually over the next four years, the probable failure to reëstablish multilateralism will deprive the United States of a large proportion of the gains made by Europe.

4. Mistaken United States policy may well account for part of the difficulties. Overzealous in pruning Europe's investment program, the government may make a good showing over the next few years; but Europe, hampered by inadequate and antiquated plant, may not raise her output and exports adequately, with the result that trade deficits will continue much longer. American experts, too optimistic concerning the favorable effects of exchange revaluation, are correspondingly neglectful of the more important problem of inadequacy of output, the allocation of output among consumption, investment and exports, and in general the important part played by control of prices and of markets. In the European economies at the present time, controls are much more important than exchange rates in determining the international position.

5. In their zeal to keep down the costs of the program to the American citizen, the experts have transferred too large a part of the real costs to the other Americas, who are asked to carry much greater burdens relative to their resources than those put upon the American economy. The financial costs on our economy are large; but the plans call for a relatively much heavier *real* burden on the other Americas.

6. This leads to another point. The ERP will require sacrifices of the American people. Administrative leaders (for example, Secretary Anderson) are too disposed to belittle the adverse effects upon the American economy. In an over-employed economy, the difference made by exporting $4 to $5 billion yearly to purchase scarce commodities, plus the new billions to be spent

EUROPEAN RECOVERY PROGRAM

under the rearmament program, are bound to have adverse effects. It is, however, possible to contain the adverse effects; but nowhere does Congress show a greater disposition to increase the *real* costs than in its utter failure to introduce a comprehensive anti-inflation program, inclusive of appropriate tax and allocation policies. Especially in order to stabilize the markets for iron and steel and oil, allocations are a must.

7. Finally, the ECA operations in Europe will require a combination of firmness, tact, and a grasp of political and economic realities which the ECA may not be able to achieve. In the substantial control over blocked currencies, over inflation and exchange policies, over trading arrangements, over the re-export of commodities obtained in whole or in part under the ERP — in all of these, the United States has arrogated to itself powers which may fructify the ERP dollars; but the unskillful exercise of this authority might prove to be a major disaster.

Abbreviations

JOURNALS, etc.

    E.J.   Economic Journal
    F.R.B.   Federal Reserve Bulletin
    J.P.E.   Journal of Political Economy
    R.E.S.   Review of Economics and Statistics
    S.C.B.   Survey of Current Business

SPECIAL

    CEEC   Committee of European Economic Cooperation
    ECA   European Cooperation Administration
    ERP   European Recovery Program
    IMF   International Monetary Fund
    FA Act   Foreign Assistance Act of 1948
    U.N.   United Nations

PUBLICATIONS

    CEEC: Committee of European Economic Cooperation, volume I, General Report; volume II, Technical Reports, September 1947

    CEA: The Impact of Foreign Aid upon the Domestic Economy: A Report to the President by the Council of Economic Advisers, October 1947

    EC Europe: Survey: A Survey of the Economic Situation and Prospects of Europe, Prepared by the Economic Commission for Europe, UN Economic and Social Council, March 1948 (United States Edition, 1948)

    Ec. Rep. Pres.: The Economic Report of the President Transmitted to the Congress, January 1948

EUROPEAN RECOVERY PROGRAM

ERP Com. Rep.: Commodity Report, European Recovery Program, 13 volumes (and numerous supplementary studies), by the State Department, 1947-48

ERP Country Studies: European Recovery Program: Country Studies, 17 volumes, by the State Department, 1947

ERP: House Hear.: United States Foreign Policy for a Post-War Recovery Program, Hearings Before the Committee on Foreign Affairs, House of Representatives, Parts I and II, 1948

ERP: House Rep.: Foreign Assistance Act of 1948, Report of the Committee on Foreign Affairs on S. 2202, House Report No. 1585, March 1948

ERP: Sen. Docs.: The European Recovery Program, Basic Documents by Senate and House Foreign Relations Committee, 1947

ERP: Sen. Hear.: European Recovery Program, Hearings before the Committee on Foreign Relations, United States Senate, Parts I, II, and III, 1948

ERP: Sen. Rep.: Report of the Committee on Foreign Relations on S. 2202, Senate Report No. 935, February 1948

ERP State: Outline of European Recovery Program, Draft Legislation and Background Information, Submitted by the Department of State for the Use of the Senate Foreign Relations Committee, 1947

FA Act of 1948: Public Law 472, 80th Congress, Foreign Assistance Act of 1948, April 3, 1948

Final Report, House: Final Report on Foreign Aid of the Select Committee on Foreign Aid Pursuant to H. Res. 296, A Resolution Creating a Select Committee on Foreign Aid, 1948

ABBREVIATIONS

Harriman: European Recovery and American Aid, a Report by the President's Committee on Foreign Aid, 2 volumes, November 1947

Krug: National Resources and Foreign Aid, Report of J. A. Krug, Secretary of the Interior, October 9, 1947

NAC: Foreign Assets and Liabilities of the United States and Its Balance of International Transactions, a Report to the Senate Committee on Finance by the National Advisory Council on International Monetary and Financial Problems, December 18, 1947 (1948)

State Dept. Est. Imp. etc.: European Recovery Program — Estimated Commodity Imports and Exports of the Participating Countries by Value and Quantity, April 1, 1948 to June 30, 1948 and July 1, 1948 to June 30, 1949

State Dept. Est. Bal. Payments: European Recovery Program — Estimated Balance of Payments on Current Account of the Participating Countries, April 1, 1948 to June 30, 1949

State Dept. Proposed Distribution: European Recovery Program: Proposed Distribution of Economic Cooperation Act Financing by Country and Commodity, April 8, 1948

SOURCES OF FIGURES

1, 2, 3, 9	Executive Branch — published by Senate Committee on Foreign Relations in *ERP: Sen. Hear.*
4	Federal Reserve Board in *F.R.B.*, 1948.
5, 6, 7	Economic Commission for Europe in *EC Europe: Survey*.
8, 11	Council of Economic Advisers in *CEA*.
10	Ec. Rep. Pres., 1948.
12	Executive Branch in *ERP Com. Rep.*, Iron and Steel.

Notes

HIGHLIGHTS

[1] *EC Europe: Survey*, pp. 1, 26–29.
[2] *Harriman*, I, 5–6; *EC Europe: Survey*, p. 25.
[3] Cf. *ERP: House Hear.*, pp. 458–461.
[4] Cf. Chapter 9.
[5] Figures from *ERP Com. Rep. Petroleum*, pp. G–13, G–29, G–30.
[6] See *ERP State*, p. 111.
[7] *ERP: Sen. Hear.*, p. 297.
[8] *EC Europe: Survey*, p. 16.
[9] *CEEC*, II, 461–522.
[10] *ERP: Sen. Hear.*, pp. 423–427.
[11] The analysis of the Commission here conflicts with the materials in their master table. I assume the analysis is correct, cf. *EC Europe: Survey*, pp. 40–43 and 68–69. The CEEC put the prewar deficit of the *participating* countries at $2 billion. *CEEC*, I, 108.
[12] Cf. *EC Europe: Survey*, pp. 40–43, 60, 68–69.
[13] Cf. R. Hinshaw in S. E. Harris, ed., *Foreign Economic Policy for the United States* (1948); also see *EC Europe: Survey*, p. 69.
[14] *EC Europe: Survey*, p. 68.
[15] *EC Europe: Survey*, pp. 69–76.
[16] Cf. *ERP State*, p. 111.
[17] *EC Europe: Survey*, pp. 40–44.
[18] *ERP State*, p. 111.

CHAPTER 1

[1] *Public Law* 472, 80th Congress, Sec. 114, A–C.
[2] For some relevant information, see pp. 104–106.
[3] *EC Europe: Survey*, pp. 1–16.
[4] *EC Europe: Survey*, p. 1.
[5] *ERP: Sen. Hear.*, p. 158. (Presumably these are dollars of constant purchasing power; if they are not, virtually no gain would have been made from 1945 to 1947.)

EUROPEAN RECOVERY PROGRAM

[6] *ERP: Sen. Hear.* III, p. 1005; cf. also U. N. *Monthly Bulletin of Statistics, passim,* for latest estimates of national income in domestic currencies; also see *NAC,* pp. 127–137. The reader should consult pp. 87–91 of this book, where reasons for differences in dollar estimates of European national incomes are explored. Perhaps the most important explanation is the difficulty of converting income totals expressed in local currencies into dollar equivalents.

[7] *EC Europe: Survey,* pp. 9–10; *ERP: Sen. Hear.,* p. 336. Cf. *CEEC,* I, 16.

[8] H. M. Stationery Office: *Economic Survey for 1948,* p. 45; cf. *National Income and Expenditure of the United Kingdom* (1947), pp. 5–6.

[9] *NAC,* p. 168.

[10] *F.R.B.,* February 1948, p. 138; April 1948, pp. 376, 378.

[11] U. N.: *Survey of Current Inflationary and Deflationary Tendencies,* September 1947, pp. 40–42.

[12] *EC Europe: Survey,* p. 135.

[13] *EC Europe: Survey,* pp. 7–8.

[14] Roy Harrod, *Are these Hardships Necessary?* (1947), 2nd ed., pp. 34–35, 41, 73–75; *U.K. Economic Survey for 1948,* p. 39; *National Income and Expenditure of the United Kingdom* (1947), p. 5.

[15] Sir Hubert Henderson, "Cheap Money and the Budget," *E.J.,* September 1947, pp. 267–269.

[16] Cf. also *Foreign Economic Policy for the United States (1948),* Chapter 1.

[17] D. H. Robertson, "The Economic Outlook," *E.J.,* December 1947, p. 435.

[18] J. R. Hicks, "The Empty Economy," *Lloyd's Bank Monthly Review,* July 1947, pp. 1–4; Harrod, *Are These Hardships Necessary?* pp. 27–29; L. Robbins, "Inquest on the Crisis," *Lloyd's Bank Monthly Review,* October, 1947, p. 13; L. Robbins, *The Economic Problem in Peace and War* (1947) pp. 59–60.

[19] Robbins, *The Economic Problem in Peace and War,* pp. 61–62, and Harrod, *Are These Hardships Necessary?* pp. 124–128.

[20] Harrod, *Are These Hardships Necessary?* p. 78.

[21] See, especially, the *EC Europe: Survey,* pp. 81–84, and House Select Committee on Foreign Aid, *Inflation and Methods of Financing Any Foreign Aid Program* (1948), pp. 15–18.

[22] U. N.: *Survey of Current Inflationary and Deflationary Tendencies* (1947), p. 43.

[23] Cf. U. N.: *Survey of Current Inflationary and Deflationary Tendencies,* p. 26; *Monthly Bulletin of Statistics,* February 1948, pp. 149–159; U. K.: *Economic Survey for 1948,* pp. 51–52; U. K.: *National Income and Expenditure of the United Kingdom* (1947), p. 8.

NOTES

[24] *EC Europe: Survey*, p. 80. (Allowance should be made for changes in territory.)

[25] Cf. *EC Europe: Survey*, pp. 86-88.

[26] *EC Europe: Survey*, pp. 36–37, 90–91.

[27] Roy Harrod, *Are These Hardships Necessary?* pp. 42–43, also p. 136; and G. Haberler in Seymour E. Harris, (ed.), *Foreign Economic Relations of the United States* (1948).

[28] Also, see my article "Dollar Scarcity," *E.J.*, June 1946.

[29] The reader will find the relevant facts in Chapter 4.

[30] H. Hazlitt, *Will Dollars Save the World?* (1947), pp. 18–19.

[31] *EC Europe: Survey*, pp. 57–59.

[32] *ERP State*, p. 42.

[33] *CEA*, p. 12.

[34] *CEA*, pp. 55–56; *ERP: Sen. Hear.*, p. 79.

[35] In the United Kingdom, the adverse balance of £70 million in 1938 is to be compared with one of £675 million in 1947. The government accounts for 40 per cent of the rise by the greater increase of import prices. (This probably includes both changes in the terms of trade and the rise of import deficit.) In addition, the invisible balance which had been £232 million (credit) in 1938, was adverse by £226 million in 1947. Price movements accounted for $1\frac{2}{3}$ times the increased trade deficits, and the losses on invisible account, for 3 times the rise in trade deficit. U. K.: *Economic Survey for 1948*, pp. 7, 14.

[36] *F.R.B.*, February 1948, p. 139.

[37] *EC Europe: Survey*, pp. 65–66.

[38] *ERP: Sen. Hear.*, pp. 391–401, 1007–1008.

[39] *ERP State*, pp. 111–113.

[40] *F.R.B.*, February 1948, p. 145; and *ERP State*, pp. 111–112.

[41] Calculated from U. N.: *Economic Report, 1945–47*, p. 126.

[42] Calculated from *F.R.B.*, February, 1948, p. 138.

[43] *Economic Report, 1945–47*, p. 176.

[44] *Economic Report, 1945–47*, p. 178.

[45] *ERP State*, p. 101; cf. *EC Europe: Survey*, pp. 98, 104.

[46] Calculated from *EC Europe: Survey, passim;* U. K.: *Economic Survey for 1948*, p. 14; and *ERP Country Studies, France*, p. 30.

[47] *EC Europe: Survey*, p. 63.

[48] *S. C. B.*, March 1948, pp. 19, 21.

[49] *EC Europe: Survey*, pp. 60–63.

EUROPEAN RECOVERY PROGRAM

CHAPTER 2

[1] Secretary Marshall has said as much (*ERP: House Hear.*, p. 71). Also see the interesting statements by Henry Wallace and the Communist Party, *ibid*, II, pp. 1436–38 and 1588–1600.

[2] *ERP: Sen. Docs.*, p. 79.

[3] Dept. of State: *The Development of the Foreign Reconstruction Policy of the United States, March–July, 1947*, Sept. 1947, pp. 8–9.

[4] *ERP: Sen. Rep.*, p. 13.

[5] *ERP: House Rep.*, p. 12; also see, pp. 5–8.

[6] *FA Act of 1948*, Sec. 102 (a).

[7] *FA Act of 1948*.

[8] *ERP: Sen. Docs.*, pp. 151–57.

[9] *ERP: Sen. Docs.*, pp. 155–58.

[10] *The Development of the Foreign Reconstruction Policy of the United States*, pp. 6–7.

[11] *ERP: Sen. Hear.*, p. 297.

[12] House Select Committee on Foreign Aid, *Latin America and the European Recovery Program*, Preliminary Report Twenty-Three (1948), pp. 15–20.

[13] House Select Committee on Foreign Aid, *Report on the United Kingdom*, Preliminary Report Eighteen (March 1948), pp. 19–20.

[14] *ERP State*, pp. 51–52.

[15] The Communist Party interprets the ERP as a deterrent to the resumption of East-West trade. *ERP: House Hear.*, II, 1437.

[16] All calculations based on *EC Europe: Survey*, pp. 40–43. (1947 data frequently incomplete.)

[17] House Select Committee on Foreign Aid, *The Eastern European Economy in Relation to the European Recovery Program*, Preliminary Report Twenty, p. 62.

[18] House Select Committee on Foreign Aid, *The Eastern European Economy in Relation to the European Recovery Program*, Preliminary Report Twenty (March 1948), p. 62.

[19] House Select Committee on Foreign Aid, *The Eastern European Economy in Relation to the European Recovery Program*, Preliminary Report Twenty, pp. 3–9, 52.

[20] House Select Committee on Foreign Aid, *The Eastern European Economy in Relation to the European Recovery Program*, pp. 30, 62.

[21] House Select Committee on Foreign Aid, *The Place of the United States in European Industrial Development*, Supplement to Preliminary Report Fourteen (April 1948), p. 8; also see pp. 1–7; also *Report on the United Kingdom*, Preliminary Report Eighteen (March 7, 1948), pp. 3–6.

NOTES

[22] *ERP: Sen. Rep.*, p. 54; and *ERP: Sen. Hear.*, pp. 516–520. (In the latter, Secretary Snyder explained why the National Advisory Council was opposed to taking action to help foreign nations obtain access to concealed assets held by their nationals in this country.)

[23] Cf. *ERP: Sen. Hear.*, pp. 173, 314.

[24] *ERP: House Hear.*, II, 1858–59.

[25] *ERP: Sen. Rep.*, pp. 16–17.

[26] These considerations largely explain the decision to set up an independent organization to administer the ERP even though difficult problems of integration with state and other departments are involved. Cf. Report of Senate Foreign Relations Committee, *Administration of United States Aid for a European Recovery Program* (January 1948); House Select Committee on Foreign Aid, *Comparative Analysis of Suggested Plans of Foreign Aid*, Preliminary Report Eleven (November 1947); and *Proposed Principles and Organization for any Program of Foreign Aid*, Preliminary Report Eight (November 1947), pp. 8–10; also frequent discussions in House and Senate Hearings on ERP, and ERP House Report, pp. 42–45, 47.

[27] Cf. Paul Sweezy, *Socialism* (New York, 1948); *ERP: House Hear.*, II, 1591–93.

[28] Henry Wallace charges the government with obstructing nationalization programs in Europe. *ERP: House Hear.*, II, 1591–93.

[29] *CEEC*, I, 13; *ERP: Sen. Hear.*, pp. 60–70, 189, 227–32; *ERP: Sen. Rep.*, pp. 43–45; *ERP: House Rep.*, pp. 11, 25.

[30] Cf. the statement of Secretary Snyder on the United States opposition to the French policy of discrimination introduced in her devaluation of January 1948. *ERP: House Hear.*, II, 1994–95.

[31] *ERP: House Hear.*, II, 410, 455–56; cf. II, 1527.

[32] Cf. *ERP: Sen. Hear.*, pp. 510–516, and *EC Europe: Survey*, pp. 102–114.

[33] Cf. *ERP: Sen. Hear.*, pp. 39, 162–63, 224–226; House Select Committee on Foreign Aid, *Foreign Aid and Exhaustion of Natural Resources in Relation to a Stockpiling Program* (November 1947).

[34] Dr. Riefler developed the argument fully. *ERP: House Hear.*, pp. 1364–70.

[35] This problem is discussed fully in Chapter 8.

[36] *ERP: House Hear.*, pp. 354–359, 1098–1105; cf. also House Report No. 1225, *Dismantlement and Removal of Plants for Germany* (December 1947).

[37] For a review of measures which Europe might take to help itself, and progress made, see *Final Report, House*, pp. 21–41.

[38] The reader will find a full discussion of the many administrative problems raised in two studies of the Herter Committee under the very

EUROPEAN RECOVERY PROGRAM

able guidance of Professor Elliott, the Staff Director: House Select Committee on Foreign Aid, *Comparative Analysis of Suggested Plans of Foreign Aid* (November 22, 1947), and *Proposed Principles and Organization for any Program of Foreign Aid* (November 22, 1947); also see *Harriman*, Section O; *ERP State*, pp. 54–61; also see numerous discussions in ERP: Senate and House Hearings, especially *ERP: Sen. Hear.*, II, 855–860 and *Administration of United States Aid for a European Recovery Program*, Report to Senate Foreign Relations by the Brookings Institution (January 22, 1948).

CHAPTER 3

[1] $\frac{40}{7} = 9 \times \frac{60}{93}$

[2] Based on *Ec. Rep. Pres.*, pp. 109, 113.

[3] Cf. pp. 34–36.

[4] Cf., however, Clark's figure in table. Dr. Baran finds that the purchasing power parity in 1937 yields a figure of 9.73 rubles = 1 dollar (official rate: 5 rubles = 1 dollar). National income per capita in the USSR for 1940 is estimated at $153 dollars, or one-quarter of that of the United States. Paul A. Baran, "National Income and Product of the U.S.S.R. in 1940," *R. E. S.*, November 1947, pp. 230–31.

[5] The International Bank estimated the national income of the ERP countries in 1946 at $99 billion, their population at 260 millions. Per capita income was $381, or roughly one-quarter of the per capita income of this country in the third quarter of 1947. *ERP: Sen. Hear.*, p. 1005.

[6] Cf. Table 1, Chapter 1, however.

[7] Pp. 31–32.

[8] Cf. pp. 30–31.

[9] Cf. U. N.: Economic Report, 1945–47, pp. 133-34; cf. *ERP: Sen. Doc.*, p. 19.

[10] Based on U. N. *Monthly Bulletin of Statistics*, February 1948, pp. 24–27. *EC Europe: Survey*, p. 1.

CHAPTER 4

[1] Based on *ERP State*, p. 111 and *NAC*, pp. 130–35.

[2] *ERP State*, p. 84; *CEC*, p. 16; *ERP Sen. Docs.*, pp. 12, 20.

[3] Cf. *ERP: House Hear.*, II, 2198. Here the State Department estimates that the ERP will yield about 875 calories per capita for human consumption or about 35 per cent of urban per capita consumption.

NOTES

[4] The reader should compare a preliminary discussion of this problem in Chapter 1, pp. 46–47.

[5] R. Harrod, *Are These Hardships Necessary?* p. 61 and Chapters II, III, IV, and V. Cf. also Chapter I, pp. 36–41, where British views on overinvestment are discussed fully.

[6] *Harriman*, pp. C-8 – C-10; *ERP State*, pp. 35–36.

[7] The next ten paragraphs are based largely on my article "Dollar Scarcity," *E. J.*, June, 1947.

[8] These figures for gold, unlike those given later, are not adjusted to a uniform $35 value for gold.

[9] For early discussion of the phenomenon of dollar scarcity the reader should consult C. Kindleberger in S. E. Harris (ed.), *Postwar Economic Problems*, (1943), pp. 379–95; also see U. S. Dept. of Commerce, *United States in the World Economy* (1943).

[10] U. S. Board of Governors, Federal Reserve System, *Banking and Monetary Statistics*, (1943), p. 536. (The price of gold was $20.67 per ounce through January 1934 and $35 thereafter.)

[11] *Banking and Monetary Statistics*, p. 34, and *F.R.B.*, November 1944, p. 1046. These figures are, of course, subject to some margin of error; but they clearly indicate the big movements.

[12] In his *Tract on Monetary Reform* (pp. 167–69, 173–76, 199–204) Lord Keynes saw the wisdom of the United States policy better than other European economists, although even he failed to note the large monetary inflation developing. Even in the *Treatise on Money* (II, 306) Keynes defended the United States policy of sterilization and also stressed the gold absorption power of the United States which was related to the unusual expansion of deposits (II, 259). When the British finally were driven off gold, however, Keynes made his most severe criticism of American and French monetary policy, which had contributed so importantly to British restrictive measures (*Essays in Persuasion*, 292–93). Except for his most recent statements, Keynes over the years was well aware of the problem of chronic shortages of gold or dollars. In the *Revision of the Treaty* (pp. 159–62) he emphasized the difficulties confronting the United States in balancing its commercial accounts. In the interwar period he again and again urged extreme measures for dealing with the gold shortages facing the United Kingdom (for example, *Persuasion*, pp. 284–87), and brought home to all that there had been long periods of disequilibrium (*Treatise* I, 347).

[13] *Banking and Monetary Statistics*, p. 19.

[14] *Banking and Monetary Statistics*, p. 481; *F.R.B.*, November 1944, p. IIII.

[15] U. S. Dept. of Labor, *Handbook of Labor Statistics*, 1941 edition, vol.

EUROPEAN RECOVERY PROGRAM

II, *Wages and Wage Regulation*, p. 13; cf. F. C. Mills, *Economic Tendencies in the United States* (1932), pp. 384–404.

[16] Dept. of Commerce, *United States in the World Economy*, p. 89, and Table I.

[17] *United States in the World Economy*, Table I; cf. Lord Keynes, *E.J.*, June 1946, pp. 174–178.

[18] Reference was made earlier to Harrod's appraisal of dollar shortage. Professor Haberler also presents with some effectiveness the case against dollar shortage, a case which rests primarily on the assumption that the shortage results from inflationary policies of European countries and that recourse to the classical medicine would generally correct the situation. Professor Haberler also contends that the adverse balance of payments on current account in the interwar period was manageable; but he arrives at this conclusion only by excluding the large exports of capital from this country in the twenties, as part of the magnitudes involved and by deducting from the inflow of gold in the thirties the inflow of short-term capital. Surely he underestimates the difficulties involved in achieving the required cost, price, and demand adjustments, though he rightly emphasizes the importance of political resistance to taking appropriate action. See Professor Haberler's essay (and my comments — Chapter 1) in S. E. Harris (ed.), *Foreign Economic Relations of the United States*. A view similar to Professor Haberler's is also well expressed in F. A. Lutz, *The Marshall Plan and European Economic Policy* (1948), pp. 3–12.

[19] *EC Europe: Survey*, p. 63.

[20] *NAC*, p. 168. Total *government transfers* amounted to $12.6 billion. Cf. *CEA*, pp. 7, 14, 15, 92–102.

CHAPTER 5

[1] Cf. Chapter 1, pp. 48–49 for a preliminary discussion of this problem.

[2] Cf. C. Gutt and A. G. B. Fisher in S. E. Harris (ed.), *Foreign Economic Policy for the United States*.

[3] Cf. Chapter 1, pp. 48–49 for an argument in support of this position; also cf. Lutz, *The Marshall Plan and European Economic Policy*, pp. 4–11.

[4] Cf. *ERP: House Hear.*, pp. 410–11, 455–460.

[5] *CEEC*, I, 121–22.

[6] Chapter 1, p. 49.

[7] Chapter 1, pp. 50–51.

[8] Cf. Chapter 6, pp. 123–124.

[9] *ERP State*, p. 70.

[10] *CEEC*, I, 122.

NOTES

[11] *ERP: Sen. Hear., passim.*
[12] *Harriman*, pp. L3b, L8–L10; *ERP State*, pp. 93–96.
[13] *Harriman*, pp. C11–12, M3–M11; *ERP State*, pp. 47–48.

CHAPTER 6

[1] For an early espousal of the dollar shortage thesis, see S. E. Harris (ed.), *The New Economics* (1947), pp. 261, 293.
[2] Some may even be content with reading only the last section.
[3] *See* pp. 52–57.
[4] *CEEC*, I, 108–09; *ERP: Sen. Hear.*, p. 79.
[5] Chapter 1, pp. 49–51, and Chapter 5, pp. 116–119.
[6] See especially *EC Europe: Survey*, pp. 30, 59; *CEA*, pp. 88, 90; *ERP: Sen. Hear.*, p. 79–80; *CEEC*, I, 52; *ERP: State*, p. 70.
[7] *EC Europe: Survey*, p. 32.
[8] Cf. *CEEC*, I, 54, 112, 118; *Harriman*, Parts I–II, p. L10, and Part III, pp. R1–R2; *ERP: Sen. Hear.*, pp. 419–20.
[9] *CEEC*, I, 132–134. "This system would make it possible to abandon the existing procedure for a bilateral balance of trade, and to deal only with the disequilibrium of the trade of a given country in relation to other countries of Europe taken together."
[10] Cf. *ERP: Sen. Hear.*, p. 427.
[11] *EC Europe: Survey*, pp. 36–37.
[12] *ERP Sen. Docs.*, pp. 24–25.
[13] *CEA*, p. 7.
[14] *Ec. Rep. Pres.*, p. 92.
[15] *CEA*, pp. 12, 15.
[16] *CEA*, p. 83.
[17] *CEA*, p. 83.
[18] *CEA*, pp. 93, 95. For the two and a half years ending December 31, 1947, the ERP countries received $11.7 billion of assistance from this country. *F.R.B.*, February 1948, p. 138.
[19] *NAC*, pp. 57, 65–66.
[20] *F.R.B.*, April 1948, pp. 376, 378.
[21] *NAC*, pp. 51–57.
[22] Data in this paragraph from *CEEC*, I, 42–44.
[23] Data in this paragraph from *CEEC*, I, 51–53.
[24] Data from *CEEC*, I, 54–56.
[25] *CEEC*, I, 112–113.
[26] *Harriman*, pp. L1–L12, cf. also *ERP: House Hear.*, II, 1504.
[27] *ERP State*, pp. 36–37.

EUROPEAN RECOVERY PROGRAM

[28] *ERP State*, pp. 42–43.
[29] *ERP State*, p. 44.
[30] Cf. again *ERP: Sen. Hear.*, III, 1003–1008 and *ERP: House Hear.*, II, 1504. These explain the differences in estimates.
[31] Cf. *ERP State*, pp. 75–91.
[32] *ERP: Sen. Hear.*, III, 1007–1021.
[33] *NAC*, p. 177.
[34] *CEA*, p. 62.

PART THREE — INTRODUCTION

[1] *ERP: Sen. Hear.*, pp. 58–59, 276, 320–321; Senate Banking Committee: *Hearings on National Stabilization* (1948), I, 140–143; also cf. my statement, *ibid.*, II, 575–581.
[2] *ERP: House Rep.*, p. 31.
[3] *Budget for Fiscal Year 1949*, p. A4; *Ec. Rep. Pres.*, pp. 31–119.
[4] House Select Committee on Foreign Aid, *Inflation and Methods of Financing Foreign Aid* (January 1948), pp. 7–11; *ERP: House Rep.*, pp. 32–33.
[5] *S.C.B.*, March 1948, p. 19; *ERP: Sen. Hear.*, pp. 256, 280.
[6] *ERP: Sen Hear.*, p. 252.
[7] *ERP: Sen. Hear.*, pp. 315–25; *F. A. Act*, S. 112.
[8] Cf. *ERP: Sen. Hear.*, pp. 40–41; *ERP: Sen. Rep.*, pp. 36–37; *ERP: House Rep.*, p. 35; *F. A. Act*, S. 111 (a), (2). See especially evidence of CIO and Mr. Joseph Curran of the National Maritime Union, *ERP: Sen. Hear.*, III, 1303, 1314–23; also *ERP: House Hear.*, II, 1516–17, 2264–81. Here the fear that transfers may result in losses of jobs is revealed; and also the conflict of views of Secretary Forrestal who saw no serious effects of transfers on defense, and the Maritime Commission, which strongly opposed them.
[9] *ERP Sen. Hear.*, III, pp. 1220–21.
[10] Cf. *ERP: Sen. Hear.*, pp. 274, 329.
[11] Senate American Small Business Committee, Interim Report on *Steel Supply and Distribution Problems*, Sen. Rep. No. 825 (January 1948), p. 11.
[12] House Select Committee on Foreign Aid, *United States Steel Requirements and Availabilities*, Preliminary Report Six (1947).
[13] *State Dept. Est. Imp., etc.*, pp. 6–7.
[14] *ERP: Sen. Hear.*, pp. 219–20, 359–67, 380–81. Cf. *Petroleum Requirements and Availabilities*, Preliminary Report Five of House Select Committee on Foreign Aid (1947).
[15] *ERP: Sen. Hear.*, p. 297.

NOTES

CHAPTER 7

[1] Cf. the excellent statement by Dr. Bissell, where he explains the overall differences largely by varying coverage and techniques for financing goods on order but not shipped. He also describes disagreements on components. *ERP: House Hear.*, p. 1504.

[2] *ERP State*, pp. 100, 111; *CEEC*, I, 51–54; and *ERP: Sen. Hear.*, pp. 1002–1003.

[3] *ERP: Sen. Docs.*, pp. 74–75; *CEEC*, I, 41, 52–53; for an official explanation of procedure see *ERP: House Hear.*, pp. 1346–1348, 1514. The United States Government checked on the CEEC estimates by studying past trade and output figures.

[4] Cf. State Department: *Proposed Distribution*, April 18, 1948, p. 7. The British allocation was reduced 1½ per cent of the total of $6702 million, and the French and Italian increased by ½ per cent each.

[5] *ERP: Sen. Hear.*, p. 1005; *CEEC*, I, 53; and *Final Report House*, p. 90; *State Dept. Est. Bal. Payments*, p. 2.

[6] The State Department indicated the manner of estimating the cost of ERP. "In food, requirements included calories needed by the urban worker both to sustain life and to provide sufficient energy to enable him to work effectively . . . In addition to calories, attention was paid to the minimum basic needs for protein and fats and oils. And finally, the historic differences between standards of living among the countries of Europe, as well as the practical limitations on increasing consumption standards rapidly, were taken into account. As indicated below, availabilities, especially at the start of the program, are far short of the screened requirements.

"In items other than food, requirements were derived in part from the physical requirements of reconstruction and in part from the interrelations of production programs . . ." *ERP: Sen. Hear.*, p. 1456.

Assistant Secretary Thorp of the State Department said it was necessary to provide the aid which would bring the ERP countries back to approximately prewar standards and would cover deficits in the balance of payments. *ERP: House Hear.*, p. 82.

[7] For several countries, the percentages in columns 2 and 3 are raised somewhat by the inclusion of dependencies in the allotment figures.

[8] *State Dept. Proposed Distribution*, p. 7; and *State Dept. Est. Bal. Payments*, p. 3.

[9] *ERP: Sen. Hear.*, p. 116.

[10] *ERP: Sen. Hear.*, pp. 95, 132–33, 220–21, and 1003; also see *ERP: House Hear.*, pp. 2196–97, where the State Department suggests that the estimate of $700 million of aid from the executive branch was excessive.

EUROPEAN RECOVERY PROGRAM

[11] For more recent estimates which do not, however, invalidate the generalizations, see State Dept. *Est. Bal. Payments*, p. 2.
[12] Cf. *ERP: Sen. Hear.*, p. 113.
[13] *ERP: Sen. Hear.*, pp. 271–72; cf. also pp. 1007–08.
[14] *ERP: Sen. Rep.*, pp. 48–49.
[15] *ERP: Sen. Rep.*, p. 46.
[16] *ERP: House Rep.*, pp. 18–22; *ERP: Sen. Hear.*, p. 1003.
[17] *ERP: Sen. Hear.*, p. 495.
[18] *ERP: House Rep.*, p. 36; *ERP: Sen. Hear.*, pp. 64–66, 290–93.
[19] "The character and purpose of the assistance" is not defined, nor is its relation to the last sentence clarified.
[20] *ERP: Sen. Rep.*, p. 48; cf. *ERP: Sen. Hear.*, p. 176. For Ambassador Douglas the primary criterion is capacity to pay; the secondary, the purpose for which the loan is made.
[21] Cf. Ch 2, pp. 71–75.
[22] *ERP: Sen. Hear.*, pp. 117–118.
[23] The impatient reader may prefer to skip pp. 168–171, which deals in some detail with reconciling aid under the ERP according to conflicting criteria.
[24] Under revised allocations, the United States reduces its exports of oil and iron and steel and increases grain exports; cf. *State Dept. Est. Imp., etc.*, pp. 6–7.

CHAPTER 8

[1] *ERP: House Hear.*, pp. 775–776.
[2] 3(b) – 2 (b) in table.
[3] Cf. the opening chapter, "Highlights," pp. 16–18. There the excessive burden proposed for the other Americas is discussed.
[4] *ERP State*, p. 93.
[5] *ERP State*, p. 55.
[6] Cf. the sensible views of Congressman Herter; *ERP: House Hear.*, II, 1858.
[7] Cf. *ERP State*, pp. 44–45.
[8] *ERP: House Hear.*, II, 1658–1661, 1852.
[9] The State Department discusses the reasons for special conditions for ERP loans by the Export-Import Bank under the FA Act. *ERP: House Hear.*, II, 2201; *FA Act*, Sec. 111 (c) (2).
[10] For a discussion of the problems raised by relying upon the Export-Import Bank and the International Bank, see especially *Harriman*, pp. M5–M7; *ERP State*, pp. 45–47 and House Committee on Foreign Aid,

NOTES

Comparative Analysis of Suggested Plans of Foreign Aid (1947), pp. 14–16. (One problem raised is the subservience of the Export-Import and the International Bank to the ECA.)

[11] *Harriman*, pp. M8–M9.

[12] *Proposed Principles and Organization for any Program of Foreign Aid*, p. 9.

[13] *ERP State*, pp. 49–50.

[14] *ERP: House Hear.*, I, 268; II, 1436.

[15] *ERP: House Hear.*, p. 1853.

[16] *National Income and Expenditure of the United Kingdom, 1947* (1948) Cmd. 7371, p. 5.

[17] House Select Committee on Foreign Aid, *Foreign Aid and Exhaustion of National Resources in Relation to a Stock Piling Program* (November 22, 1947), pp. 1–11.

CHAPTER 9

[1] Figures from *CEA*, p. 7; *Harriman*, p. 9; and *ERP State*, pp. 39, 42–43.

[2] Cf. pp. 214–220.

[3] The political issues are well put in *Harriman*, Parts one and two, Section B; cf. Chapter 2 of this volume.

[4] Parts of the remainder of this chapter are based on a statement and evidence by the writer before the Senate Committee on Banking and Currency, *Hearings on National Stabilization* (January 1948), Part 2, pp. 559–581. The reader should also consult *Joint Economic Report*, Report of the Joint Committee on Economic Report (May 18, 1948), especially pp. 2–9, 21–31.

[5] For 1947 the rise was $4.3 billion. *F.R.B.*, May 1948, p. 536.

[6] See *F.R.B.*, December 1947, pp. 1455–68; cf. *Joint Economic Report*, May 1948, pp. 23–26.

[7] In a later section, I discuss briefly the relation of the budget and the ERP.

[8] Cf. *Joint Economic Report*, pp. 28–31.

[9] *CEA*, pp. 68–70; *Harriman*, pp. N10–N11; House Select Committee on Foreign Aid, (1) *Inflation and Methods of Financing any Foreign Aid Program*, especially pp. 6–7; and (2) *Governmental Control Powers Affecting the Foreign-Aid Program* (1948), pp. 7–12, and S. 1873 (Senator Capehart), S. 1888 (Senator Barkley), S. 1923 (Senator Taylor), and S. 1967 (Senator Morse); Hearings, Senate Banking and Currency Committee, *National Stabilization* (948), Parts 1 and 2.

EUROPEAN RECOVERY PROGRAM

[10] *Governmental Control Powers Affecting the Foreign-Aid Program*, pp. 11–12.
[11] See my *Price and Related Controls in the United States*, (1944), Chapter XV.
[12] *Governmental Control Affecting Foreign-Aid Program*, pp. 26–27.
[13] *ERP: Sen. Hear.*, p. 297.
[14] See the excellent statement by Edwin George, *ERP: House Hear.*, II, 1767–1778.
[15] For the full argument, see *Hearings on National Stabilization* (1948), pp. 579–80.
[16] *The Budget of the U. S. Government for Fiscal Year Ending June 30, 1949*, p. A4.
[17] In such a period, the case for tying our grants to exports from this country is stronger than in 1947.

CHAPTER 10

[1] The reader will find very useful analyses of commodities in short supply in *Final Report on Foreign Aid*.
[2] For a brief and preliminary discussion see the introduction to this part.
[3] *ERP State*, pp. 115–118.
[4] *ERP State*, p. 89.
[5] *ERP: Sen. Hear.*, pp. 319ff.
[6] *ERP: Sen. Hear.*, p. 319.
[7] *ERP: Sen. Hear.*, pp. 340–341.
[8] *ERP State*, pp. 38–39; *S.C.B.*, May 1948, p. 4.
[9] *CEA*, pp. 21–25.
[10] *Governmental Control Powers Affecting the Foreign-Aid Program*, p. 23.
[11] This section is based primarily on *CEEC*, Chapters 3, 6; *ERP State*, pp. 75–77, 84–87; *Harriman*, Chapter E; *Commodity Report, ERP*, Chapter A (1948); *Report of Cabinet Committee on World Food Programs* (September 22, 1947); reprinted in *ERP: Sen. Docs.*, pp. 127–131.
[12] See Table 30.
[13] *ERP Com. Rep.*, p. A1.
[14] *ERP State*, p. 84.
[15] Especially *State Dept. Est. Imp. etc.*, pp. 6–7; also see *State Dept, Est. Bal. Payments* and *State Dept. Proposed Distribution*.
[16] *ERP: Sen. Docs.*, p. 129; cf. however, *ERP: Sen. Hear.*, pp. 310–311. Exports of bread grains were 2 million tons higher in 1947–48; but of all grains, 1½ million tons less.

NOTES

[17] *ERP Com. Rep.*, p. A19.
[18] *ERP Com. Rep.*, pp. A23–A38.
[19] *ERP Com. Rep.*, pp. A28–A33.
[20] *ERP Com. Rep.*, pp. A33–A39; *Agricultural Outlook Charts* (1948), pp. 26–27.
[21] *ERP Com. Rep.*, pp. A41–A55.
[22] *ERP Com. Rep.*, pp. A58–A63; and *Agricultural Outlook Charts* (1947), pp. 43, 47.
[23] *ERP State*, pp. 77–80, 87–89; *ERP Com. Rep.*, Chapter G, "Petroleum," pp. 1–43, tables and appendix; and *Harriman*, Chapter G.
[24] *ERP Com. Rep.*, pp. G36–G37.
[25] *ERP Com. Rep.*, p. G1.
[26] *ERP Com. Rep.*, pp. G1, G11, G13.
[27] *ERP Com. Rep.*, pp. G3, G16.
[28] *ERP Com. Rep.*, p. G2.
[29] *ERP Com. Rep.*, pp. G2, G3.
[30] *ERP Com. Rep.*, pp. G29–G30.
[31] *ERP: Com. Rep. (Iron and Steel)*, pp. H1–H6 and H22–H27.
[32] *ERP Com. Rep.*, pp. H10–H12; and *Harriman*, p. F7.
[33] *ERP: Com. Rep.* H16–H19.

CHAPTER 11

[1] *CEEC*, Vol. I, especially pp. 11–25 and Vol. II.
[2] *CEEC*, I, 11.
[3] *CEEC*, I, 11.
[4] *CEEC*, I, 54–56.
[5] Especially *Harriman*, Chapters C and L; *ERP State*, especially pp. 28–36 and 69–83.
[6] *ERP State*, p. 75.
[7] *ERP State*, pp. 75–76.
[8] *ERP State*, pp. 75–83.
[9] Cf. opening Chapter, pp. 20–21.
[10] *ERP State*, pp. 54, 55.
[11] *CEEC*, I, 56; *ERP State*, p. 112.
[12] *Harriman*, p. L8.
[13] *State Dept. Est. Imp. etc.*, p. 7; *ERP Sen. Hear.*, III, 1007–1008; *ERP State*, pp. 111–112.
[14] *ERP State*, pp. 70–74.
[15] *ERP State*, pp. 71–75; *Harriman*, pp. C6–C15; *ERP: Sen. Hear.*, III, 1006–1007; cf. pp. 35–41 of this book.

EUROPEAN RECOVERY PROGRAM

[16] Based on materials in *NAC*, pp. 131, 135–136, and unpublished sources by E. M. Doblin; cf. *ERP Sen. Hear.*, III, 1005.

[17] *CEEC*, I, 51–53.

[18] U. N., *Economic Report, 1945–1947*, p. 124.

[19] Improvement continued in 1948.

[20] *Economic Report, 1945–1947*, pp. 134–141.

[21] *EC Europe: Survey*, p. 9.

[22] *Economic Report, 1945–1947*, pp. 148–49.

[23] *Economic Report, 1945–1947*, p. 149.

[24] *Economic Report, 1945–1947*, p. 193.

[25] The reader will find a brief discussion of inflation, and in particular, the effects on output, distribution, government, and trade in pp. 41–45.

[26] Based on materials in *Economic Report, 1945–1947*, pp. 158–168, and *Monthly Bulletin of Statistics*, February 1948.

[27] *Economic Report*, pp. 166–67.

[28] I have relied especially on the following: Executive Branch, *ERP Country Studies: The United Kingdom;* H. M. S., *Economic Survey for 1947* (1947); *Economic Survey for 1948* (1948); *National Income and Expenditure of the United Kingdom, 1938 to 1946* (April 1947); *Capital Investment in 1948* (December 1947); House Select Committee on Foreign Aid, *Report on the United Kingdom* (March 7, 1948); U. N., *Survey of Current Inflationary and Deflationary Tendencies* (September 1947).

[29] *National Income and Expenditure of the U. K., 1938 to 1946*, pp. 18–19; *Economic Survey for 1948*, p. 45.

[30] See especially p. 32.

[31] *ERP Country Studies: The United Kingdom*, p. 3; U. N., *Survey of Current Inflationary and Deflationary Tendencies*, p. 24.

[32] Cf. my introduction to *Foreign Economic Relations of the United States*.

[33] *Survey of Current Inflationary and Deflationary Tendencies*, p. 26. Cf. Chapter 1, pp. 42–43, where it is suggested that these statistics exaggerate the redistribution effected.

[34] U. N., *Monthly Bulletin of Statistics*, February 1948, pp. 141, 151.

[35] *Economic Survey for 1948*, p. 52.

[36] *ERP Country Studies: United Kingdom*, pp. 15–16.

[37] *Economic Survey for 1948*, pp. 48–50; *Survey of Current Inflationary and Deflationary Tendencies*, p. 27; *Capital Investment in 1948*, p. 5.

[38] *Economic Survey for 1948*, pp. 7–17, 56–57.

[39] *Ibid.*, pp. 32–37.

[40] *Economic Survey for 1947 (The Battle for Output)*, p. 27; *Economic Survey for 1948*, p. 9.

[41] *ERP Country Studies: France*, p. 75.

[42] *ERP Country Studies: France*, pp. 12–18; U. N., *Survey of Current*

NOTES

Inflationary and Deflationary Tendencies, pp. 39–41; *Monthly Bulletin of Statistics*, February 1948, p. 25.

[43] *Survey of Current Inflationary and Deflationary Tendencies*, p. 43; *Monthly Bulletin of Statistics*, February 1948.

[44] IMF: *International Financial Statistics*, January 1948, pp. 62–63; *ERP Country Studies: France*, pp. 25–26, 68–78.

[45] *Survey of Current Inflationary and Deflationary Tendencies*, p. 42.

[46] *ERP Country Studies: France*, pp. 20–22, 60–62.

[47] *ERP Country Studies: France*, pp. 40–59.

[48] Especially *ERP Country Studies: Italy*, and *Survey of Current Inflationary and Deflationary Tendencies*, pp. 44–53.

[49] *ERP Country Studies: Italy*, p. 51.

[50] *Survey of Current Inflationary and Deflationary Tendencies*, pp. 47–48.

[51] *ERP Country Studies: Italy*, pp. 9–10.

[52] *Survey of Current Inflationary and Deflationary Tendencies*, pp. 47–52; and *ERP Country Studies: Italy*, pp. 15, 16, 50.

[53] *ERP Country Studies: Italy*, pp. 25–42.

[54] *ERP Country Studies: Germany*, p. 18.

[55] *Harriman*, Part III, pp. Q1–Q2, and *ERP Country Studies: Western Germany*, pp. 49–51; *CEEC*, I, 53.

[56] See especially U. S. State Department, *United States Economic Policy Towards Germany, 1946; JCS 1067: Directive to Commander in Chief of United States Forces of Occupation Regarding the Military Government of Germany* (April 1945); *The Potsdam Agreement* (Released August 2, 1946); *Plan of Allied Control Council for Reparations and the Level of Post-War German Economy* (April 1, 1946); *State Department Bulletin*, July 15, 1947, No. 582; Office of Military Government for Germany, *A Year of Potsdam* (1946); The U. S. Strategic Bombing Survey, *The Effects of Strategic Bombing on the German War Economy* (October 1945); *Harriman*, Part III, p. Q2; J. K. Galbraith in S. E. Harris (ed.), *Foreign Economic Relations of the United States*.

[57] Based on *ERP Country Studies: Western Germany*, pp. 1–28.

[58] *ERP Country Studies: Western Germany*, pp. 29–45.

[59] *ERP Country Studies: The Netherlands*.

[60] The reader should compare variations in estimates by executive branch. *ERP State*, pp. 100, 111.

Postscript

THE FIRST SIX MONTHS OF THE ECA

On the whole, the ERP has progressed reasonably well in the period of almost six months that has passed since the passage of the Foreign Assistance Act of 1948. The fact that total production in Europe, both on the farm and in industry, advanced in the latter part of 1947 and the first half of 1948 has contributed to the favorable developments in the ERP. On the credit side we should also mention the able personnel chosen by Messrs. Hoffman, Harriman, and Bissell to operate the ECA. Recent developments do not, however, suggest that Europe is reconciled to interference by the United States in her internal affairs, or that much progress has been made in contending with inflation, or with the adverse balance of payments.

First, we comment on output. In the last quarter of 1947, according to the United Nations (*Selected World Economic Indices* — issued in July 1948), world agricultural output was but 93 (1938 = 100) and industrial output, 130–135. For the world, exclusive of the United States, the latter figure is 97. For most Western European countries, late 1947 and (a fortiori early 1948) industrial output greatly exceeded that of the prewar period. For thirteen ERP countries, industrial output (unweighted mean) in 1947 exceeded that of 1946 by 15 per cent; but food production in 1946–47 was still 11 per cent below the prewar level. In the early months of 1948, British industrial output was running one-fourth to one-fifth in excess of 1946, and output in the crucial coal and steel industries was very satisfactory. In Italy, however, national income (stable currency) in 1947 was but 77 per cent of that in

EUROPEAN RECOVERY PROGRAM

1938; and industrial output in France and Germany was below the prewar figure.

Inflation remains a crucial problem. Undoubtedly, the high level of investments is a factor. Five of the ERP countries used 27 per cent of their gross product for investment in 1947, as compared with 18 per cent in 1938.

Even the United Kingdom suffered a rise of prices: the increase was 9 per cent in the first half of 1948. A doubling in the cost of social security with the introduction of a comprehensive program in July 1948, and a food subsidy program costing about £ 470 million annually (20 per cent of the average earnings of workers), will make control of inflation more difficult. In France, the wholesale price level increased almost 40 per cent in the first six months of 1948, and the cost of living, 20 per cent. Despite anticipated aid of 150 billion francs from the ERP and despite a moderation of their investment program, the French expect a budgetary deficit of 200 billion francs in the current fiscal year. Even Italy, successful in stabilizing her price level in the first half of 1948, faces a rising budgetary deficit. On the other hand, many of the smaller countries seem to have the inflationary situation under control. Seven ERP countries suffered a rise in wholesale prices of less than 2 per cent in the first quarter of 1948.

Related to the domestic inflation is the failure of the international accounts to improve. The crucial importance of the British situation explains my concentration on it; but one has but to read Mr. Reynaud's statement of August 19, 1948, on the French budgetary situation, the absence of savings, the excessive investment, to realize that Britain is not alone. In the first six months of 1948, the British adverse balance on trade account was substantially below the 1947 deficit, but much in excess of the planned deficit; and that despite a diversion of imports from hard-currency countries. The difficulty was not a failure to realize export plans but rather the high value of imports, to which a rise of 10 per cent in

POSTSCRIPT

import prices in the first six months of 1948 contributed. (The rise was but 3 per cent for export prices.) Sir Stafford Cripps warned the country that only £ 300–400 million would be available in 1948 to meet the adverse balance, whereas in 1947 the country had consumed £ 1,000 billion of reserves and loans. It is no wonder that the *Economist* wrote of a permanent dollar shortage and Mr. Hawtrey urged a rise in the dollar value of the pound sterling, both as a means of improving the terms of trade and of freeing the British economy from the inflationary effects of rising prices in the United States.

Little progress was made on the cooperation front. European experts are not so enthusiastic as in July 1947. In a dispatch to the *New York Times of* September 12, 1948, Mr. Michael Hoffman reminds us of the failure to achieve much cooperation.

Resentment against intrusion in Europe's internal affairs by the United States persists. Thus the British *Banker's Magazine* in June 1948 warned American experts, overenthusiastic in urging European devaluation, to await internal monetary reforms. In a dispatch to the *New York Times* of August 1, 1948, Harold Callender from Paris reminded the American public that Europe was balking at planning imposed by the ECA. On the very next day, the Vienna correspondent of the *New York Times* informed us that the Austrian National Bank was annoyed with the release of large amounts of schillings by the ECA, with attendant inflationary effects.

Finally, there is the problem of alloting the aid. After months of wrangling, on September 11, 1948, the Office of European Economic Cooperation (OEEC), entrusted with the responsibility of dividing ERP funds, subject to approval by ECA, announced its distribution schedule. The allotment to Germany and the use of ERP funds to finance intra-European trade were the most perplexing problems.

It is interesting that, except for a large reduction of aid to Ger-

EUROPEAN RECOVERY PROGRAM

many, the distribution of the OEEC conformed closely to that of the executive branch made in the latter part of 1947. The percentage of the total aid distributed in 1948-49 to the five most important countries follows:

	15-Month Period — Executive Branch (Late 1947)	12-Month Period — OEEC September, 1948
United Kingdom	25.7	25.8
France	21.0	20.4
Germany — Trizonia	14.5	10.6
Italy	12.7	12.3
Netherlands	10.3	10.2

(Sources: Page 165, above, and *New York Times*, September 12, 1948.)

In summary, the probable outcome of the ERP is almost as beclouded late in September as it was early in April 1948. The most perplexing unknown is the course of inflation, both in Europe and in the United States. A solution of the inflation problem will contribute greatly to that of production and to that of dollar scarcity. Finally, we shall have to practice continued caution, in our interference in domestic European problems. It needs scarcely to be added how important are Russian policy and, in general, the clarification of the political situation.

Index

Acheson, Dean, quoted on Russian interference with recovery, 61
Administration, of ERP, 80–82
Agricultural machinery, exports of, to ERP countries, 208, 210
Agricultural markets, ERP and, 221–228
Agriculture, European production, 33, 250–251
Allocations, need for, in anti-inflationary attack, 146–147, 197–198
Anderson, Clinton P., 144, 148, 273; quoted on ERP exports and prices, 214–216
Anti-inflation, need for program of, in United States, 146–147
Argentina, noncooperation in ERP, 65–66
Austin, Warren R., 64
Austria, 247; inflation, 19; per capita income, 88, 90; food production and requirements, 96; multilateral payment arrangement, 125; ERP aid, 165; national income, 248

Balance of payments, European deficit, 20–24, 53, 247–248, 272–273; effect of U. S. inflation, 50–51; financing of, 51–52, 126–132; causes of deficit, 122–126, 139; Paris program and revisions, 132–139; factors summarized, 139–142; in allocation of ERP funds, 156–163. See also Trade deficit.
Baldwin, Raymond, 178

Bank of France, gold holdings, 111
Belgium, inflation, 19, 191; ratio of imports and foreign assistance, 55; exports to United States, 56; per capita income, 88, 89–90; industrial production, 92, 93; multilateral payments arrangement, 125; factors in ERP aid, 157, 158, 160, 165; financing of imports, 169; agricultural output, 250; cost of living, 251
Bissell, Dr. Richard, 163
Bizonal Germany, financing of imports, 169; trends in economic recovery, 247, 266–269. See also Germany, Western Germany
Board of Economic Warfare, 82
Bridges, Styles, 81
Budget, United States, and ERP, 203–205
Bulgaria, 70; changing pattern of trade, 56

Caloric intake, United States and ERP countries, 221–222
Canada, repercussion of ERP, 65
Capital movements, United States long-term, 105–106
Capitalism, ERP as support of, 15–16
CEA. See Council of Economic Advisers
CEEC. See Committee of European Economic Cooperation
Chemicals, 199
China, 64

[301]

INDEX

Coal, exports of, to ERP countries, 208, 209, 210; European requirements, 228–229
Committee of European Economic Cooperation, 7, 13, 18, 21, 67, 116, 117, 118, 119, 123, 124, 125, 179; estimates governing aid to Europe, 134–139, 150–152, 155, 158, 163; import programs, 209–214; agricultural program, 222; objectives, 242–247
Commodity Report, ERP, 226
Communism, ERP as weapon against, 6, 16, 60–63, 173, 272
Consumption, ERP countries, 251; United Kingdom, 253–255
Controls, U. S. imposition of, in Europe, 11–12; in operation of ERP, 197–203, 207
Conversion rates, 89
Cooperation, of ERP countries, 75–80
Cost of living, in ERP countries, 251–252
Cotton, 148; exports of, to participating countries, 208, 210
Council of Economic Advisers, 123, 141, 198
Credit. *See* Money and credit
Credits and grants, 1914–1947, 104–106
Cripps, Sir Stafford, 47
Cripps program, 257
Crisis of 1947, background of, 85–86
Currencies, overvaluation, 48–49, 110–112; French devaluation policy, 78, 114–116; local, under ERP, 79, 179–184; hard and soft, 99, 124. *See also* Foreign exchange
Customs unions, in ERP countries, 78–79

Czechoslovakia, 70; investment program, 36; exports to United States, 56; dollar income, 88, 90; inflation, 191; cost of living, 251; monetary purge, 252

Dairy products, 228; exports of, to ERP countries, 208, 210
Deficits. *See* Trade deficit
Demand, potential deficiency of, in United States, 149; reduction of, as solution to inflation, 192
Denmark, inflationary problem, 44; changing pattern of trade, 56, 57; dollar income, 88, 90; industrial production, 92, 93; multilateral payment arrangement, 125; ERP aid, 157, 159, 160, 161
Depression, unlikelihood of, in United States, 60–61
Disinvestment, European, 34–35. *See also* Investment
Dollar shortage, problem of, 46–47, 96–99, 106–108; defined, 99–101; United States gold stock, 101–103; motivating factors, 103–104
Douglas, Lewis, 31, 35, 163, 181

Eastern Europe, ERP in trade with Western Europe, 67–71; interwar period, 86. *See also* Europe
ECA. *See* European Cooperation Administration
Eccles, Marriner S., 194
ECE. *See* Economic Commission for Europe
Economic Commission for Europe, 105, 123
Economic Journal, 103
Economic relations, international: dollar scarcity, 46–47; unrealistic exchange rates, 48–49; terms of trade and import prices, 49–51;

INDEX

financing deficit in balance of payments, 51–52; variations among countries, 52–57; summary, 57–59
Economist, London, 191
Elliott, W. Y., 147
Energy sources, outlays under ERP, 228–232
England. *See* United Kingdom
ERP. *See* European Recovery Program
ERP countries, production, 8; inflation problem, 18–20, 272; trade deficits, 21–23, 51–52, 247–248; national income, 31–33, 248; terms of trade, 49; changing patterns of trade, 56–57; cooperation with ERP, 75–80; balance of payments, 122–123, 272–273; exports among, 125; gold, dollar balances, and investments in United States, 130–131; import requirements, 132; recovery goals, 241–242; objectives of CEEC, 242–247; industrial output, 248–250; agricultural output, 250–251; consumption, 251; cost of living, 251–252. *See also* Europe *and* countries by name
Europe, inflation problem, 18–20, 42–43; trade deficit, 20–24, 132–135; industrial output, 30–31, 91–94, 127; national income, 31–33, 86–91, 93–94; disinvestment abroad, 34–35; investment programs, 36–41; international economic position, 46–59; terms of trade, 49–51, 123–124; balance of payments, 50–51, 53; financing of trade deficits, 51–52; import and export trade, 54, 124, 130; ratio of imports and foreign assistance, 55; changing patterns of trade, 56–57; interwar period and 1947 crisis, 85–86; ratio of taxes to income, 88, 90–91; need for recovery program, 95–96; dollar shortage, 96–99; ratio of exports to production, 126; estimates governing aid to, 135–139. *See also* Eastern Europe, ERP countries *and* countries by name
European Cooperation Administration, 15, 72, 74, 75, 78, 82
European Recovery Program, nature of, 3–5; objectives, 5–6; potential contributions, 6–7; pitfalls, 9–18; inflation problem, 13–14, 18–20, 145–148, 185, 189–190; European trade deficit, 20–24; problems summarized, 24–25; as weapon against communism, 60–64, 173, 272; repercussions on nonparticipating countries, 64–66; problem of re-exports, 66–67; in West-East European trade, 67–71; as weapon against socialism, 71–75; administration, 80–82; ratio of payments to income and imports, 95; estimates governing aid, 134–139, 150–152, 155, 158, 163; controls in operation of, 146–147, 158–164, 197–203, 207; as subsidizing program, 148–149; impact on particular markets, 150–153; effects on distribution of United States exports, 152–154; standards of aid, 155–158, 173; loans and capacity to repay, 164–166; import structure and manner of financing, 166–171; costs to United States, 173–176; method of purchasing, 176–177; question of goods or dollars, 177–178; problems of finance summarized, 178–179; control of local currency,

[303]

INDEX

179–184; national income and cost of, 185–188; budgetary problem and, 203–205; export drains, 208–214; exports and prices, 214–220; agricultural markets, 221–228; outlays for energy sources, 228–232; iron and steel requirements, 232–236; United States policy, 273–274

Exchange. *See* Foreign exchange

Export-Import Bank, 115, 160, 164, 175, 179

Exports, in European trade balance, 20–24; European, 68–71, 124; of ERP countries, 125; ratio of European, to production, 126; to ERP countries, 130, 208–214; effects of ERP on United States, 152–154; control of, 198–203; ERP, and price increase, 214–220. *See also* Trade

Far East, foodstuffs requirements, 221

Farm products, 207

Fats and oils, imports by ERP countries, 209, 210, 216

Federal Reserve banks, 194

Fertilizer, financing of, under ERP, 170

Fiscal policy, objectives of, 195–197

Five-Year Plans, in Soviet Russia, 86

Food, 197; European production and requirements, 95–96; financing of, under ERP, 170; exports of, to participating countries, 208, 210

Foreign Assistance Act of 1948, 10, 41, 48, 62, 64, 72, 74, 75, 79, 82, 135, 167, 176, 181; passage of, 29; agreements of participating countries 76–78

Foreign Economic Administration, 82

Foreign exchange, revaluation of rates, 10–11; unrealistic rates, 48–49; French devaluation policy, 78, 114–116, 121; conversion rates, 89; rate problems, 109–110; overvaluation of currencies, 110–112; stabilization, 112–114, 119–121; exchange rates and terms of trade, 116–119

France, inflation, 18, 19, 42–43, 44, 191; investment program, 35–36; terms of trade, 49; ratio of imports and foreign assistance, 55; changing pattern of trade, 56, 57, 58; devaluation of currency, 78, 114–116, 121; interwar period, 86; per capita income, 88, 90; conversion rate, 89; industrial production, 91, 92; food production and requirements, 96; overvaluation of currency, 110–111; multilateral payments arrangement, 125; ERP aid, 156, 157, 159, 160, 161, 162, 165; financing of imports, 169, 170; problem of ECA currency control, 182–183; trends in economic recovery, 247, 258–263, 271; national income, 248; agricultural output, 250; monetary inflation and price movements, 252

Fruits, 148

Fuel, financing of, under ERP, 170

Germany, interwar period, 85; per capita income, 88, 90; industrial production, 93; overvaluation of currency, 111; control of local currencies, 181; meat requirements, 227, 228; agricultural output, 250; monetary purge, 252; monetary

[304]

INDEX

system, 271. *See also* Bizonal Germany, Western Germany
Gold, United States stock, 101-103, 107; Bank of France holdings, 111; reserves of ERP countries, 131
Government bond market, and monetary control, 194-195
Grain, 150, 197; need for allocation system, 148; imports by ERP countries, 209, 210, 216
Grants. *See* Credits and grants
Greece, inflation, 18, 19, 42, 190-191; ratio of imports and foreign assistance, 55; trade with United States, 56, 57; ERP aid, 157, 158, 159, 160; financing of imports, 169, 170; problem of ECA currency control, 182-183; national income, 248; agricultural output, 250; monetary inflation and price movements, 252
Great Britain. *See* United Kingdom
Guillotine Committee, 262

Harriman, W. Averell, 74, 145, 146
Harriman Committee, 60, 97, 117-118, 119, 125, 176, 179, 181, 198, 222, 245; estimates governing aid to Europe, 133-139 *passim*, 155, 163
Herter, Christian A., 73, 178, 182
Herter Committee, 65-66, 67, 70, 79, 80, 81, 151, 179, 180, 181, 198
Hickenlooper, Bourke, 166, 215-216
Hitler, Adolf, 85
Hoffman, Paul, 74
Holland. *See* Netherlands
Hungary, investment program, 36; inflationary problem, 42, 191; changing pattern of trade, 56; per capita income, 88, 90; monetary purge, 252

Iceland, 247
Imports, in European trade balance, 20-24; ratio of foreign assistance and, 55; European, 68-71, 124, 130; requirements of ERP countries and Western Germany, 132; financing of, under ERP, 166-171. *See also* Trade
Income, national, of ERP countries, 31-33, 248; European disinvestment abroad, 34-35; prewar and postwar, in United States and Europe, 86-91, 93-94; United Kingdom, 253-254
Industry, European output, 30-31, 91-94, 127, 248-251, 258-260; investment and non-investment in Europe, 37-38
Inflation, problem of, in ERP, 13-14, 18-20; open and suppressed, 42-43; adverse effects, 44-45; U. S., and European balance of payments, 50-51; overvalued currency in solution of, 111; effects of ERP, 145-148, 185, 189-190; need for anti-inflation program, 147-148; national income and cost of ERP, 185-188; corrective measures, 190-203, 205-206; resulting injustices, 192-193; expansion of money and credit, 193-194; monetary control and government bond market, 194-195; United Kingdom, 255-256; France, 260-262; Italy, 264
International Bank, 132, 134, 175; estimate governing aid to Europe, 138-139, 155, 163
International Monetary Fund, 78, 109, 119
Investment, problem of, in Europe, 9; Monnet Plan, 19, 35; European programs, 36-41

[305]

INDEX

Ireland, 247; cost of living, 252
Iron and steel, 151, 152, 178, 197; need for allocation system, 148; exports of, to ERP countries, 208, 209, 211; problem of, under ERP, 232–236
Iron Curtain countries, postwar trade, 70–71; United States loans to, 130
Italy, inflation, 18, 19, 42, 44; ratio of imports and foreign assistance, 55; changing pattern of trade, 56; per capita income, 88, 90; industrial production, 91, 92; multilateral payment arrangement, 125; ERP aid, 156–162 *passim*; financing of imports, 169; trends in economic recovery, 247, 264–266, 270–271; national income, 248; agricultural output, 250; monetary inflation and price movements, 252

Keynes, John Maynard, 101, 102, 103
Krug, Julius A., 151

Lard, 149
Latin America, 270; contribution to ERP, 16–18; repercussions of ERP, 64–66
Lend-Lease, 82
Loans, United States, to Europe, 55–56, 130; ERP, and capacity to repay, 164–166
Lumber, 197; need for allocation system, 148
Luxemburg, 247; exports to United States, 56; multilateral payments arrangement, 125

McCloy, John J., 32
Machine tools, 178

Machinery, 151, 197; imports by ERP countries, 209, 210, 211
Marshall, George C., 29, 76, 145, 155–156, 163; quoted on non-cooperation, 61
Marshall Plan, 47, 186, 215
Marx, Karl, 72
Meat, 150; imports by ERP countries, 209, 210; European requirements, 227
Middle East, repercussion of ERP, 65
Molotov, V. M., 6, 61, 63
Monetary control, and government bond market, 194–195
Monetary policy, limits of, 195
Monetary purges, 252
Money and credit, expansion of, 193–194
Monnet Plan, 19, 35
Multilateralism, in ERP countries, 79, 125

National Advisory Council on International and Financial Problems, 10, 109, 130
Nationalization, industrial, 71, 74–75
Naval stores, 149
Netherlands, inflation, 19, 44; ratio of imports and foreign assistance, 55; trade with United States, 56, 57; industrial production, 92, 93; food production and requirements, 96; multilateral payment arrangement, 125; ERP aid, 157, 158, 160, 165; financing of imports, 169; trends in economic recovery, 247, 269–270; national income, 248; agricultural output, 250; cost of living, 251, 252
Netherlands East Indies, 269
New York Times, 194

[306]

INDEX

Norway, inflation, 42; ratio of imports and foreign assistance, 55; trade with United States, 56; dollar income, 88, 90; industrial production, 92, 93, 249; food production and requirements, 96; multilateral payment arrangement, 125; ERP aid, 157, 159, 160; agricultural output, 250; cost of living, 251, 252

Oil. *See* Petroleum

Paris Conference countries, United States loans to, 130
Paris Conference of Foreign Ministers (1947), 61, 63-64, 242, 245
Paris Report, 132-133; revisions, 133-139
Petroleum, 65, 197; problem of, in ERP, 14-15, 151, 228-232; need for allocation system, 148; exports of, to ERP countries, 208, 211
Poland, investment program, 36; ratio of imports and foreign assistance, 55; changing pattern of trade, 56; per capita income, 88, 90; cost of living, 252
Population, ratio of income to (1946), 86
Portugal, 158, 169, 247
Prices, import, and terms of trade, 49-51; influence of ERP exports, 214-220
Private enterprise, ERP as support of, 15-16, 71-75
Production, industrial, in Europe, 30-31, 91-94, 127, 248-251; ratio of European exports to, 126; industrial, in France, 258-260
Purchasing, method of, under ERP, 176-177

Reciprocal Trade Agreements, 13; extension of, 79
Reconstruction Finance Corporation, 82
Recovery, inflation problem, 13-14, 18-20; European trade deficit, 20-24; European industrial output, 30-31, 91-94, 127, 248-251; Russian obstruction, 61-63; European goals, 241-242, 272; objectives of CEEC, 242-247; economic trends in ERP countries, 248-252; United Kingdom, 252-258; France, 258-263; Italy, 264-266; Bizonal Germany, 266-269; Netherlands, 269-270
Re-exports, problem of, under ERP, 66-67
RFC, 82
Rice, 149
Russia. *See* Union of Soviet Socialist Republics

Sabotage, communist, of ERP, 16, 272
Scandinavian countries, national income, 248; cost of living, 251. *See also* countries by name
Select Committee on Foreign Aid. *See* Herter Committee
Shipping, proposed transfer to foreign charters, 149
Snyder, John W., 11
Socialism, ERP as weapon against, 71-75
South America. *See* Latin America
Sovereignty, of ERP countries, 76, 181
Stabilization, of foreign exchange, 119-120
State Department, in administration of ERP, 81-82
Steel. *See* Iron and steel

[307]

INDEX

Stock piles, availability of, in ERP countries, 79; United States program, 180
Subsidization, ERP as program for, 12–13, 149
Sugar, 226–227
Surplus products, dumping of, under ERP, 12–13
Sweden, inflation, 19; changing pattern of trade, 56, 57; per capita income, 88, 90; industrial production, 92, 93; multilateral payment arrangement, 125; ERP aid, 157, 158; financing of imports, 169; agricultural output, 250; cost of living, 252
Switzerland, changing pattern of trade, 56; food production and requirements, 96; balance of payment, 160; financing of imports, 169; national income, 248; agricultural output, 250; cost of living, 252

Taber, John, 15, 81
Taxes, ratio of, to income in European countries, 88, 90–91; fiscal policy and, 195–197
Taylor, Glen H., 198
Taylor, Henry, 173
Terms of trade, overvaluation and, 48–49; problem of, 49–51, 123–124; exchange rates and, 116–119
Timber, imports by ERP countries, 209, 211
Tobacco, 149, 208, 210, 228
Trade, international, effect of inflation on, 44–45; terms of, 48–51, 116–119, 123–124; changing patterns of, in Europe, 56–57; ERP in West-East European, 67–71; United States, with Europe, 130. *See also* Exports, Imports

Trade deficit, problem of, in Europe, 9–10, 20–24; European, and U. S. inflation, 50–51; financing of, 51–52; European, with Americas, 132–135; European, summary of factors involved, 139–142. *See also* Balance of payments
Truman, Harry S., 146
Turkey, 247

Union of Soviet Socialist Republics, solution of dollar problem, 47, 98; in European recovery, 61–63; attitude toward ERP, 63–64, 272; trade with United Kingdom, 69; interwar period, 86; per capita income, 88, 89, 90; capital levy on money, 191
United Kingdom, inflation, 19, 42, 43, 191; national income, 1947, 32; disinvestment, 34; investment program, 36, 38–41; terms of trade, 49, 55, 117; ratio of imports and foreign assistance, 55; changing pattern of trade, 56, 57, 58; trade with Eastern Europe, 69; nationalization program, 71, 74–75; interwar period, 85; income controls, 87–88; per capita income, 88, 90; industrial production, 92, 93; food production and requirements, 96; dollar shortage, 97; multilateral payment arrangement, 125; ERP aid, 156–162 *passim*, 165; financing of imports, 169, 170; policy of ECA currency control, 182–183; meat requirements, 227; coal output, 229; trends in economic recovery, 247, 252–258, 270–271; agricultural output, 250; cost of living, 251
United Nations, 64

[308]

INDEX

United Nations Relief and Rehabilitation Administration, 64
United States, prewar and postwar income, 86–91, 93–94; ratio of taxes to income, 91; gold stock, 101–103, 107; capital movements and transfers, 105–106; deterioration of terms of trade, 123; balance of payments, 128–129; trade with Europe, 130; gold, dollar balances, and foreign investments in, 130–131; need for liberal economic policies, 140–141; costs of ERP, 173–176; stock-piling program, 180; corrective measures against inflation, 190–203, 205–206; policy toward ERP, 273–274

United States Stabilization Fund, 119
USSR. *See* Union of Soviet Socialist Republics

Vandenberg-Brookings proposal, administration of ERP, 81–82
Vegetables, 149

Wallace, Henry A., 6
Western Germany, inflation, 18; ERP aid, 157, 158, 159, 160; financing of imports, 169. *See also* Bizonal Germany, Germany
Wheat, 149, 215

Yugoslavia, monetary purge, 252